EDUCATION IN A COMPETITIVE AND GLOBALIZING WORLD

TECHNOLOGY IN EDUCATION: FUTURE READY LEARNING AND SCHOOLS

EDUCATION IN A COMPETITIVE AND GLOBALIZING WORLD

Additional books in this series can be found on Nova's website under the Series tab.

Additional e-books in this series can be found on Nova's website under the e-book tab.

EDUCATION IN A COMPETITIVE AND GLOBALIZING WORLD

TECHNOLOGY IN EDUCATION: FUTURE READY LEARNING AND SCHOOLS

AUSTIN CARLSON
EDITOR

New York

Copyright © 2016 by Nova Science Publishers, Inc.

All rights reserved. No part of this book may be reproduced, stored in a retrieval system or transmitted in any form or by any means: electronic, electrostatic, magnetic, tape, mechanical photocopying, recording or otherwise without the written permission of the Publisher.

We have partnered with Copyright Clearance Center to make it easy for you to obtain permissions to reuse content from this publication. Simply navigate to this publication's page on Nova's website and locate the "Get Permission" button below the title description. This button is linked directly to the title's permission page on copyright.com. Alternatively, you can visit copyright.com and search by title, ISBN, or ISSN.

For further questions about using the service on copyright.com, please contact:
Copyright Clearance Center
Phone: +1-(978) 750-8400   Fax: +1-(978) 750-4470   E-mail: info@copyright.com.

NOTICE TO THE READER

The Publisher has taken reasonable care in the preparation of this book, but makes no expressed or implied warranty of any kind and assumes no responsibility for any errors or omissions. No liability is assumed for incidental or consequential damages in connection with or arising out of information contained in this book. The Publisher shall not be liable for any special, consequential, or exemplary damages resulting, in whole or in part, from the readers' use of, or reliance upon, this material. Any parts of this book based on government reports are so indicated and copyright is claimed for those parts to the extent applicable to compilations of such works.

Independent verification should be sought for any data, advice or recommendations contained in this book. In addition, no responsibility is assumed by the publisher for any injury and/or damage to persons or property arising from any methods, products, instructions, ideas or otherwise contained in this publication.

This publication is designed to provide accurate and authoritative information with regard to the subject matter covered herein. It is sold with the clear understanding that the Publisher is not engaged in rendering legal or any other professional services. If legal or any other expert assistance is required, the services of a competent person should be sought. FROM A DECLARATION OF PARTICIPANTS JOINTLY ADOPTED BY A COMMITTEE OF THE AMERICAN BAR ASSOCIATION AND A COMMITTEE OF PUBLISHERS.

Additional color graphics may be available in the e-book version of this book.

Library of Congress Cataloging-in-Publication Data

ISBN: 978-1-53610-234-5

Published by Nova Science Publishers, Inc. † New York

CONTENTS

Preface		**vii**
Chapter 1	Future Ready Learning: Reimagining the Role of Technology in Education *Office of Educational Technology*	**1**
Chapter 2	Future Ready Schools: Building Technology Infrastructure for Learning *Office of Educational Technology*	**133**
Related Nova Publication		**217**
Index		**219**

PREFACE

Technology can be a powerful tool for transforming learning. It can help affirm and advance relationships between educators and students, reinvent our approaches to learning and collaboration, shrink long-standing equity and accessibility gaps, and adapt learning experiences to meet the needs of all learners. Our schools, community colleges, and universities should be incubators of exploration and invention. Educators should be collaborators in learning, seeking new knowledge and constantly acquiring new skills alongside their students. Education leaders should set a vision for creating learning experiences that provide the right tools and supports for all learners to thrive. However, to realize fully the benefits of technology in our education system and provide authentic learning experiences, educators need to use technology effectively in their practice. Furthermore, education stakeholders should commit to working together to use technology to improve American education. These stakeholders include leaders; teachers, faculty, and other educators; researchers; policymakers; funders; technology developers; community members and organizations; and learners and their families. This book reviews the role of technology in education as well as building technology infrastructure for learning.

In: Technology in Education
Editor: Austin Carlson

ISBN: 978-1-53610-234-5
© 2016 Nova Science Publishers, Inc.

Chapter 1

FUTURE READY LEARNING: REIMAGINING THE ROLE OF TECHNOLOGY IN EDUCATION[*]

Office of Educational Technology

INTRODUCTION

If the technology revolution only happens for families that already have money and education, then it's not really a revolution.—*Arne Duncan, U.S. Secretary of Education*

Technology can be a powerful tool for transforming learning. It can help affirm and advance relationships between educators and students, reinvent our approaches to learning and collaboration, shrink long-standing equity and accessibility gaps, and adapt learning experiences to meet the needs of all learners.

Our schools, community colleges, and universities should be incubators of exploration and invention. Educators should be collaborators in learning, seeking new knowledge and constantly acquiring new skills alongside their students. Education leaders should set a vision for creating learning experiences that provide the right tools and supports for all learners to thrive.

However, to realize fully the benefits of technology in our education system and provide authentic learning experiences, educators need to use

---

[*] This is an edited, reformatted and augmented version of a document issued by the U.S. Department of Education, Office of Educational Technology, January 2016.

technology effectively in their practice. Furthermore, education stakeholders should commit to working together to use technology to improve American education. These stakeholders include leaders; teachers, faculty, and other educators; researchers; policymakers; funders; technology developers; community members and organizations; and learners and their families.

About This Plan

The National Education Technology Plan (NETP) sets a national vision and plan for learning enabled by technology through building on the work of leading education researchers; district, school, and higher education leaders; classroom teachers; developers; entrepreneurs; and nonprofit organizations. The principles and examples provided in this document align to the Activities to Support the Effective Use of Technology (Title IV A) of Every Student Succeeds Act as authorized by Congress in December 2015.

a call to action

a vision for learning enabled through technology

a collection of recommendations & real-world examples

WRITTEN FOR...

Teachers

Policymakers

Administrators

Teacher preparation professionals

To illustrate key ideas and recommendations, the plan includes examples of the transformation enabled by the effective use of technology. These examples include both those backed by rigorous evidence as well as emerging innovations. The identification of specific programs or products in these examples is designed to provide a clearer understanding of innovative ideas and is not meant as an endorsement. The NETP also provides actionable recommendations to implement technology and conduct research and development successfully that can advance the effective use of technology to support learning and teaching.

Intended to be useful for any group or individual with a stake in education, the NETP assumes as its primary audiences teachers; education leaders; those responsible for preparing teachers; and policymakers at the federal, state, and local levels. The concepts, recommendations, and examples are also applicable to post-secondary institutions, community organizations, and state-level initiatives. The NETP focuses on using technology to transform learning experiences with the goal of providing greater equity and accessibility (see Section 1: Learning).

Equity and Accessibility

Equity in education means increasing all students' access to educational opportunities with a focus on closing achievement gaps and removing barriers students face based on their race, ethnicity, or national origin; sex; sexual orientation or gender identity or expression; disability; English language ability; religion; socio-economic status; or geographical location.[1]

Accessibility refers to the design of apps, devices, materials, and environments that support and enable access to content and educational activities for all learners. In addition to enabling students with disabilities to use content and participate in activities, the concepts also apply to accommodating the individual learning needs of students, such as English language learners, students in rural communities, or students from economically disadvantaged homes. Technology can support accessibility through embedded assistance—for example, text-to-speech, audio and digital text formats of instructional materials, programs that differentiate instruction, adaptive testing, built-in accommodations, and other assistive technology tools.[2]

When carefully designed and thoughtfully applied, technology can accelerate, amplify, and expand the impact of effective teaching practices.

However, to be transformative, educators need to have the knowledge and skills to take full advantage of technology-rich learning environments (see Section 2: Teaching). In addition, the roles of PK–12 classroom teachers and post-secondary instructors, librarians, families, and learners all will need to shift as technology enables new types of learning experiences.

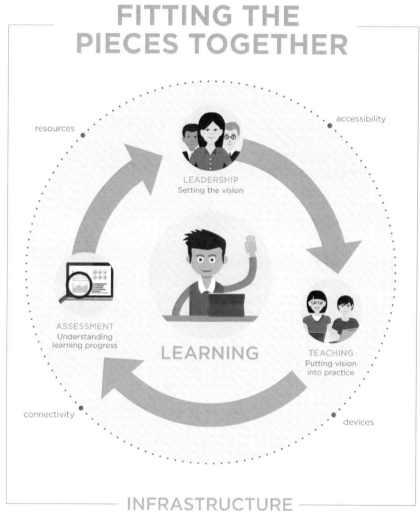

For these systemic changes in learning and teaching to occur, education leaders need to create a shared vision for how technology best can meet the needs of all learners and to develop a plan that translates the vision into action (see Section 3: Leadership).

Technology-enabled assessments support learning and teaching by communicating evidence of learning progress and providing insights to teachers; administrators; families; and, most importantly, the learners themselves. These assessments can be embedded within digital learning activities to reduce interruptions to learning time (see Section 4: Assessment).

Learning, teaching, and assessment enabled by technology require a robust infrastructure (see Section 5: Infrastructure). Key elements of this infrastructure include high-speed connectivity and devices that are available to teachers and students when they need them. Aside from wires and devices, a comprehensive learning infrastructure includes digital learning content and other resources as well as professional development for educators and education leaders.

Recent Progress and the Road Ahead

Since the 2010 NETP, the United States has made significant progress in leveraging technology to transform learning in a variety of ways.

- The conversation has shifted from *whether* technology should be used in learning to *how* it can improve learning to ensure that all students have access to high-quality educational experiences.[3]
- Technology increasingly is being used to personalize learning and give students more choice over what and how they learn and at what pace, preparing them to organize and direct their own learning for the rest of their lives.
- Advances in the learning sciences have improved our understanding of how people learn and illuminated which personal and contextual factors most impact their success.
- Research and experience have improved our understanding of what people need to know and the skills and competencies they need to acquire for success in life and work in the 21st century. Through pre-service teacher preparation programs and professional learning, educators are gaining experience and confidence in using technology to achieve learning outcomes.

- Sophisticated software has begun to allow us to adapt assessments to the needs and abilities of individual learners and provide near real-time results.
- Nationally, progress has been made toward ensuring that every school has high-speed classroom connectivity as a foundation for other learning innovations.
- The cost of digital devices has decreased dramatically, while computing power has increased, along with the availability of high-quality interactive educational tools and apps.
- Technology has allowed us to rethink the design of physical learning spaces to accommodate new and expanded relationships among learners, teachers, peers, and mentors.

Although we can be proud of the progress of the last five years, there is still much work to do. Now, a look at the work ahead:

- A digital use divide continues to exist between learners who are using technology in active, creative ways to support their learning and those who predominantly use technology for passive content consumption.
- Research on the effectiveness of technology-enabled programs and resources is still limited, and we should build capacity to generate evidence of individual-, program-, and community-level outcomes.
- Many schools do not yet have access to or are not yet using technology in ways that can improve learning on a daily basis, which underscores the need—guided by new research—to accelerate and scale up adoption of effective approaches and technologies.
- Few schools have adopted approaches for using technology to support informal learning experiences aligned with formal learning goals.
- Supporting learners in using technology for out-of-school learning experiences is often a missed opportunity.
- Across the board, teacher preparation and professional development programs fail to prepare teachers to use technology in effective ways.
- Assessment approaches have evolved but still do not use technology to its full potential to measure a broader range of desired educational outcomes, especially non-cognitive competencies.
- The focus on providing Internet access and devices for learners should not overshadow the importance of preparing teachers to teach

effectively with technology and to select engaging and relevant digital learning content.

- As students use technology to support their learning, schools are faced with a growing need to protect student privacy continuously while allowing the appropriate use of data to personalize learning, advance research, and visualize student progress for families and teachers.

Digital Use Divide

Traditionally, the digital divide referred to the gap between students who had access to the Internet and devices at school and home and those who did not.[4,5] Significant progress is being made to increase Internet access in schools, libraries, and homes across the country. However, a digital use divide separates many students who use technology in ways that transform their learning from those who use the tools to complete the same activities but now with an electronic device (e.g., digital worksheets, online multiple-choice tests). The digital use divide is present in both formal and informal learning settings and across high- and low-poverty schools and communities.[6,7,8]

The NETP is a common vision and action plan that responds to an urgent national priority. It describes specific actions the United States should take to ensure learners of all ages have opportunities for personal growth and prosperity and remain competitive in a global economy.

Non-Cognitive Competencies

Non-cognitive competencies (also referred to as social and emotional Learning) include a range of skills, habits, and attitudes that facilitate functioning well in school, work, and life. They include self-awareness, self-management, social awareness, and relationship skills as well as perseverance, motivation, and growth mindsets.[9,10,11]

---

1. LEARNING - ENGAGING AND EMPOWERING LEARNING THROUGH TECHNOLOGY

GOAL: All learners will have engaging and empowering learning experiences in both formal and informal settings that prepare them to be active, creative, knowledgeable, and ethical participants in our globally connected society.

To be successful in our daily lives and in a global workforce, Americans need pathways to acquire expertise and form meaningful connections to peers and mentors. This journey begins with a base of knowledge and abilities that can be augmented and enhanced throughout our lives. Fortunately, advances in learning sciences have provided new insights into how people learn.[1] Technology can be a powerful tool to reimagine learning experiences on the basis of those insights.

Historically, a learner's educational opportunities have been limited by the resources found within the walls of a school. Technology-enabled learning allows learners to tap resources and expertise anywhere in the world, starting with their own communities. For example:

- With high-speed Internet access, a student interested in learning computer science can take the course online in a school that lacks the budget or a faculty member with the appropriate skills to teach the course.
- Learners struggling with planning for college and careers can access high-quality online mentoring and advising programs where resources or geography present challenges to obtaining sufficient face-to-face mentoring.
- With mobile data collection tools and online collaboration platforms, students in a remote geographic area studying local phenomena can collaborate with peers doing similar work anywhere in the world.
- A school with connectivity but without robust science facilities can offer its students virtual chemistry, biology, anatomy, and physics labs—offering students learning experiences that approach those of peers with better resources.
- Students engaged in creative writing, music, or media production can publish their work to a broad global audience regardless of where they go to school.
- Technology-enabled learning environments allow less experienced learners to access and participate in specialized communities of practice, graduating to more complex activities and deeper participation as they gain the experience needed to become expert members of the community.[2]

These opportunities expand growth possibilities for all students while affording historically disadvantaged students greater equity of access to high-quality learning materials, expertise, personalized learning, and tools for planning for future education.[3,4] Such opportunities also can support increased capacity for educators to create blended learning opportunities for their students, rethinking when, where, and how students complete different components of a learning experience.

Personalized Learning

Personalized Learning refers to instruction in which the pace of learning and the instructional approach are optimized for the needs of each learner. Learning objectives, instructional approaches, and instructional content (and its sequencing) all may vary based on learner needs. In addition, learning activities are meaningful and relevant to learners, driven by their interests, and often self-initiated.

What People Need to Learn

To remain globally competitive and develop engaged citizens, our schools should weave 21st century competencies and expertise throughout the learning experience. These include the development of critical thinking, complex problem solving, collaboration, and adding multimedia communication into the teaching of traditional academic subjects.[5] In addition, learners should have the opportunity to develop a sense of **agency** in their learning and the belief that they are capable of succeeding in school.

Blended Learning

In a blended learning environment, learning occurs online and in person, augmenting and supporting teacher practice. This approach often allows students to have some control over time, place, path, or pace of learning. In many blended learning models, students spend some of their face-to-face time with the teacher in a large group, some face-to-face time with a teacher or tutor in a small group, and some time learning with and from peers. Blended learning often benefits from a reconfiguration of the physical learning space to facilitate learning activities, providing a variety of technology-enabled learning zones optimized for collaboration, informal learning, and individual-focused study.

10 Office of Educational Technology

Beyond these essential core academic competencies, there is a growing body of research on the importance of non-cognitive competencies as they relate to academic success.[7,8,9] Non-cognitive competencies include successful navigation through tasks such as forming relationships and solving everyday problems. They also include development of self-awareness, control of impulsivity, executive function, working cooperatively, and caring about oneself and others.

Building Non-Cognitive Competencies:
Providing Opportunities for Practice

Interacting with peers, handling conflicts, resolving disputes, or persisting through a challenging problem are all experiences that are important to academic success.

Digital games can allow students to try out varied responses and roles and gauge the outcomes without fear of negative consequences.[28] Accumulating evidence suggests that virtual environments and games can help increase empathy, self-awareness, emotional regulation, social awareness, cooperation, and problem solving while decreasing the number of behavior referrals and in-school suspensions.[29]

Games such as Ripple Effects and The Social Express use virtual environments, storytelling, and interactive experiences to assess a student's social skill competencies and provide opportunities to practice. Other apps help bridge the gap between the virtual environment and the real world by providing just-in-time supports for emotional regulation and conflict resolution. A number of apps are available to help students name and identify how they are feeling, express their emotions, and receive targeted suggestions or strategies for self-regulation. Examples include Breathe, Think, Do with Sesame; Smiling Mind; Stop, Breathe and Think; Touch and Learn—Emotions; and Digital Problem Solver.

Agency in Learning

Learners with agency can "intentionally make things happen by [their] actions," and "agency enables people to play a part in their self-development, adaptation, and self-renewal with changing times."[6] To build this capacity, learners should have the opportunity to make meaningful choices about their learning, and they need practice at doing so effectively. Learners who successfully develop this ability lay the foundation for lifelong, self-directed learning.

Fostering Growth Mindset:
Technology-Based Program to Fuel Student Achievement

A key part of non-cognitive development is fostering a growth mindset about learning. Growth mindset is the understanding that abilities can be developed through effort and practice and leads to increased motivation and achievement. The U.S. Department of Education has funded several growth mindset–related projects, including a grant to develop and evaluate SchoolKit, a suite of resources developed to teach growth mindset quickly and efficiently in schools.

Jill Balzer, a middle school principal in Killeen, Texas, has seen success from using SchoolKit in her school. Balzer spoke with an eighth grader who achieved academic distinction for the first time in five years after using the using the program. "When I asked him what the difference was," recalled Balzer, "he said that now he understood that even though learning was not always going to come easy to him it didn't mean he was stupid, it just meant he needed to work harder on that subject."[30]

District of Columbia Public Schools also have made the SchoolKit available to all middle schools. Principal Dawn Clemens of Stuart-Hobson Middle School saw increases in reading scores for their seventh-grade students after using the program. "With middle-schoolers, there are always excuses," Clemens said. "But this shifts the language to be about payoff from effort, rather than 'the test was too hard' or 'the teacher doesn't like me.'"[31]

12　　　　　　　　　Office of Educational Technology

Increased connectivity also increases the importance of teaching learners how to become responsible digital citizens. We need to guide the development of competencies to use technology in ways that are meaningful, productive, respectful, and safe. For example, helping students learn to use proper online etiquette, recognize how their personal information may be collected and used online, and leverage access to a global community to improve the world around them can help prepare them for successfully navigating life in a connected world. Mastering these skills requires a basic understanding of the technology tools and the ability to make increasingly sound judgments about the use of them in learning and daily life. For the development of digital citizenship, educators can turn to resources such as Common Sense Education's digital citizenship curriculum or the student technology standards from the International Society for Technology in Education (ISTE).

Technology-Enabled Learning in Action

Learning principles transcend specific technologies. However, when carefully designed and thoughtfully applied, technology has the potential to accelerate, amplify, and expand the impact of powerful principles of learning. Because the process of learning is not directly observable, the study of learning often produces models and conclusions that evolve across time. The recommendations in this plan are based on current assumptions and theories of how people learn even while education researchers, learning scientists, and educators continue to work toward a deeper understanding.

The NETP focuses on how technology can help learners unlock the power of some of the most potent learning principles discovered to date. For example, we know that technology can help learners think about an idea in more than one way and in more than one context, reflect on what is learned, and adjust understanding accordingly.[10,11] Technology also can help capture learners' attention by tapping into their interests and passions.[12] It can help us align *how* we learn with *what* we learn.

Following are five ways technology can improve and enhance learning, both in formal learning and in informal settings. Each is accompanied by examples of transformational learning in action.

1. Technology can enable personalized learning or experiences that are more engaging and relevant. Mindful of the learning objectives, educators might design learning experiences that allow students in a class to choose from a menu of learning experiences—writing essays, producing media, building websites, collaborating with experts across the globe in data collection—assessed via a common rubric to demonstrate their learning. Such technology-enabled learning experiences can be more engaging and relevant to learners.

Scaling up Personalized Learning: Massachusetts' Innovation Schools Create Multiple Pathways to Learning

As part of Massachusetts' Achievement Gap Act of 2010, funding was set aside to give schools the opportunity to implement innovative strategies to improve learning. Through this legislation, educators can create Innovation Schools that can operate with increased flexibility in key areas such as schedule, curriculum, instruction, and professional development.[32]

As of 2015, there were 54 approved Innovation Schools and Academies in 26 school districts across Massachusetts. Some schools implemented a science, technology, engineering, and mathematics (STEM) or STEM-plus-arts model, and others implemented a combination of one or more of the following educational models: multiple pathways, early college, dual-language immersion, or expanded learning time.

Students in a Safety and Public Service Academy combine rigorous college-style coursework available in a variety of formats (in class, online, blended learning, off-site for internships and job shadows) in areas such as forensics, computer science, criminal law, crisis management, psychology, and video production. Students at the Arts Academy may combine their coursework with off-site learning opportunities at local universities, combining high-tech design skills and knowledge of the creative arts to prepare them for post-secondary education and a career in the arts.

Pentucket Regional School District's program has scaled their innovation approach to every elementary school in the district. Their approach is centered on student choice and the use of opportunities for learning that extend beyond the classroom walls. Through the redesign of the school day and year, students engage in hands-on experiential learning with in-class lessons; online and blended coursework; and off-campus academic opportunities, internships, and apprenticeships.

---

2. Technology can help organize learning around real-world challenges and project-based learning using a wide variety of digital learning devices and resources to show competency with complex

14 Office of Educational Technology

concepts and content. Rather than writing a research report to be read only by her biology teacher and a small group of classmates, a student might publish her findings online where she receives feedback from researchers and other members of communities of practice around the country. In an attempt to understand the construction of persuasive arguments, another student might draft, produce, and share a public service announcement via online video streaming sites, asking his audience for constructive feedback every step of the way.

Project-Based Learning

Project-based Learning takes place in the context of authentic problems, continues across time, and brings in knowledge from many subjects. Project-based learning, if properly implemented and supported, helps students develop 21st century skills, including creativity, collaboration, and leadership, and engages them in complex, real-world challenges that help them meet expectations for critical thinking.[13]

Engaged Creation: Exploratorium Creates a Massive Open Online Course (MOOC) for Exploring Circuits and Electricity

In the summer of 2015, the Exploratorium in San Francisco launched its first MOOC, working with Coursera, called Tinkering Fundamentals to inspire STEM-rich tinkering; introduce a set of high-quality activities that could be replicated easily in the classroom; and foster robust discussions of the learning.

The six-week course included a blend of hands-on activities, short videos of five to eight minutes each, an active discussion forum, live Web chats, social media, and other resources. Each week the videos highlighted an introduction to a new tinkering activity, the learning goals, and tips for facilitation; step-by-step instructions for how to build and support others to build the tinkering contraption; classroom video and interviews with teachers about classroom implementation and student learning; profiles of artists; and comments by learning experts. Reflective prompts generated extensive conversation in the discussion forums.

To facilitate these online activities, the Exploratorium integrated multiple platforms, including Coursera and live video streaming tools. Instructors used these online platforms and spaces to reflect on the week's activities and forum posts and to provide real-time feedback to participants.

Future Ready Learning

In videoconferences, the instructors positioned themselves as questioners rather than as experts, enhancing a strong sense of camaraderie and collaborative exploration.

The Exploratorium used a social media aggregator to showcase photos and videos of participants' tinkering creations, underscoring the hands-on and material nature of the work of the MOOC. The course attracted more than 7,000 participants from 150 countries, of whom approximately 4,400 were active participants, resulting in more than 66,000 video views and 6,700 forum posts. For more information, visit the Exploratorium and Coursera on the Web.

Building Projects for Real Audiences: National Parks Service Deepens Engagement through Technology

Journey Through Hallowed Ground is a partnership project of the National Park Service that encourages students to create rich connections to history through project-based learning, specifically making videos about their visits to historical sites. The students take the roles of writers, actors, directors, producers, costume designers, music directors, editors, and filmmakers with the support of professional video editors. The videos allow the students to speak about history in their own words as well as share their knowledge with their peers. In addition to learning about history, participating in the projects also teaches students to refine their skills of leadership and teamwork. All videos become official material of the National Park Service and are licensed openly for use by other students and teachers around the world.

---

3. Technology can help learning move beyond the classroom and take advantage of learning opportunities available in museums, libraries, and other out-of-school settings. Coordinated events such as the Global Read Aloud allow classrooms from all over the world to come together through literacy. One book is chosen, and participating classrooms have six weeks in which teachers read the book aloud to students and then connect their classrooms to other participants across the world. Although the book is the same for each student, the interpretation, thoughts, and connections are different. This setting helps support learners through the shared experience of reading and builds a perception of learners as existing within a world of readers. The shared experience of connecting globally to read can lead to deeper understanding of not only the literature but also of their peers with whom students are learning.

Upskilling Adult Learners: At Peer-to-Peer University (P2PU), Everyone Is a Teacher and a Learner

P2PU and the Chicago Public Library (CPL) have partnered to pilot Learning Circles— lightly facilitated study groups for adult learners taking online courses together at their local library. In spring 2015, the partnership ran a pilot program in two CPL branches, facilitating in-person study groups around a number of free, online courses. The pilot program has expanded to 10 CPL branches in fall 2015, with the ultimate goal of developing an open-source, off-the-shelf solution that can be deployed by other public libraries, allowing all libraries and their communities to harness the potential of blended learning for little to no expertise or cost.

Meeting once a week in two-hour sessions, a non-content expert librarian helps facilitate a peer-learning environment, with the goal that after six weeks the Learning Circles become self-sustainable. P2PU has designed a number of software tools and guidelines to help onboard learners and facilitators, easing administrative burdens and integrating deeper learning principles into existing online learning content. Initial results suggest that students in Learning Circles have far higher retention than do students in most online courses, participants acquire non-cognitive skills often absent from pure online learning environments, and a diverse audience is participating. By working with libraries and building in additional learning support, P2PU also is able to reach first-time online learners, many of whom do not have a post-secondary degree.

P2PU measures success in terms of both the progress of individual learners and the viability of the model. In addition to the number of branches involved, cost per user, and number of learners, attributes such as retention, returning to additional Learning Circles, advancing from the role of learner to that of facilitator, and transitioning from Learning Circles into other fields (formal education, new job) are all other factors that contribute to success. Furthermore, P2PU designs for and measures academic mindsets (community, self-efficacy, growth mindsets, relevance) as a proxy for learner success.

Future Ready Learning 17

Helping Parents Navigate a Technological World:
A Resource for Making Informed Technology Decisions

Family Time With Apps: A Guide to Using Apps With Your Kids is an interactive resource for parents seeking to select and use apps in the most effective ways with their children.[33] The guide informs parents of the variety of ways that apps can support children's healthy development and family learning, communication, and connection with eight strategies. These strategies are playing games together, reading together every day, creating media projects, preparing for new experiences, connecting with distant family, exploring the outside world, making travel more fun, and creating a predictable routine. Tips on how to find the best apps to meet a child's particular needs and an explanation of how and why to use apps together also are included.

The guide references specific apps, which connect parents with the resources to select appropriate apps for their children. This online community is connected with various app stores and gives parents a menu for app selection on the basis of learning topic, age, connectivity, and device capability. Information also is included that describes exactly what other elements are attached to each app—for example, privacy settings, information collection, advertisements allowed, related apps, and so on.

The Joan Ganz Cooney Center at Sesame Workshop also recommends the Parents' Choice Award Winners as a tool for selecting child-appropriate apps. These apps, reviewed by the Parents' Choice Awards Committee within the Parents' Choice Foundation, have gone through a rigorous, multi-tiered evaluation process. The committee looks for apps that help children grow socially, intellectually, emotionally, and ethically while inspiring creativity and imagination and connecting parents and children.

---

4. Technology can help learners pursue passions and personal interests. A student who learns Spanish to read the works of Gabriel García Márquez in the original language and a student who collects data and creates visualizations of wind patterns in the San Francisco Bay in anticipation of a sailing trip are learning skills that are of unique interest to them. This ability to learn topics of personal interest teaches students to practice exploration and research that can help instill a mindset of lifelong learning.

Leveraging the Power of Networks: Cultivating Connections between Schools and Community Institutions

Cities of LRNG helps close the opportunity gap by connecting young people with a wide range of learning opportunities throughout their cities. The program makes learning activities from hundreds of community organizations easily discoverable to youth and their families on a single online platform.

Each LRNG city has a website where partner organizations can make their offerings visible. Young people receive recommended activities on the basis of their personal passions. For example, in Chicago through the local Chicago Cities of Learning initiative, more than 120 organizations have provided a collective 4,500 engaging learning opportunities for tens of thousands of young people in all areas of the city through the its platform.

As students participate in learning activities, they earn digital badges that showcase their skills and achievements. These digital badges signify mastery of a skill—for example, coding, games, design, or fashion—giving out-of-school learning greater currency by documenting and archiving learning wherever it occurs. Each time a young person earns a badge, he or she is recommended additional learning experiences and invited to broaden or deepen skills to propel him or her along academic, civic, or career trajectories. Because digital badges contain in-depth information about each individual's learning experiences, schools and potential employers can gain a comprehensive view of each person's interests and competencies.

Hive Learning Networks, a project of the Mozilla Foundation, organize and support city-based, peer-to-peer professional development networks and champion connected learning, digital skills, and Web literacy in youth-serving organizations in urban centers around the world. Using a laboratory approach and catalytic funding model, Hive re-imagines learning as interest based and empowers learners through collaboration with peer educators, youth, technology experts, and entrepreneurs.

Similar to Cities of LRNG, Hive networks are made up of community-based organizations, including libraries; museums; schools; after-school programs; and individuals, such as educators, designers, and artists. Hive participants work together to create learning opportunities for youth within and beyond the confines of traditional classroom experiences, design innovative practices and tools that leverage digital literacy skills for greater impact, and advance their own professional development.

The Hive model supports three levels of engagement:

Future Ready Learning

> 1. Events. Organizations with shared learning goals unite to provide fun, engaging events, such as maker parties, as a first step toward exploring longer term collaborations.
> 2. Learning Communities. Community organizers with an interest in Hive's core principles come together in regular meet-ups and events to explore how to apply connected learning tools and practices. Learning communities are in seven cities in the United States, Canada, and India.
> 3. Learning Networks. With an operational budget and staff, Hive Learning Networks commit to promoting innovative, open-source learning models in partnership with a community's civic and cultural organizations, businesses, entrepreneurs, educators, and learners. Learning Networks are in New York, Chicago, and Pittsburgh.

5. Technology access when equitable can help close the digital divide and make trans-formative learning opportunities available to all learners. An adult learner with limited physical access to continuing education can upskill by taking advantage of online programs to earn new certifications and can accomplish these goals regardless of location.

> **Building Equal Experiences:**
> **Black Girls Code (BGC) Informs and Inspires**
>
> Introducing girls of color to technology at an early age is one key to unlocking opportunities that mostly have eluded this underserved group. BGC, founded in 2001 by Kimberly Bryant, an electrical engineer, aims to "increase the number of women of color in the digital space by empowering girls of color to become innovators in STEM subjects, leaders in their communities, and builders of their own futures through exposure to computer science and technology."[34]
>
> Through a combination of workshops and field trips, BGC gives girls of color a chance to learn computer programming and connects them to role models in the technology space. BGC also hosts events and workshops across the country designed to help girls develop a wide range of other skills such as ideation, teamwork, and presenting while exploring social justice issues and engaging in creating solutions to those issues through technology.[35] One example of such an event occurred at DeVry University where 100 girls between the ages of 7 and 17 learned how to build a

20 Office of Educational Technology

webpage in a day. Tech industry volunteers led sessions in how to code using HTML, change the look and formatting of webpages using CCS, and design a basic Web structure. The girls developed web-pages that integrated text, images, videos, and music, according to their interests and creativity. Toward the end of the day, participants presented their websites to cheering parents, volunteers, and other attendees. Between 10 and 12 similar events by BGC are held in Oakland each year.[36]

BGC is headquartered in San Francisco, and BGC chapters are located in Chicago; Detroit; Memphis; New York; Oakland; Raleigh; and Washington, D.C., with more in development.

Creating for Access: Hello Navi for the Visually Impaired

When Maggie Bolado, a teacher at Resaca Middle School in Los Fresnos, Texas, was approached about the unique challenge of helping a visually impaired student navigate the school's campus, she had not imagined the innovation that was about to happen. Bolado helped guide a group of seventh- and eighth-grade students to develop an app to navigate the school grounds called Hello Navi. Working mostly during extracurricular time, the students learned bracket coding via online tutorials that enabled them to develop the app. As they learned to program, they also were developing problem-solving skills and becoming more detail oriented.

When the app was made available for download, requests came in to tailor the app to the needs of other particular users, including one parent who wanted to know how to make it work for her two-year-old child. The students participated in a developers' forum to go through requests and questions on the app and problem-solve challenges and issues together. The students also interpreted various data sets, tracking the number of times the app was downloaded and monitoring the number of total potential users, making possible an improved next iteration of the app.

The Future of Learning Technologies

Although these examples help provide understanding of the current state of educational technologies, it is also important to note the research being done on early stage educational technology and how this research might be applied more widely in the future to learning.

As part of their work in cyberlearning, the National Science Foundation (NSF) is researching opportunities offered by integrating emerging technologies with advances in the learning sciences. Following are examples of the projects being funded by the NSF as part of this effort:

Increased use of games and simulations to give students the experience of working together on a project without leaving their classrooms. Students are involved actively in a situation that feels urgent and must decide what to measure and how to analyze data in order to solve a challenging problem. Examples include RoomQuake, in which an entire classroom becomes a scaled-down simulation of an earthquake. As speakers play the sounds of an earthquake, the students can take readings on simulated seismographs at different locations in the room, inspect an emerging fault line, and stretch twine to identify the epicenter. Another example is Robot-Assisted Language Learning in Education (RALL-E), in which students learning Mandarin converse with a robot that exhibits a range of facial expressions and gestures, coupled with language dialogue software. Such robots will allow students to engage in a social role-playing experience with a new language without the usual anxieties of speaking a new language. The RALL-E also encourages cultural awareness while encouraging good use of language skills and building student confidence through practice.

New ways to connect physical and virtual interaction with learning technologies that bridge the tangible and the abstract. For example, the In Touch With Molecules project has students manipulate a physical ball-and-stick model of a molecule such as hemoglobin, while a camera senses the model and visualizes it with related scientific phenomena, such as the energy field around the molecule. Students' tangible engagement with a physical model is connected to more abstract, conceptual models, supporting students' growth of understanding. Toward a similar goal, elementary school students sketch pictures of mathematical situations by using a pen on a tablet surface with representational tools and freehand sketching, much as they would on paper. Unlike with paper, they easily copy, move, group, and transform their pictures and representations in ways that help them to express what they are learning about mathematics. These can be shared with the teacher, and, via artificial intelligence, the computer can help the teacher see patterns in the sketches and support the teacher's using student expression as a powerful instructional resource.

Interactive three-dimensional imaging software, such as zSpace, is creating potentially transformational learning experiences. With three-dimensional glasses and a stylus, students are able to work with a wide range of images from the layers of the earth to the human heart. The zSpace program's noble failure feature allows students constructing a motor or building a battery to make mistakes and retry, learning throughout the process. Although the content and curriculum are supplied, teachers can customize and tailor lesson plans to fit the needs of their classes. This type of versatile technology allows students to work with objects schools typically would not be able to afford, providing a richer, more engaging learning experience.

Augmented reality (AR) as a new way of investigating our context and history. In the Cyberlearning: Transforming Education EXP project, researchers are addressing how and for what purposes AR technologies can be used to support the learning of critical inquiry strategies and processes. The question is being explored in the context of history education and the Summarizing, Contextualizing, Inferring, Monitoring, and Corroborating (SCIM-C) framework developed for historical inquiry education. A combined hardware and software platform is being built to support SCIM-C pedagogy. Students use a mobile device with AR to augment their "field" experience at a local historical site. In addition to experiencing the site as it exists, AR technology allows students to view and experience the site from several social perspectives and to view its structure and uses across several time periods. Research focuses on the potential of AR technology in inquiry-based fieldwork for disciplines in which analysis of change across time is important to promote understanding of how very small changes across long periods of time may add up to very large changes.

Across these examples, we see that learning is not contained within screens or classrooms and that technology can enrich how students engage in the world around them.

To see additional examples of cyberlearning, visit The Center for Innovative Research in CyberLearning.[14]

Bringing Equity to Learning through Technology

Closing the Digital Use Divide

Traditionally, the *digital divide* in education referred to schools and communities in which access to devices and Internet connectivity were either unavailable or unaffordable.[15] Although there is still much work to be done, great progress has been made providing connectivity and device access. The modernization of the federal **E-rate program** has made billions of dollars available to provide high-speed wireless access in schools across the country.

Future Ready Learning

> **E-Rate Program: Source of Funding for Connectivity**
>
> The Schools and Libraries Universal Service Support Program, commonly known as the E-rate program, is a source of federal funding for Internet connectivity for U.S. schools and libraries. Created by Congress in 1996, E-rate provides schools and libraries with discounted Internet service on the basis of need. The program was modernized in 2014 to ensure there is sufficient funding available to meet the need for robust wireless connectivity within schools and high-speed connectivity to schools. For more information about E-rate, visit the website of the Federal Communications Commission (FCC).

DIGITAL USE DIVIDE

While essential, closing the digital divide alone will not transform learning. We must also close the digital use divide by ensuring all students understand how to use technology as a tool to engage in creative, productive, life-long learning rather than simply consuming passive content.

However, we have to be cognizant of a new digital divide—the disparity between students who use technology to create, design, build, explore, and collaborate and those who simply use technology to consume media passively.[16,17,18,19]

On its own, access to connectivity and devices does not guarantee access to engaging educational experiences or a quality education.[20] Without thoughtful intervention and attention to the way technology is used for learning, the digital use divide could grow even as access to technology in schools increases.[21,22,23,24]

Providing Technology Accessibility for All Learners

Learning experiences enabled by technology should be accessible for all learners, including those with special needs. Supports to make learning accessible should be built into learning software and hardware by default. The approach of including accessibility features from the beginning of the development process, also known as *universal design*, is a concept well established in the field of architecture. Modern public buildings include features such as ramps, automatic doors, or braille on signs to make them accessible by everyone. In the same way, features such as text-to-speech, speech-to-text, enlarged font sizes, color contrast, dictionaries, and glossaries should be built into educational hardware and software to make learning accessible to everyone.

Three main principles drive application of universal design for learning (UDL)[25,26,27]:

1. **Provide multiple means of representation so that students can approach information in more than one way.** Examples include digital books, specialized software and websites, and screen readers that include features such as text-to-speech, changeable color contrast, alterable text size, or selection of different reading levels.
2. **Provide multiple means of expression so that all students can demonstrate and express what they know.** Examples include providing options in how they express their learning, where appropriate, which can include options such as writing, online concept mapping, or speech-to-text programs.
3. **Provide multiple means of engagement to stimulate interest in and motivation for learning.** Examples include providing options among several different learning activities or content for a particular competency or skill and providing opportunities for increased collaboration or scaffolding.

Digital learning tools can offer more flexibility and learning supports than can traditional formats. Using mobile devices, laptops, and networked systems, educators are better able to personalize and customize learning experiences to align with the needs of each student. They also can expand communication with mentors, peers, and colleagues through social media tools. Digital tools also can make it possible to modify content, such as raising or lowering the complexity level of a text or changing the presentation rate.

At a higher level of engagement, digital tools such as games, websites, and digital books can be designed to meet the needs of a range of learners, from novices to experts. Learners with little understanding might approach the experience first as a novice and then move up to an intermediate level as they gain more knowledge and skills. One example is McGill University's The Brain From Top to Bottom. The site includes options to engage with the content as a beginner, intermediate, or advanced learner and adjusts the learning activities accordingly.

To help in the selection of appropriate universally designed products and tools, the National Center on Universal Design for Learning has developed a resource linking each guideline to information about digital supports that can help a teacher put UDL into practice.

Reaching All Learners:
Tools For Udl

Developed with support from the U.S. Department of Education, the tools listed here were designed to help educators implement UDL principles into classroom practice and make learning activities more accessible:

- Nimble Assessment Systems developed Nimble Tools to deliver standard versions of assessment instruments that are tailored with embedded accommodation tools to meet the specific needs of students with disabilities. Some examples of the accommodation tools include a keyboard with custom keyboard overlays, the capacity of the system to read text aloud for students, an on-screen avatar presenting questions in American Sign Language (ASL) or Signed English, and the magnification of text and images for students with visual impairments.

26 Office of Educational Technology

- The Information Research Corporation developed eTouchSciences, an integrated software and hardware assistive technology platform to support STEM learning among middle school students with (or without) visual impairments. The product includes a haptic sensing controller device to provide real-time tactile, visual, and audio feedback. See video.
- Filament Games developed the Game-enhanced Interactive Life Science suite of learning games to introduce middle school students to key scientific concepts and practices in the life sciences. These games, aligned to UDL, provide students with multiple means of representation, expression, and engagement and provide assistive features such as in-game glossaries and optional voice-over for all in-game text. See video.
- Institute for Disabilities Research and Training developed the myASL Quizmaker to provide Web-based assessments for deaf or hard of hearing students who use ASL. This product provides automatic ASL graphic and video translations for students; enables teachers to create customized tests, exams, and quizzes that are scored automatically; and provides teacher reports with grades and corrected quizzes. See video.

Design in Practice:
Indiana School District Adopts UDL for All Students

Bartholomew Consolidated School Corporation is a public school district in Columbus, Indiana, serving approximately 12,000 students. The student population consists of 13 percent in special education, 50 percent receive free or reduced-price lunch, and more than 54 languages are spoken. UDL has been helpful as a decision-making tool in the deployment of technologies such as computers and other networked devices. The UDL guidelines help educators determine what strategies, accessible technologies, and teaching methods will enable all students to achieve lesson goals.

In one instance, a social studies teacher held an online discussion during a presidential debate. Realizing that some students were not taking part in class discussions, the teacher used technology to provide multiple means of representation, expression, and engagement. Some students who were reluctant to speak up in a face-to-face setting felt safe to do so online, becoming engaged participants in the class discussion.

Since they adopted a universal design approach, graduation rates increased by 8 percent for general education students and 22 percent for special education students. Also, the number of students taking and passing Advanced Placement tests has increased.

Physical Spaces and Technology-Enabled Learning

Blended learning and other models of learning enabled by technology require educators to rethink how they organize physical spaces to facilitate best collaborative learning using digital tools. Considerations include the following:

- Are the design and layout of the physical space dynamic and flexible enough to facilitate the technology-enabled learning models and practices selected? Can a space in which an educator delivers whole-class instruction also be shifted to facilitate individual online practice and research?
- Do the physical spaces align in their ability to facilitate individual and collaborative work? When practices such as project-based learning require students to be working together with multiple devices for research and presentation building, is the space as useful as when individual learners need time and space to connect with information and experts online for personalized learning?
- Can the physical spaces and tools be shaped to provide multiple contexts and learning experiences such as Wi-Fi access for outdoor classrooms? Are library spaces able to become laboratories? Can a space used as a history lecture hall for one class become a maker space for engineering the next period?

For more information and tools for aligning physical spaces, visit the Centre for Effective Learning Environments and the Clayton Christensen Institute's Blended Learning Universe.

28   Office of Educational Technology

> **Innovation from the Ground up: Denver School for Science and Technology (DSST) Uses Space to Promote Student Achievement**
>
> The DSST is an innovative high school located in Stapleton, Colorado, a redeveloped neighborhood near downtown Denver. Behind the bright colors and unique geometry of spaces at DSST lies a relationship to the way academic subjects are taught and community is formed at the high school. The school is designed to be flexible and aims to support student achievement through the design of its physical spaces.
>
> The school features a series of gathering spaces that can be used for various academic and social purposes throughout the day. The largest of the gathering areas, near the school's entrance, is where the school's daily morning meeting for both students and faculty is held. Student and faculty announcements, skits, and other community functions are all encouraged in this communal setting.
>
> Each of the three academic pods also includes informal spaces for gathering, studying, and socializing. These academic clusters are linked by a galleria, or large open hallway, that is lined with skylights and also serves as a gathering place for students and faculty members.
>
> DSST has demonstrated results in the academic achievement of its students and in its attendance record. In 2005, the school's founding Grade 9 class was the highest scoring Grade 9 class in Denver in mathematics and the second highest scoring class in reading and writing. DSST was also the only Denver high school to earn a significant growth rating on the Colorado Student Assessment Program test scores from one year to the next. Student attendance at the school is typically about 96 percent.

Recommendations

- **States, districts, and post-secondary institutions should develop and implement learning resources that embody the flexibility and power of technology to create equitable and accessible learning ecosystems that make learning possible everywhere and all the time for all students.**

  Whether creating learning resources internally, drawing on collaborative networks, or using traditional procurement procedures, institutions should insist on the use of resources and the design of learning experiences that use UD practices to ensure accessibility and increased equity of learning opportunities.

- **States, districts, and post-secondary institutions should develop and implement learning resources that use technology to embody design principles from the learning sciences.**
Educational systems have access to cutting-edge learning sciences research. To make better use of the existing body of research literature, however, educators and researchers will need to work together to determine the most useful dissemination methods for easy incorporation and synthesis of research findings into teachers' instructional practices.

- **States, districts, and post-secondary institutions should take inventory of and align all learning technology resources to intended educational outcomes. using this inventory, they should document all possible learner pathways to expertise, such as combinations of formal and informal learning, blended learning, and distance learning.**
Without thoughtful accounting of the available tools and resources within formal and informal learning spaces within a community, matching learners to high-quality pathways to expertise is left to chance. Such an undertaking will require increased capacity within organizations that have never considered such a mapping of educational pathways. To aid in these efforts, networks such as LRNG, the Hive Learning Networks, and education innovation clusters can serve as models for cross-stakeholder collaboration in the interest of best using existing resources to present learners with pathways to learning and expertise.

- **Education stakeholders should develop a born accessible standard of learning resource design to help educators select and evaluate learning resources for accessibility and equity of learning experience.**
Born accessible is a play on the term born digital and is used to convey the idea that materials that are born digital also can and should be born accessible. If producers adopt current industry standards for producing educational materials, materials will be accessible out of the box. Using the principles and research-base of UD and UDL, this standard would serve as a commonly accepted framework and language around design for accessibility and offer guidance to ven-

30 Office of Educational Technology

dors and third-party technology developers in interactions with states, districts, and institutions of higher education.

2. TEACHING - TEACHING WITH TECHNOLOGY

GOAL: Educators will be supported by technology that connects them to people, data, content, resources, expertise, and learning experiences that can empower and inspire them to provide more effective teaching for all learners.

Technology offers the opportunity for teachers to become more collaborative and extend learning beyond the classroom. Educators can create learning communities composed of students; fellow educators in schools, museums, libraries, and after-school programs; experts in various disciplines around the world; members of community organizations; and families. This enhanced collaboration, enabled by technology offers access to instructional materials as well as the resources and tools to create, manage, and assess their quality and usefulness.

To enact this vision, schools need to support teachers in accessing needed technology and in learning how to use it effectively. Although research indicates that teachers have the biggest impact on student learning out of all other school-level factors, we cannot expect individual educators to assume full responsibility for bringing technology-based learning experiences into schools.[1,2,3,4,5] They need continuous, just-in-time support that includes professional development, mentors, and informal collaborations. In fact, more than two thirds of teachers say they would like more technology in their classrooms,[6] and roughly half say that lack of training is one of the biggest barriers to incorporating technology into their teaching.[7]

Institutions responsible for pre-service and in-service professional development for educators should focus explicitly on ensuring all educators are capable of selecting, evaluating, and using appropriate technologies and resources to create experiences that advance student engagement and learning. They also should pay special care to make certain that educators understand the privacy and security concerns associated with technology. This goal cannot be achieved without incorporating technology-based learning into the programs themselves.

For many teacher preparation institutions, state offices of education, and school districts, the transition to technology-enabled preparation and professional development will entail rethinking instructional approaches and techniques, tools, and the skills and expertise of educators who teach in these programs. This rethinking should be based on a deep understanding of the roles and practices of educators in environments in which learning is supported by technology.

Roles and Practices of Educators in Technology-Supported Learning

Technology can empower educators to become co-learners with their students by building new experiences for deeper exploration of content. This enhanced learning experience embodies John Dewey's notion of creating "more mature learners."[8] Side-by-side, students and teachers can become engineers of collaboration, designers of learning experiences, leaders, guides, and catalysts of change.[9,10] Following are some descriptions of these educator roles and examples of how technology can play an integral part.

Educators can collaborate far beyond the walls of their schools. Through technology, educators are no longer restricted to collaborating only with other educators in their schools. They now can connect with other educators and experts across their communities or around the world to expand their perspectives and create opportunities for student learning. They can connect with community organizations specializing in real-world concerns to design learning experiences that allow students to explore local needs and priorities. All of these elements make classroom learning more relevant and **authentic**.

In addition, by using tools such as videoconferencing, online chats, and social media sites, educators, from large urban to small rural districts, can connect and collaborate with experts and peers from around the world to form online professional learning communities.

Authentic Learning

Authentic learning experiences are those that place learners in the context of real-world experiences and challenges.[11]

---

32   Office of Educational Technology

Building Communities for Educators: International Education and Resource Network (iEARN) Fosters Global Collaborative Teaching and Learning

Through technology, educators can create global communities of practice that enable their students to collaborate with students around the world. Technology enables collaborative teaching regardless of geographic location, as demonstrated by the global nature of the Solar Cooking Project organized by earth and environmental science teacher Kathy Bosiak.

Bosiak teaches at Lincolnton High School in Lincolnton, North Carolina, and is a contributing educator for iEARN, a nonprofit organization made up of more than 30,000 schools and youth organizations in more than 140 countries. iEARN offers technology-enabled resources that enable teachers and students around the world to collaborate on educational projects, all designed and facilitated by teachers and students to fit their curriculum, classroom needs, and schedules.[17]

In addition to its student programs, iEARN offers professional face-to-face workshops for teachers that combine technology and continued engagement through virtual networks and online professional learning opportunities. The workshops focus on the skills needed to engage in Internet-based collaborative learning projects, including peer review, team building, joining regional and international learning communities, and developing project-based curricula that integrate national education standards.

Educators can design highly engaging and relevant learning experiences through technology. Educators have nearly limitless opportunities to select and apply technology in ways that connect with the interests of their students and achieve their learning goals. For example, a classroom teacher beginning a new unit on fractions might choose to have his students play a learning game such as Factor Samurai, Wuzzit Trouble, or Sushi Monster as a way to introduce the concept. Later, the teacher might direct students to practice the concept by using manipulatives so they can start to develop some grounded ideas about equivalence.[12]

To create an engaging and relevant lesson that requires students to use content knowledge and critical thinking skills, an educator might ask students to solve a community problem by using technology. Students may create an online community forum, public presentation, or call to action related to their proposed solution. They can use social networking platforms to gather information and suggestions of resources from their contacts. Students can draft and present their work by using animated presentation software or through multimedia formats such as videos and blogs. This work can be shared in virtual discussions with content experts and stored in online learning portfolios.

A school without access to science labs or equipment can use virtual simulations to offer learners experiences that are currently unavailable because of limited resources. In addition, these simulations are safe places for students to learn and practice effective processes before they conduct research in the field. Just as technology can enhance science learning for schools lacking equipment, it can enable deep learning once students are in the field as well. Students can collect data for their own use via mobile devices and probes and sync their findings with those of collaborators and researchers anywhere in the world to create large, authentic data sets for study.

Educators can lead the evaluation and implementation of new technologies for learning. Lower price points for learning technologies make it easier for educators to pilot new technologies and approaches before attempting a school-wide adoption. These educators also can lead and model practices around evaluating new tools for privacy and security risks, as well as compliance with federal privacy regulations. (For more on these regulations, see Section 5: Infrastructure). Teacher-leaders with a broad understanding of their own educational technology needs, as well as those of students and colleagues, can design short pilot studies that impact a small number of students to ensure the chosen technology and the implementation approach have the desired outcomes. This allows schools to gain experience with and confidence in these technologies before committing entire schools or districts to purchases and use.

Teacher-leaders and those with experience supporting learning with technology can work with administrators to determine how to share their learning with other teachers. They also can provide support to their peers by answering questions and modeling practical uses of technology to support learning.

Evaluating Technology through Rapid Cycle Technology Evaluations

As schools continue to invest heavily in education technology, there is a pressing need to generate evidence about the effectiveness of these investments and also to develop evaluation tools that developers and practitioners can use to conduct their own evaluations that take less time and incur lower costs than do traditional evaluations. The U.S. Department of Education is funding a rapid cycle technology evaluation project that will design research approaches for evaluating apps, platforms, and tools; conduct pilots and disseminate the resulting short reports; and create an interactive guide and implementation support tools for conducting rapid cycle technology evaluations to be used by schools, districts, developers, and researchers.

Rapid cycle technology evaluations will help provide results in a timely manner so that evidence of effectiveness is available to school and district leaders when they need to make purchasing decisions.

Teach to Lead: Developing Teachers as Leaders

Teach to Lead, a joint program of the National Board for Professional Teaching Standards, ASCD, and the U.S. Department of Education, aims to advance student outcomes by expanding opportunities for teacher leadership, particularly opportunities that allow teachers to stay in the classroom. With the help of supporting organizations, Teach to Lead provides a platform for teacher-leaders and allies across the country (and around the world) to create and expand on their ideas.

Teach to Lead participants are invested personally in the development of their teacher leadership action plans because the ideas are their own. Participants identify a current problem within their school, district, or community and develop a theory of action to solve that problem. Since its inception in March 2014, Teach to Lead has engaged more than 3,000 educators, in person and virtually through its online platform, with more than 850 teacher leadership ideas spanning 38 states. Teach to Lead regional Teacher Leadership Summits brought together teams of teacher-leaders and supporting organizations to strengthen their teacher leadership ideas, share resources, and develop the skills necessary to make their projects a reality.

Marcia Hudson and Serena Stock, teacher-leaders at Avondale Elementary School in Michigan, identified a need for teacher-led professional development at their school and created a module for teachers to collect and analyze student outcome data to drive new professional development opportunities. The teachers now are holding engagement meetings with teacher-leaders to develop and fund professional development and data collection further.

Future Ready Learning

> Chris Todd teaches at Windsor High School in Connecticut and is a Teacher-Leaderin-Residence for the Connecticut State Department of Education. Chris's team is developing the Connecticut Educator Network, a database of teacher-leaders who are readily available to advise on policy development. The group intends to provide training and policy briefings to continue to hone the teachers' leadership skills.

Educators can be guides, facilitators, and motivators of learners. The information available to educators through high-speed Internet means teachers do not have to be content experts across all possible subjects. By understanding how to help students access online information, engage in simulations of real-world events, and use technology to document their world, educators can help their students examine problems and think deeply about their learning. Using digital tools, they can help students create spaces to experiment, iterate, and take intellectual risks with all of the information they need at their fingertips.[13,14] Teachers also can take advantage of these spaces for themselves as they navigate new understandings of teaching that move beyond a focus on *what* they teach to *how* students can learn and show what they know.

Deepening Student Understanding:
Using Interactive Video to Improve Learning

Reflective teachers can search for new ways for their students to engage with technology effectively, especially when students are not optimizing their learning experiences. Every year at Crocker Middle School, Ryan Carroll would ask his sixth-grade world history students to watch a variety of online videos for homework. He found that no matter how entertaining or interesting the videos were, his students were not retaining much of the information being presented, and often they were confused about key concepts. After learning about Zaption, a teaching tool funded by the U.S. Department of Education, Carroll realized his students could get more out of the videos he assigned. Using Zaption's interactive video platform, he added images, text, drawings, and questions to clarify tricky concepts and check for understanding as students watched the video.

Zaption's analytics allow educators to review individual student responses and class-wide engagement data quickly, giving greater insight on how students are mastering key concepts as they watch and enabling teachers to address misconceptions quickly.

Educators can help students make connections across subject areas and decide on the best tools for collecting and showcasing learning through activities such as contributing to online forums, producing webinars, or publishing their findings to relevant websites. These teachers can advise students on how to build an online learning portfolio to demonstrate their learning progression. Within these portfolios, students can catalog resources that they can review and share as they move into deeper and more complex thinking about a particular issue. With such portfolios, learners will be able to transition through their education careers with robust examples of their learning histories as well as evidence of what they know and are able to do. These become compelling records of achievement as they apply for entrance into career and technical education institutions, community colleges, and four-year colleges and universities or for employment.

Co-Learning in the Classroom: Teacher User Groups Provide Peer Learning for Adult Education Educators

Recognizing the power of virtual peer learning, the U.S. Department of Education's Office of Career, Technical, and Adult Education has funded projects that have established teacher user groups to explore the introduction of openly licensed educational resources into adult education. This model of professional development recognizes that virtual peer learning can support teachers to change their practice and provide leadership and growth opportunities. The small groups of far-flung teachers work with a group moderator to identify, use, and review openly licensed resources in mathematics, science, and English language arts.

Reviews referenced the embedded evaluation criteria in OER Commons, a repository of open educational resources (OER) that can be used or reused freely at no cost and that align to the College- and Career-Readiness mathematics and language arts and Next Generation Science Standards. They also included practice tips for teaching the content to adult learners. The reviews are posted on OER Commons and tagged as Adult Basic Education or Adult English for Speakers of Other Languages to facilitate the discovery by other teachers of these high-quality, standards-aligned teaching and learning materials.

Educators can be co-learners with students and peers. The availability of technology-based learning tools gives educators a chance be co-learners alongside their students and peers. Although educators should not be expected to know everything there is to know in their disciplines, they should be expected to model how to leverage available tools to engage content with curiosity and a mindset bent on problem solving and how to be co-creators of knowledge. In short, teachers should be the students they hope to inspire in their classrooms.[15]

> ## Learning out Loud Online: Jennie Magiera, District Chief Technology Officer and Classroom Teacher
>
> Planning a lesson on how elevation and other environmental influences affect the boiling point of water, Jennie Magiera realized that many of the students in her fourth-grade class in Cook County, Illinois, had never seen a mountain. So Magiera reached out to her network of fellow educators through social media to find a teacher in a mountainous area of the country interested in working with her on the lesson.
>
> Soon, Magiera and a teacher in Denver were collaborating on a lesson plan. Using tablets and online videoconferencing, the students in Denver showed Magiera's students the mountains that they could see outside of their classrooms every day. After a discussion of elevation, the two teachers engaged their students in a competition to see which class could boil water faster. By interacting with students in the other class, Magiera's students became engaged more deeply in the project, which led them to develop a richer understanding of ecosystems and environments than they might have otherwise.

Educators can become catalysts to serve the underserved. Technology provides a new opportunity for traditionally underserved populations to have equitable access to high-quality educational experiences. When connectivity and access are uneven, the digital divide in education is widened, undermining the positive aspects of learning with technology.

All students deserve equal access to (1) the Internet, high-quality content, and devices when they need them and (2) educators skilled at teaching in a technology-enabled learning environment. When this occurs, it increases the likelihood that learners have personalized learning experiences, choice in tools and activities, and access to adaptive assessments that identify their individual abilities, needs, and interests.

Connected Educators: Exemplars

Technology can transform learning when used by teachers who know how to create engaging and effective learning experiences for their students. In 2014, a group of educators collaborated on a report entitled, *Teaching in the Connected Learning Classroom*. Not a how-to guide or a set of discrete tools, it draws together narratives from a group of educators within the National Writing Project who are working to implement and refine practices around technology-enabled learning. The goal was to rethink, iterate on, and assess how education can be made more relevant to today's youth.

Producing Student Films with Online Audiences: Katie Mckay: Lights, Camera, Social Action!

In Katie McKay's diverse, fourth-grade transitional bilingual class, encouraging her students to work together on a project helped them build literacy skills while simultaneously giving them the opportunity to pursue culturally relevant questions related to equity.

McKay recognized that her students were searching for the language to talk about complicated issues of race, gender, power, and equity. To address the competing priorities of preparing her students for the state test and providing them with authentic opportunities to develop as readers and writers, McKay started a project-based unit on the history of discrimination in the United States.

Students worked in heterogeneously mixed groups to develop comic strips that eventually were turned into two videos, one showing micro-aggressions students commonly see today and one about the history of discrimination in the United States. The movie on micro-aggressions portrayed current scenarios that included characters who acted as agents of change, bravely and respectfully defending the rights of others.

According to McKay, students who previously were disengaged found themselves drawn into the classroom community in meaningful and engaging ways.

While reflecting on this unit, McKay wrote: "We were not only working to promote tolerance and appreciation for diversity in our community. We also were resisting an oppressive educational context. In the midst of the pressure to perform on tests that were isolating and divisive, we united in collaborative work that required critical thinking and troubleshooting. In a climate that valued silence, antiquated skills, and high-stakes testing, we engaged in peer-connected learning that highlighted 21st century skills and made an impact on our community."[18]

Just-in-Time Learning: Janelle Bence: How Do I Teach What I Do Not Know?

Texas teacher Janelle Bence was looking for new ways to engage and challenge her students, the majority of whom are English language learners from low-income families. After observing her students' motivation to persist through game challenges, she wondered if games held a key to getting them similarly engaged in classwork. After attending a session on gaming at a National Writing Project Annual Meeting, Bence was inspired to incorporate gaming into her classroom. She did not know anything about gaming and so, as is the case for many teachers seeking to bridge the gap between students' social interests and academic subjects, she had to figure out how to teach what she did not know.

Bence started by reading a book about using video games to teach literacy. As she read, she shared her ideas and questions on her blog and talked to other educators, game designers, and systems thinkers. Through these collaborations, she decided that by creating games, her students would be required to become informed experts in the content of the game as well as to become powerful storytellers.

As she explored games as a way to make academic tasks more engaging and accessible for her students, Bence found it was important to take advantage of professional learning and peer networks, take risks by moving from a passive consumer of knowledge to actually trying the tasks that she planned to use with students, and put herself in her students' shoes. Bence shared that "finding a way to connect to students and their passions—by investigating what makes them tick and bridging [those passions] to academic tasks— educators are modeling risks that encourage the same behavior in their learners."[19]

Building Student Agency: Jason Sellers: Text-Based Video Games

Aware of the popularity of video games among his students, and as a longtime fan of video games himself, teacher Jason Sellers decided to use gaming to develop his 10th-grade students' ability to use descriptive imagery in their writing. Specifically, Sellers introduced his students to text-based video games. Unlike graphics-based games in which users can view graphics and maneuver through the game by using controller buttons, text-based games require players to read descriptions and maneuver by typing commands such as "go north" or "unlock the door with a key."

Sellers decided his students could practice using descriptive imagery by developing their own text-based games.

Using tutorials and other resources found on Playfic, an interactive fiction online community, Sellers created lessons that allowed students to play and eventually create interactive fiction games. Prior to the creation of the games, Sellers's class analyzed several essays that skillfully used descriptive imagery, such as David Foster Wallace's *A Ticket to the Fair*, and composed short pieces of descriptive writing about their favorite locations in San Francisco.

Students then transferred their newly honed descriptive storytelling skills to the development of an entertaining text-based game. Because Sellers's students wanted to develop games their peers would want to play, they focused on ways to make their games more appealing, including, as Sellers described, "using familiar settings (local or popular culture), familiar characters (fellow students or popular culture), and tricky puzzles."[20]

According to Sellers, this project allowed students to work through problems collaboratively with peers from their classroom and the Playfic online community and motivated them to move beyond basic requirements to create projects worthy of entering competitions.

Rethinking Teacher Preparation

Teachers need to leave their teacher preparation programs with a solid understanding of how to use technology to support learning. Effective use of technology is not an optional add-on or a skill that we simply can expect teachers to pick up once they get into the classroom. Teachers need to know how to use technology to realize each state's learning standards from day one. Most states have adopted and are implementing college- and career-ready standards to ensure that their students graduate high school with the knowledge and skills necessary to succeed.

For states that have voluntarily adopted the Common Core State Standards, there are more than 100 direct mentions of technology expectations, and similar expectations exist in states adopting other college- and career-ready standards. Many federal, state, and district leaders have made significant investments in providing infrastructure and devices to schools. Without a well-prepared and empowered teaching force, our country will not experience the full benefits of those investments for transformative learning.

Schools should be able to rely on teacher preparation programs to ensure that new teachers come to them prepared to use technology in meaningful ways. No new teacher exiting a preparation program should require remediation by his or her hiring school or district. Instead, every new teacher should be prepared to model how to select and use the most appropriate apps and tools to support learning and evaluate these tools against basic privacy and security standards. It is inaccurate to assume that because pre-service teachers are tech savvy in their personal lives they will understand how to use technology effectively to support learning without specific training and practice. This expertise does not come through the completion of one educational technology course separate from other methods courses but through the inclusion of experiences with educational technology in all courses modeled by the faculty in teacher preparation programs.

Aligning Education with Technology Standards:
University of Michigan

Pre-service teachers at the University of Michigan School of Education are experiencing the kind of learning with technology their students will one day know. The curriculum addresses each of the five ISTE Standards for Teachers[21] and aligns with skills from the Partnership for 21st Century Skills.[22] Each standard also has related course projects designed for teacher candidates to use technology actively to demonstrate their understanding of the material through practice and feedback. For example, teacher candidates are asked to design and teach a 20-minute webinar for fourth graders that is based on Next Generation Science Standards and to design and teach a lesson that uses technology and meets the needs of their learners as part of their student teaching placement.

Preparing to Teach in Technology-Enabled Environments:
Saint Leo University

A 2006 survey of Saint Leo University teacher preparation program alumni showed satisfaction with their preparation with one notable exception—technology in the classroom. As a result, the education department established a long-term goal of making technology innovation a keystone of its program. Saint Leo faculty redesigned their program on the basis of the Technological Pedagogical and Content Knowledge model, in which pre-service teachers learned to blend content, pedagogical, and technological knowledge in their PK–12 instruction.[23]

Faculty developed their expertise with different technologies so that every course models the use of technology to support teaching and learning. The school built an education technology lab where teacher candidates can practice using devices, apps, and other digital learning resources. Students regularly reflect on their experience using technology to increase effectiveness and efficiency as well as its value in the learning process.

Perhaps most notably, Saint Leo ensures all pre-service teachers have basic technologies available at their student teaching placements. Each pre-service teacher is given a digital backpack with a tablet, portable projector, speakers, and a portable interactive whiteboard. A student response system is also available for pre-service teachers to use in their field placements.

Advancing Knowledge and Practice of Assistive Technologies for New Teachers: Illinois State University

Illinois State University's Department of Special Education is one of the largest special education training programs in the nation. Recognizing the value of assistive technology in meeting the needs of each student, the special education teacher preparation program at the University includes an extensive emphasis on selection and use of assistive technologies.

Classroom learning is brought to life through ongoing clinical and field-based experiences in schools and at the university's Special Education Assistive Technology Center. The center provides hands-on experiences to pre-service teachers enrolled in the special education programs at Illinois as well as opportunities for teachers, school administrators, family members, and businesses to learn about assistive technologies. Furthermore, faculty work in partnership with a variety of public, private, and residential schools to enhance student field experiences and provide opportunities for students to work with learners with a range of disabilities and in a variety of settings, including rural, urban, and suburban areas.

Building Digital Literacy in Teaching: University of Rhode Island (URI)

A critical aspect of ensuring that young Americans learn appropriate digital literacy skills is equipping educators at all levels with the same skills. To that end, URI offers a graduate certificate in digital literacy for graduate students, classroom teachers, librarians, and college faculty. By targeting a broad audience to participate in the program, URI is expanding the number of educators with the professional capacity to help students to learn, access, analyze, create, reflect, and take action using digital tools, texts, and technologies in all aspects of their lives.

During the program, students are introduced to key theories of digital literacy in inquiry-driven learning and given time to experiment with and explore a wide range of digital texts, tools, and technologies. In collaboration with a partner, they create a project-based instructional unit that enables them to demonstrate their digital skills in the context of an authentic learning situation. Throughout the program, students participate in hands-on, minds-on learning experiences; participants build a deeper understanding of digital literacy while developing practical skills and have time to reflect on the implications of the digital shift in education, leisure, citizenship, and society.

In its evaluation of the program, URI has found that participants experienced a dramatic increase in digital skills associated with implementing project-based learning with digital media and technology. Their understanding of digital literacy also shifted to focus more on inquiry, collaboration, and creativity.

Fostering Ongoing Professional Learning

The same imperatives for teacher preparation apply to ongoing professional learning. Professional learning and development programs should transition to support and develop educators' identities as fluent users of technology; creative and collaborative problem solvers; and adaptive, socially aware experts throughout their careers. Programs also should address challenges when it comes to using technology learning: ongoing professional development should be job embedded and available just in time.[16]

Increasing Online Professional Learning:
Connected Educator Month Builds Collaboration across the Country

Connected Educator Month, part of the U.S. Department of Education's Connected Educators project, began with a monthlong online conference that included a centralized guiding structure, kickoff and closing events, engagement resources, and an open calendar to which organizations of all types could submit professional learning events and activities. Educators used these resources and the calendar to create their own professional development plan for the month. Available activities included webinars, Twitter chats, forum discussions, and actively moderated blog discussions based on personal learning needs and interests.

In the first year, more than 170 organizations provided more than 450 events and activities, with educators completing an estimated 90,000 hours of professional learning across the month. More than 4 million people followed the #ce12 hashtag on Twitter, generating 1.4 million impressions per day.

Now led by partner organizations from the original Connected Educators project— American Institutes for Research (AIR), Grunwald Associates LLC, and Powerful Learning Practice—Connected Educator Month features more than 800 organizations and has provided more than 1,000 events and activities. Australia, New Zealand, and Norway hosted their own iterations of Connected Educator Month, and educators in more than 125 countries participated in some way.

Putting Learning in Teachers' Hands:
Denver Public Schools Personalizes Professional Development

In 2014, 80 teachers from 45 schools engaged in the pilot year of Project Cam Opener, an initiative of the Personalized Professional Learning team in Denver Public Schools. Now in its second year with 425 teachers and leaders, Project Cam Opener allows educators to record their teaching with customized video toolkits and share those videos for self-reflection and feedback within an online community of practice.

In the program's pilot year, the first 80 teachers recorded hundreds of videos using tools such as Swivls, iPads, high-definition webcams, and microphones. The videos were uploaded to private YouTube channels and shared via a Google+ community for feedback. For many of these teachers, it was the first time that they had seen the teaching practices of other teachers in their district. The videos sparked daily conversations and sharing of ideas.

Three measures are used to determine the effectiveness of Project Cam Opener: engagement, retention, and observation. In the first end-of-year survey, 90 percent of respondents said that taking part in Project Cam Opener made them more engaged in their own professional learning and

Future Ready Learning

growth. In addition, not a single teacher from the pilot group left Denver Public Schools after their year with Project Cam Opener (the overall district rate of turnover is 20 percent). Although teacher observation scores are harder to attribute to this project specifically, the growth of this cohort of teachers outpaced that of their non–Project Cam Opener counterparts, according to the district's Framework for Effective Teaching.

Micro-Credentialing Teacher Learning: Kettle Moraine Introduces Teacher-Led Professional Learning

Kettle Moraine School District in Wisconsin is creating a professional learning environment in which practicing teachers can be the masters and architects of their own learning. Using the Digital Promise educator micro-credentialing framework as a guide (for more information on Digital Promise's micro-credentialing work, see Section 4), teachers in the district take a technology proficiency self-assessment, which they use as a baseline for their personal professional growth. The teachers then work by themselves and in collaborative teams to develop specific professional learning goals aligned to district strategic goals, which they submit to district leadership for approval.

Once these goals are approved, the teachers establish measurable benchmarks against which they can assess their progress. Both the goals and benchmarks are mapped to specific competencies, which, in turn, are tied to micro-credentials that can be earned once teachers have demonstrated mastery. Demonstrations of mastery include specific samples of their work, personal reflections, classroom artifacts, and student work and reflections, which are submitted via Google Forms to a committee of 7 to 10 teachers who review them and award micro-credentials.

Currently, 49 staff members are working to earn a micro-credential for personalized learning, which requires them to conduct their own background research and engage in regularly scheduled Twitter chats as well as blogging, networking, and other forms of self-guided learning using technology. Many also have begun to engage with teachers across the country, allowing them to give and receive ideas, resources, and support.

Embracing the Unconference: Going to Edcamp

An educator attending an Edcamp event engages in a professional learning experience vastly different from traditional professional development. Sessions are built on the interests and needs of the people who attend and are created on the day by using a cloud-based collaborative application that is open to all (including those unable to participate in person). Each teacher chooses which sessions to attend on the basis of individual interests or needs.

Because using technology in learning effectively is one of the challenges facing teachers, sessions frequently are organized around sharing practices and overcoming common challenges when improving practices around the use of technology. Teachers collaborate to overcome challenges together, often making connections that lead beyond the single session or day, as partnerships are formed to engage their students with each other. The shared documents created at these events become an archive and resource for whoever attended, in person or virtually.

The first Edcamp was organized in Philadelphia by a group of local educators interested in new unconference (self-organizing) approaches to a conference for professional learning. The model took off, and five years later there have been more than 750 Edcamps all organized by local educators. The enormous popularity of the format has led to the formation of the Edcamp Foundation, a nonprofit organization that will formalize much of the ad hoc support that has been provided to Edcamp organizers until now.

RECOMMENDATIONS

- **Provide pre-service and in-service educators with professional learning experiences powered by technology to increase their digital literacy and enable them to create compelling learning activities that improve learning and teaching, assessment, and instructional practices.**

  To make this goal a reality, teacher preparation programs, school systems, state and local policymakers, and educators should come together in the interest of designing pre- and in-service professional learning opportunities that are aligned specifically with technology expectations outlined within state standards and that are reflective of the increased connectivity of and access to devices in schools. Technology should not be separate from content area learning but used to transform and expand pre- and in-service learning as an integral part of teacher learning.

- **Use technology to provide all learners with online access to effective teaching and better learning opportunities with options in places where they are not otherwise available.** This goal will require leveraging partner organizations and building institutional and teacher capacity to take advantage of free and openly licensed educational content such as that indexed on LearningRegistry.org. Adequate connectivity will increase equitable access to resources, instruction, expertise, and learning pathways regardless of learners' geography, socio-economic status, or other factors that historically may have put them at an educational disadvantage.

- **Develop a teaching force skilled in online and blended instruction.** Our education system continues to see a marked increase in online learning opportunities and blended learning models in traditional schools. To meet the need this represents better, institutions of higher education, school districts, classroom educators, and researchers need to come together to ensure practitioners have access to current information regarding research-supported practices and an understanding of the best use of emerging online technologies to support learning in online and blended spaces.

- **Develop a common set of technology competency expectations for university professors and candidates exiting teacher preparation programs for teaching in technologically enabled schools and post-secondary education institutions.** There should be no uncertainty of whether a learner entering a PK–12 classroom or college lecture hall will encounter a teacher or instructor fully capable of taking advantage of technology to transform learning. Accrediting institutions, advocacy organizations, state policymakers, administrators, and educators have to collaborate on a set of clear and common expectations and credentialing regarding educators' abilities to design and implement technology-enabled learning environments effectively.

3. LEADERSHIP - CREATING A CULTURE AND CONDITIONS FOR INNOVATION AND CHANGE

GOAL: Embed an understanding of technology-enabled education within the roles and responsibilities of education leaders at all levels and set state, regional, and local visions for technology in learning.

Taking full advantage of technology to transform learning requires strong leadership capable of creating a shared vision of which all members of the community feel a part. Leaders who believe they can delegate the articulation of a vision for how technology can support their learning goals to a chief information officer or chief technology officer fundamentally misunderstand how technology can impact learning. Technology alone does not transform learning; rather, technology helps enable transformative learning. The vision begins with a discussion of how and why a community wants to transform learning. Once these goals are clear, technology can be used to open new possibilities for accomplishing the vision that would otherwise be out of reach. Moving to learning enabled by technology can mean a shift in the specific skills and competencies required of leaders. Education leaders need personal experience with learning technologies, an understanding of how to deploy these resources effectively, and a community-wide vision for how technology can improve learning.[1]

Although leadership in technology implementation is needed across all levels of the education system, the need in PK–12 public schools is acute. The 2015 Consortium for School Networking (CoSN) Annual E-rate and Infrastructure Survey found that 55 percent of school systems have not fully met the FCC's short-term goal of 100 megabits per second of Internet bandwidth per 1,000 students. Although we still have progress to make, this is a significant improvement from 19 percent reaching the goal in 2013.[2] Recent changes to the federal E-rate program make funding available to increase connectivity to the remaining schools; however, these transitions will not happen without strong leadership at state, district, and school levels.

Setting National Priorities: President Obama's ConnectED Initiative

In June 2013, President Obama announced the ConnectED initiative, designed to enrich K–12 education for every student in America. ConnectED has four goals:

> 1. Within five years, connect **99** percent of America's students through next-generation broadband and high-speed wireless in their schools and libraries
> 2. Empower teachers with the best technology and training to help them keep pace with changing technological and professional demands
> 3. Provide students with feature-rich educational devices that are price competitive with basic textbooks
> 4. Empower students with digital learning content and experiences aligned with college- and career-ready standards being adopted and implemented by states across America
>
> WhiteHouse.gov has more information on ConnectED. For guidance on how these goals are being operationalized, see the U.S. Department of Education's Future Ready Schools: Building Technology Infrastructure for Learning and the White House's ConnectED resources.

Future Ready Leaders

To help support leaders' move toward creating the technical infrastructure and human capacity necessary to fully implement this vision for transformative learning enabled by technology, the U.S. Department of Education partnered with the Alliance for Excellent Education and more than 40 other partner organizations to launch Future Ready in November 2014. The department also challenged superintendents to indicate their commitment to transform teaching and learning in their districts by signing the Future Ready Pledge. To review the Future Ready Pledge and see which districts have signed, visit http://www.futurereadyschools.org/take-the-pledge.

Future Ready Focus Areas

Selected by synthesizing the best available research and practice knowledge, the four focus areas of Future Ready are collaborative leadership, personalized student learning, robust infrastructure, and personalized professional learning.[3]

Collaborative Leadership

- Education leaders develop a shared vision for how technology can support learning and how to secure appropriate resources to sustain technology initiatives. Leaders seek input from a diverse team of stakeholders to adopt and communicate clear goals for teaching, leading, and learning that are facilitated by technology. They model tolerance for risk and experimentation and create a culture of trust and innovation.

- Leaders communicate with all stakeholders by using appropriate media and technology tools and establish effective feedback loops. While implementing the vision through a collaboratively developed strategic plan, leaders use technology as a learning tool for both students and teachers. Leaders are creative and forward thinking in securing sustainable streams of human and capital resources to support their efforts, including appropriate partnerships both within their institutions and beyond.

Facilitating Open Communication: Chula Vista Elementary School District (CVESD) Develops Mobile APP For Communicating with Parents

CVESD recognized that it needed to do better in reaching the families of its approximately 30,000 students across 45 schools, more than 50 percent of whom are enrolled in the free or reduced-price lunch program and 30 percent of whom are English language learners. CVESD's traditional e-mail and newsletter communications were more accessible to their higher income families than to their lower income families, so CVESD reached out to district families to understand how they might be able to communicate more effectively.

Through their conversations, CVESD discovered that 99 percent of families had consistent access to a smartphone and that most used social media often. Working closely with parents, CVESD created a Facebook page, Twitter accounts, and a mobile app. Parent suggestions, such as the ability to check cafeteria account balances so they could track the money they gave their children for lunch and the ability to import school events to personal calendars, were incorporated into the CVESD Mobile App, launched in November 2014. Families have the option of receiving this and other information through the mobile app in Spanish.

Personalized Student Learning

Technology enables personalized pathways for student learning through active and collaborative learning activities. Clearly defined sets of learning outcomes guide instruction. The outcomes, and the aligned curriculum, instruction, and assessment, reflect the multidisciplinary nature of knowledge; prepare students for our participatory culture through attention to digital literacy and citizenship; and attend to general skills and dispositions, such as reflection, critical thinking, persistence, and perseverance.

Leaders ensure that policies and resources equip teachers with the right tools and ongoing support to personalize learning in their classrooms.

Teachers collaborate to make instructional decisions based on a diverse data set, including student and teacher observations and reflections, student work, formative and summative assessment results, and data from analytics embedded within learning activities and software aided by real-time availability of data and visualizations, such as information dashboards. Leadership policy and teacher methods support student voice and choice in the design of learning activities and the means of demonstrating learning. Students frequently complete a series of self-directed, collaborative, multidisciplinary projects and inquiries that are assessed through a profile or portfolio. Technology is integral to most learning designs, used daily within and beyond the classroom for collaboration, inquiry, and composition, as well as for connecting with others around the world. In the classroom, teachers serve as educational designers, coaches, and facilitators, guiding students through their personalized learning experiences.

Robust Infrastructure

- A robust technology infrastructure is essential to Future Ready learning environments, and leaders need to take ownership of infrastructure development and maintenance. The 2015 CoSN Annual E-rate and Infrastructure Survey found that affordability remains the primary obstacle for robust connectivity; network speed and capacity pose significant challenges for schools; and, finally, too many school systems report a lack of competition for broadband services in many parts of the United States, particularly in rural areas.[4] Leaders are responsible for meeting these challenges and ensuring ubiquitous access among administrators, teachers, and students to connectivity and devices and for supporting personnel to ensure equipment is well maintained. Future Ready leaders take direct responsibility to ensure infrastructure remains up-to-date (both in terms of security and relevant software, apps, and tools) and open to appropriate Web content and social media tools to enable collaborative learning. Leaders also recognize the importance of building capacity among those responsible for creating and maintaining the technology infrastructure. Future Ready leaders support all of these efforts through careful planning and financial stewardship focused on long-term sustainability.

Personalized Professional Learning
- Leaders ensure the availability of ongoing, job-embedded, and relevant professional learning designed and led by teachers with support from other experts. Leaders develop clear outcomes for professional learning aligned with a vision for student learning.
- In Future Ready schools, teachers and leaders engage in collaborative inquiry to build the capacity of both the participating staff and the school as a whole through face-to-face, online, and blended professional learning communities and networks. Leaders ensure that professional learning planning is participatory and ongoing. Leaders learn alongside teachers and staff members, ensuring that professional learning activities are supported by technology resources and tools, time for collaboration, and appropriate incentives.

To support the unique needs of superintendents and district leaders, the U.S. Department of Education identified and then filmed eight Future Ready districts that exemplified these four Future Ready focus areas. The resulting collection of 47 research-based, short videos break down specific actions taken by these district leaders to transform teaching and learning. Superintendents can take a short survey that results in a personalized, on-demand video playlist of Future Ready leadership in action. For more information about the Future Ready Leaders project and access to the survey and videos, visit the U.S. Department of Education Future Ready Leaders website at http://tech.ed.gov/leaders.

Implementation Is Key

Although vision is critical to transforming teaching and learning, a strategic implementation plan is key to success. In some states, districts or schools will develop their own technology implementation plans; in others, state education leaders take the lead and districts follow. The Future Ready website includes free online assessment tools to be completed by district teams. The resulting reports are designed to help district teams create a comprehensive implementation plan that accounts for the four Future Ready focus areas and support strategies.

In addition to working with teams within educational organizations to create an implementation plan, leaders also should solicit input and feedback from a broad range of influencers: administrators, teacher-leaders experienced in using technology to support learning, professional organizations, boards of education, knowledgeable members of the community, business leaders, cultural institutions, colleagues in other districts, and parents.[5]

Leading by Example: Van Henri White, School Board President

Many school board members assume their responsibilities mostly focus on approving budgets and making hiring decisions. Van Henri White, Rochester, New York, School Board President and Council of Urban Boards Education Chair, sees transforming teaching and learning as the responsibility of all educational leaders, including and beyond a district's superintendent. White believes part of leading a board means learning and leveraging the same technology tools he hopes his district's teachers are using to support learning in classrooms. For example, during Rochester's observance of Martin Luther King Day in 2015, White joined Rochester educators, students, and staff as they engaged in a videoconference session with districts across the country, including New York City; Miami-Dade; and Ferguson, Missouri, for a structured conversation about race and civil rights in America.

White also believes in the importance of establishing connectivity beyond a district's facilities. He and other district leaders in Rochester have begun conversations with local city and county leaders to provide wireless Internet access for homes and families throughout the district. He sees such access to technology and connectivity as more than a district tool—as one to be leveraged for family learning as well. White hopes district-wide wireless access will mean parents will be able to help their students by looking up cademic content they may not understand and will provide equitable access to district-provided tools such as its online communication portal.

54 Office of Educational Technology

For more information on Future Ready and to access a growing set of curated resources that align to the Future Ready framework from more than 40 partners, such as CoSN's Certified Education Technology Leader certification for school district leaders, visit http://www.futurereadyschools.org/futureready.

Setting an Agenda for Change: Howard-Winneshiek (Howard-Winn) Community School District

John Carver, Superintendent of Howard-Winn Community School District, faced less than optimal conditions when he initiated a digital learning transformation project modeled on Future Ready Schools. The district was experiencing declining enrollment and was failing to meet the standards of No Child Left Behind in reading comprehension, and almost half of the district's students qualified for free or reduced-priced lunch. Many districts face similar challenges; what set Howard-Winn apart was the district's decision to view failure as an opportunity to learn and improve.

Despite a lack of funding and community reluctance to change, Carver successfully gained support by working closely with teachers, the school board, and the district's School Improvement Advisory Committee to set an ambitious goal: By the year 2020, children in Howard-Winn will be the best prepared, most recruited kids on the planet.[6]

Creating a new brand, 2020 Howard-Winn, helped Carver communicate the district vision of technology embedded in all parts of instruction, social and online systems of support for district professionals, and active community buy-in and participation.

Behind these three pillars are leadership attributes essential to change: the courage to identify challenges and create a sense of urgency; openness to invest time, build trust, and cultivate relationships with stakeholders; and constant availability, visibility, and ownership as the drivers and face of change.

Although the implementation is still in its early stages, the district has acquired 1,300 laptops and implemented a 1:1 program. Teachers are challenged to be digital explorers and are asked to seek professional development opportunities proactively by using technology and to teach their students to be good digital citizens.

Since implementing these measures, student attendance at Howard-Winn schools has improved 90 percent, and a tech-enabled partnership with

Northeast Iowa Community College has saved students between $9,000 and $10,000 in tuition fees by allowing district students to access college coursework while still in high school. The district also has seen a 17 percent increase in students meeting and exceeding summative assessment benchmarks. With more than $250,000 in support from stakeholders, the district also has been able to implement sustainable and cost-saving measures such as solar-powered Wi-Fi routers and propane-powered buses.

As the district continues to implement its vision of digital learning, Carver says he and other leaders have been driven by the following question: Do we love our kids enough to stop doing the things that do not work anymore?

Providing Statewide Leadership:
North Carolina Digital Learning Plan

To accelerate progress toward the goal of providing equitable access to high-quality learning for all K–12 students in the state, North Carolina asked the Friday Institute for Educational Innovation at North Carolina State University to develop the North Carolina Digital Learning Plan. Beginning in June 2014, the Friday Institute engaged in a multi-faceted planning process, building on prior research and work on digital learning initiatives, with schools and districts across North Carolina.

The planning process included site visits to 18 districts and various charter schools and included 164 focus groups and interviews with superintendents, principals, teachers, technology directors, curriculum and instruction directors, chief financial officers, professional development directors, instructional technology facilitators, technicians, parents, and students.

In addition, Friday Institute researchers met with the deans of education of both the University of North Carolina system and independent colleges and universities across North Carolina, local school board members, legislators, business leaders, nonprofit education organizations, and other stakeholders. The researchers gathered data and analyzed the technology infrastructure of all of North Carolina's K–12 public schools, using the information to help prepare the state's E-rate application.

Friday Institute staff also conducted reviews of existing research on digital learning programs and gathered information about initiatives and strategies from other states and large districts. In May 2015, at the request of the North Carolina State Board of Education, all 115 districts and 120

> charter schools completed the North Carolina Digital Learning Progress Rubric. The resultant rubric data provide an overview of progress throughout the state in five categories: leadership, professional learning, content and instruction, technology and infrastructure, and data and assessment. The North Carolina Digital Learning Plan can be found here.

Budgeting and Funding for Technology

Districts often are challenged financially when it comes to implementing technology initiatives and programs. Once a vision for the use of technology is in place, district superintendents and school leaders first should examine existing budgets to identify areas in which spending can be reduced or eliminated to pay for learning technologies. They also should consider all possibilities for creative funding of these programs. The following approaches are recommended for consideration as districts review their budgets and funding.

Eliminate or Reduce Existing Costs

As technology enables new learning opportunities and experiences, it also can render existing processes and tools obsolete, freeing up funds to pay for technology. Three obvious examples are copy machines (and related supplies and services contracts), dedicated computer labs, and replacing commercially licensed textbooks with **openly licensed educational resources**. In September 2015, U.S. Secretary of Education Arne Duncan challenged schools to begin this process by replacing just one book as a first step in appreciating the cost savings and developing an understanding of what would be necessary to implement such a change school- or district-wide.

Openly Licensed Educational Resources

Openly licensed educational resources are teaching, learning, and research resources that reside in the public domain or have been released under a license that permits their use, modification, and sharing with others. Open resources may be full online courses or digital textbooks or more granular resources such as images, videos, and assessment items.

Future Ready Learning

> **Turning Toward Open: Illinois School District Embraces Openly Licensed Digital Resources**
>
> Many schools are freeing up funds for digital resources by transitioning away from textbooks. The state of Illinois offered Williamsfield Community Unit School District 210 three options when tasked with selecting instructional materials aligned with new mathematics standards: valid and reliable outside sources of material that aligned with standards, a mathematics model scope and sequence developed by the Illinois State Board of Education, or a textbook series.
>
> With a limited budget of $10,000, the district decided to forgo traditional textbook adoption and instead began the process of creating and using openly licensed content. The district relied on a mathematics scope and sequence framework openly provided by the Dana Center and used a variety of open source content through OER Commons and Learning Registry. With the money previously allotted for textbooks, the district purchased low-cost, cloud-based laptop computers. In addition, leadership allocated federal Rural Education Achievement Program and Title II funding to procure devices and upgrade connectivity infrastructure.
>
> Recognizing a need to build professional capacity around these new resources, district leadership dedicated professional development time, including pullout days with class coverage, to help teachers better understand how to curate, collaborate, and house digital content. In addition, the teachers are using collaborative cloud-based storage to house their repository of content. The approach has spread beyond mathematics instruction into other subjects as well, setting a tone and track for the district's growing STEM initiative.
>
> The district routinely evaluates the user experience of the openly licensed resources. Follow-up efforts will encourage the district's most innovative teachers to remix or contribute original openly licensed learning resources, leveraging the Illinois Shared Learning Environment OER tool set to do so.

Partner with Other Organizations

Partnership options for securing resources include local businesses and other organizations, alumni, internal and nearby teacher experts to provide professional development, and curriculum development arrangements with other districts. Some school districts have formed partnerships with local and county governments, sharing technology infrastructure and technical staff to keep costs down by jointly funding chief technology officer roles and taking advantage of the economies of scale when building and purchasing broadband access together. These economies of scale also can be realized through consortium purchasing such as the Kentucky Valley Educational Cooperative, which represents several districts and higher education institutions at once and helps decide issues of resource allocation.

Make Full Use of Federal Funds

The E-rate program provides substantial price discounts for infrastructure costs for schools and public libraries and is one source of technology funding. In addition, for funding beyond connectivity, a U.S. Department of Education Dear Colleague letter, published in November 2014, provides guidance and examples for leveraging existing federal funds for technology-related expenditures.

Using Federal Funds: U.S. Department of Education Dear Colleague Letter on Acceptable Uses of Federal Funding for Technology

The purpose of the Dear Colleague letter prepared by the U.S. Department of Education in November 2014 was to help state, district, and eligible partnership grantees better understand how they may be able to use their federal grant funds to support innovative technology-based strategies to personalize learning. The letter includes examples of how funds from the Elementary and Secondary Education Act (Titles I, II, and III) and Individuals with Disabilities Education Act (IDEA) may support the use of technology to improve instruction and student outcomes. Examples were limited to the Elementary and Secondary Education Act and IDEA because of the scale of these programs, but funds from many other formula and competitive grant programs that are administered by the U.S. Department of Education also may be used for this purpose.

The examples do not depart from previous U.S. Department of Education guidance but rather clarify opportunities to use federal grant funds to support digital learning, including improving and personalizing professional learning and other supports for educators, increasing access to high-quality digital content and resources for students, facilitating educator collaboration and communication, and providing devices for students to access digital learning resources. Funding these four areas is important because technology itself is not a panacea.

> **Creative Funding Solutions: Edgecombe County Public Schools Goes Digital and Combines Funding Sources to Pay for It**
>
> Edgecombe County Public Schools in North Carolina has one of the highest dropout rates in the state and three of the lowest performing elementary schools, and during the past few years nearly 700 students (of 6,200 students served) have left the district in favor of other options. To change these staggering statistics, Edgecombe County Public School leaders made a district-wide commitment to an evidence-based global education approach that is supported by technology and funded through an innovative model that combines federal funding with the use of free online educational resources.
>
> The revised district-wide technology plan, which includes statewide access to free digital teaching and learning resources, now also reflects the North Carolina State Board of Education's goal of Future Ready Schools for the 21st century. The plan focuses on four priorities: (1) updating infrastructure; (2) providing universal access for students and staff to devices; (3) online professional development opportunities for all staff; and (4) a shared services model to reduce redundancies and consolidate systems, applications, and infrastructure.
>
> To fund the plan, the district applied for and received E-rate funding and also sought out alternatives to print-based textbook purchases. Not only is this latter decision cost- effective but it provides students and staff with high-quality, up-to-date resources for learning. Instead of print-based textbooks—which quickly go out of date—the district now uses North Carolina's WiseOwl to access free online resources as well as the University of North Carolina's Learn NC repository of learning resources and professional development resources.

Rethink Existing Staff Responsibilities

As part of their technology implementation plans, many districts, schools, and higher education institutions are rethinking the roles and responsibilities of existing staff members to support technology in learning. For example, some are expanding the role of librarians to become evaluators and curators of learning technology resources, an activity that taps into their existing skill sets. Other districts and schools have adopted shared leadership and staffing models, enabling them to expand what they can offer students by sharing expensive resources. Another option for districts and schools is to partner with other organizations to staff specific technology in learning programs.

60 Office of Educational Technology

Whatever approach is adopted, organizations are well served to make sure they are fully staffing to meet needs rather than simply adding additional work to existing positions.

Building Nonprofit Partnerships: Code in the Schools Helps Schools Build Computer Science Capacity

To increase capacity, schools can partner with organizations to source instructors and provide professional development to build teacher skills and confidence. Many schools in the greater Baltimore area have partnered with Code in the Schools to provide support for their teachers and librarians who wanted to introduce project-based computer science in the classroom by using low-cost equipment, such as Raspberry Pi, Arduino, and Makey Makey, and learning to use free browser-based resources to start teaching code in the classroom by using Scratch, Code.org, and MIT App Inventor.

Some teachers also worked with Code in the Schools to teach video game and app development in their classrooms. For example, Liberty Elementary School Principal Joseph Manko partnered with Code in the Schools to develop a PK–5 computational skills curriculum, conduct professional development for teachers, and provide direct instruction both during the school day in the library's maker space and in the after-school program.

Ensure Long-Term Sustainability

Technology investments are not onetime expenses. Although onetime grants and other supplemental funding sources can serve as catalysts for establishing technology in learning efforts, they are not sustainable as schools and districts build toward a long-term vision and plan. When devices reach the end of life and infrastructure equipment becomes obsolete, districts and schools should have a reliable means to replace or upgrade them. Leaders should consider technology an ongoing, line-item expense from the very beginning of planning technology implementation.

Recommendations

- **Establish clear strategic planning connections among all state, district, university, and school levels and how they relate to and are supported by technology to improve learning.**

Although some of these efforts are supported by summits organized at the federal level by Future Ready Schools, state and local authorities are uniquely suited to understand the needs and resources available within their local education ecosystems. Broad, coordinated strategic planning requires a commitment from all parties involved to collaborate consistently across organizational boundaries. These conversations and connections need proactive champions who will invest in working at this level and who can take advantage of existing state and regional conferences to further this work.

- **Set a vision for the use of technology to enable learning such that leaders bring all stakeholder groups to the table, including students, educators, families, technology professionals, community groups, cultural institutions, and other interested parties.**
  Although not all parties will be responsible for the execution of a vision for the use of technology to enable learning, by making certain all involved stakeholder groups are part of the vision-setting process, leaders will ensure better community support and the establishment of a plan for learning technology that reflects local needs and goals.
- **Develop funding models and plans for sustainable technology purchases and leverage openly licensed content while paying special attention to eliminating those resources and tasks that can be made obsolete by technology.**
  Rather than viewing technology as an add-on component to support learning, leaders should take stock of current systems and processes across learning systems and identify those that can be augmented or replaced by existing technologies. During the planning process, they also should identify systems and processes for which no replacement currently exists within the district, school, or college and set goals for developing more efficient solutions.
- **Develop clear communities of practice for education leaders at all levels that act as a hub for setting vision, understanding research, and sharing practices.**
  Building on the model of the education innovation clusters, state, district, university, and community organization leaders should establish cohesive communities of practice—in person and online—to create virtuous cycles for sharing the most recent research and effective practices in the use of educational technology.

62 Office of Educational Technology

4. ASSESSMENT - MEASURING FOR LEARNING

GOAL: At all levels, our education system will leverage the power of technology to measure what matters and use assessment data to improve learning.

Measuring learning is a necessary part of every teacher's work. Teachers need to check for student understanding, and parents, students, and leaders need to know how students are doing overall in order to help them successfully prepare for college and work. In addition to supporting learning across content areas, technology-enabled assessments can help reduce the time, resources, and disruption to learning required for the administration of paper assessments.[1] Assessments delivered using technology also can provide a more complete and nuanced picture of student needs, interests, and abilities than can traditional assessments, allowing educators to personalize learning.

Through embedded assessments, educators can see evidence of students' thinking during the learning process and provide near real-time feedback through learning dashboards so they can take action in the moment.[2] Families can be more informed about what and how their children learned during the school day. In the long term, educators, schools, districts, states, and the nation can use the information to support continuous improvement and innovations in learning.

Technology-enabled tools also can support teacher evaluation and coaching. These tools capture video and other evidence of qualities of teaching such as teamwork and collaboration. They provide new avenues for self-reflection, peer reflection and feedback, and supervisor evaluation.

Educators and institutions should be mindful of whether they are measuring what is easy to measure or what is most valuable to measure. Traditional assessments in schools and post-secondary institutions today rely largely on multiple-choice questions and fill-in-the-bubble answers.[3] Many assessments also happen after learning has occurred and with results delivered months later, usually after the course has ended. Assessments are more instructionally useful when they afford timely feedback.

Continued advances in technology will expand the use of ongoing, formative, and embedded assessments that are less disruptive and more useful for improving learning. These advances also ensure that all students have the best opportunity to demonstrate their knowledge and skills on statewide assessments that increasingly focus on real-world skills and complex demonstrations of understanding. Statewide assessment—coupled with meaningful accountability—is an essential part of ensuring students have equitable access to high-quality educational experiences. At the same time, it is crucial to focus time and effort on tests worth taking—those that reflect the kind of instructional experiences students need and that provide actionable insight.

64 Office of Educational Technology

As technology gives us the capability to improve on long-standing assessment approaches, our public education system has a responsibility to use the information we collect during assessment in ways that can have the greatest impact on learning. This means using assessments that ask students to demonstrate what they have learned in meaningful ways. And students and parents know there is more to a sound education than picking the right answer on a multiple-choice question or answering an extended-response question outside of the context of students' daily lives. All learners deserve assessments that better reflect what they know and are able to do with that knowledge.

Approaches to Assessment

Various types of assessments are appropriate for different uses and at different times. Summative assessments measure student knowledge and skills at a specific point in time. Summative assessments often are administered in common to a group of students, whether an entire class, grade level at a school, or grade level across a district. These assessment results can help to determine whether students are meeting standards in a given subject and to evaluate the effectiveness of an instructional curriculum or model.[4]

Many PK–12 schools administer formal summative tests at the end of the year, which they may augment with interim tests earlier in the year. These assessments provide system-wide data on student achievement as well as data by sub-groups of learners.[5] The data can provide valuable insights regarding the achievement and progress of all students, including efforts to promote equitable access to excellent educational opportunities and to narrow achievement gaps.

In contrast, formative assessments are frequent, instructionally embedded checks for understanding that provide quick, continual snapshots of student progress across time. Formative assessments provide information during the instructional process, before summative assessments are administered. Both teachers and students can use the results from formative assessments to determine what actions to take to help promote further learning. These assessments help identify students' understanding, inform and improve the instructional practice of teachers, and help students track their own learning.[6]

Optimally, a comprehensive assessment system balances multiple assessment approaches to ensure that students, families, educators, and policymakers have timely and appropriate information to support individual learners and to make good decisions to strengthen educational systems overall.

Using Assessment Data to Support Learning

In almost all aspects of our daily lives, data help us personalize and adapt experiences to our individual needs. However, there is much work remaining to realize the full potential of using assessment data to improve learning. One recent study of teacher perceptions of the use of data revealed a range of frustrations with many current implementations. These frustrations include being overwhelmed with large amounts of data from disparate sources, incompatibility of data systems and tools that make data analysis unnecessarily time-consuming, inconsistency in the level of detail and quality of data, and delays in being able to access data in time to modify instruction.[7]

Education data systems do not always maximize the use of interoperability standards that would enable easy and secure sharing of information with educators, schools, districts, states, students, and their families. As a result, educators are missing out on significant opportunities to use data to improve and personalize learning. With improved educational data systems, leaders can leverage aggregate data to improve the quality and effectiveness of technology-enabled learning tools and resources.

For example, it is now possible to gather data during formative and summative assessments that can be used to create personalized digital learning experiences. In addition, teachers can use these data to inform interventions and decisions about how to engage individual students; personalize learning; and create more engaging, relevant, and accessible learning experiences for all learners.

Assessment data can be made available directly to students. When they have access to their data, students can play a larger role in choosing their own learning pathways.[8] The data also can be made available to family members so students' advocates can play a more active role in supporting their children's education. Moreover, data can be used to support teachers' efforts—individually or in teams, departments, or schools—to improve professional practice and learning.[9] For personalized learning systems to reach their full potential, data systems and learning platforms should include seamless interoperability with a focus on data security and issues related to privacy.

In many cases, pre-service teaching candidates do not receive sufficient instruction on understanding and using data. At the same time, in-service teachers can benefit from ongoing professional development on the integration of technology to enhance their teaching. According to the Data Quality Campaign, as of February 2014, just 19 states included the demonstration of data literacy skills as a requirement for teacher licensure.[10] Although data from technology-based assessments and data systems hold great potential, they are meaningful only when educators use them effectively. Teachers deserve ongoing support to strengthen their skills in how to use data to meet the needs of students better.

Addressing these challenges will take a three-pronged approach: (1) preparing and supporting educators in realizing the full potential of using assessment data, (2) encouraging the development of data assessment tools that are more intuitive and include visualizations that clearly indicate what the data mean for instruction, and (3) ensuring the security and privacy of student data within these systems.

For a more complete discussion of student data safety and privacy, see Section 5: Infrastructure.

How Technology Transforms Assessment

Technology can help us imagine and redefine assessment in a variety of ways. These tools can provide unobtrusive measurements for learners who are designing and building products, conducting experiments using mobile devices, and manipulating parameters in simulations. Problems can be situated in real-world environments, where students perform tasks, or include multi-stage scenarios that simulate authentic, progressive engagement with the subject matter. Teachers can access information on student progress and learning throughout the school day, which allows them to adapt instruction to personalize learning or intervene to address particular learning shortfalls. The unique attributes of technology-based assessments that enable these activities include the following.

Enable Enhanced Question Types
Technology-based assessments allow for a variety of question types beyond the limited multiple-choice, true-or-false, or fill-in-the-blank options that have characterized traditional assessments. Examples of enhanced question types include the following:

- Graphic response, which includes any item to which students respond by drawing, moving, arranging, or selecting graphic regions
- Hot text, in which students select or rearrange sentences or phrases within a passage
- Equation response, in which students respond by entering an equation

- Performance-based assessments, in which students perform a series of complex tasks

Technology-enhanced questions allow students to demonstrate more complex thinking and share their understanding of material in a way that was previously difficult to assess using traditional means.

In particular, performance-based assessments are designed so that students must complete a series of complex skills that ask them to synthesize information from multiple sources, analyze that information, and justify their conclusions. For example, a performance task in English language arts might include reading passages from primary documents, analyzing the set of passages, and writing an essay in response to a prompt. In a mathematics class, a performance task might ask students to analyze a graph based on actual data and describe the linear relationship between the quantities. Because performance-based assessments allow students to construct an original response rather than selecting the right answer from a list, they can measure students' cognitive thinking skills and their ability to apply their knowledge to solve realistic, meaningful problems.[11]

Using the technology offered in performance-based assessments, students can enter their responses in the online interface. For tasks that require hand scoring, scores can be merged with machine-scored items in the same system, thus providing complete test results. For example, the Partnership for Assessment of Readiness for College and Careers and the Smarter Balanced Assessment Consortium evaluate students' ability to excel at classroom speaking and listening assignments in addition to more traditional machine-scored prompts.

Measure Complex Competencies

A recent convening of the National Research Council (NRC) underscored the importance of broadening the focus of assessment to include non-cognitive competencies and the importance of technology in measuring knowledge, skills, and abilities.[12]

As an example, the NRC highlighted the work of the international comparative assessment, **Programme for International Student Assessment (PISA)**. PISA administers a novel technology-based assessment of student performance in creative problem solving designed to measure students' capacity to respond to non-routine situations to achieve their potential as constructive and reflective citizens. The NRC also highlighted the SimScientists simulation-based curriculum unit and assessments, which are designed to use technology to measure middle school students' understanding of ecosystems and scientific inquiry.

Similarly, the National Assessment of Educational Progress (NAEP) recently announced plans to expand its testing program to begin to include measures of students' motivation, mindset, and perseverance in an effort to build the evidence base for more widespread use.

PISA

PISA is a triennial international survey that aims to evaluate education systems worldwide by testing the skills and knowledge of 15-year-old students. For additional information, visit www.oecd.org/pisa/.

Technology Enables Assessment of Growth Mindset

With funding from the U.S. Department of Education's Small Business Innovation Research program, Mindset Works developed SchoolKit, an app designed to strengthen academic and social and emotional success. Through animations, assessments, and classroom activities, students learn a growth mindset—the understanding that ability develops with effort. Pilot research in nine middle schools showed significant increases in student growth mindset, which related to increases in learning goals, positive beliefs about effort, and positive academic habits and behaviors (such as resilient responses to failure and better learning strategies).[19]

These changes also related to increases in students' grade point averages. Since launching in 2012, SchoolKit has been used by tens of thousands of students around the country, including all middle schools in Washington, D.C. The app is based on Carol Dweck's research on growth mindsets.[20]

Provide Real-Time Feedback

Technology-based formative assessments can offer real-time reporting of results, allowing stakeholders to understand students' strengths and weaknesses, while guiding them to make valid, actionable interpretations of the assessment data. Such assessments can enable educators to see, evaluate, and respond to student work more quickly than can traditional assessments. Similarly, learners and their families can access this information almost in real time. Technology-based summative assessments also facilitate faster turnaround of results.

Some of today's technology-based assessments also allow for a richer menu of approaches to feedback than do traditional or even first-generation online assessments. Certain formative assessment platforms allow educators to provide feedback to students via in-line comments (through video, audio, or text), engage in online chats, e-mail feedback directly to families and learners, and connect learners to additional resources for practicing specific skills or developing key understandings.

These technologies also can increase the efficiency of the process of giving feedback, allowing educators more time to focus on areas of greatest need. For example, for giving feedback on areas of frequent concern, educators can pre-populate a menu of responses to use as comments, allowing them to shift focus to areas of feedback unique to each student. Automated responses can be generated as well when assignments are late or incomplete. Although this is still nascent technology, in recent years, advances have occurred in automated scoring of essays that may make it a more powerful tool to generate timely feedback.

Increase Accessibility

Advances in technology grounded in UD and systems that align to UDL have made assessments more accessible and valid for a greater number of students, including those with diverse abilities and language capabilities. These advances have allowed a greater proportion of the population access to assessments.

Special features include the ability to increase font sizes and change color contrast, text-tospeech, bilingual dictionaries, glossaries, and more. These features can be embedded in assessments and made available to students, depending on what the assessment is measuring and identified learner needs. Seamless accessibility features embedded in technology-based assessments reduce the need to single out individual students for extra supports, providing an added benefit for students and educators alike.

Similarly, assistive technology, such as text-to-speech, alternate response systems, and refresh-able braille, supports students with disabilities in accessing learning. These technologies continue to advance and can make it possible for students to interact with digital learning resources in ways that would be impossible with standard print-based assessments. When both assistive technologies and assessments effectively interoperate, students are better able to demonstrate what they know and how to apply this knowledge.

Office of Educational Technology

Adapt to Learner Ability and Knowledge

Computer adaptive testing has facilitated the ability of assessments to estimate accurately what students know and can do across the curriculum in a shorter testing session than would otherwise be necessary. Computer adaptive testing uses algorithms to adjust the difficulty of questions throughout an assessment on the basis of a student's responses. For example, if the student answers a question correctly, a slightly more challenging item is presented next; if the student answers incorrectly, he or she receives another opportunity to demonstrate knowledge in a different manner.

Because adaptive tests target content and test items aligned with each student's ability level, the adaptation leads to more precise scores for all students across the achievement continuum in a greatly reduced time period. Achieving the same level of precision in a traditional paperand-pencil test would require students to answer many more questions, potentially impacting instructional time. Moving forward, these assessments can benefit from increased interoperability so that the data from these adaptive measures can be pulled into a centralized dashboard that allows a more integrated understanding of student performance.

Embedded with the Learning Process

Embedded assessments are woven directly into the fabric of learning activities students undertake. Such assessments may be technology driven or simply a part of effective instruction, and they may appear in digital learning tools and games. They are generally invisible to the instructional process because they are embedded in the regular classroom activities. Embedded assessments have the potential to be useful for diagnostic and support purposes in that they provide insights into *why* students are having difficulties in mastering concepts and provide insights into how to personalize feedback to address these challenges.[13]

Game-based assessment is designed to leverage parallels between video game design and next-generation learning and assessment.[14,15] Recent research has focused on promising ways that digital learning can support formative assessment practices[16]—including wraparound features such as annotation tools and dashboards—and ways that games can identify more nuanced conclusions about student learning outcomes.[17]

Future Ready Learning

Incorporating Student Interests: Games and Assessment

GlassLab creates and supports high-impact games that make learning visible by creating games, conducting research, and building infrastructure that lowers entry costs for new developers. For example, GlassLab has conducted a number of studies investigating the efficacy of games as a tool for learning and unobtrusive assessment.

Students using GlassLab's games regularly report that they persist in the face of challenging academic content in the games and that they feel ownership over their learning. SimCityEDU: Pollution Challenge!, one of GlassLab's digital games, provides educators with the tools and content to engage students in real-world challenges faced by countries globally. The game focuses on the countries' need to reduce dependence on cheaper, pollution-generating resources such as coal while at the same time growing their economies.

In SimCityEDU: Pollution Challenge!, students play the role of a city mayor faced with a growing pollution problem and a shrinking economy. While learning how economic and environmental issues influence one another, students are assessed on their ability to problem-solve and understand relationships in complex systems. The GlassLab assessment system gathers evidence for students' problem-solving and systems-thinking skills unobtrusively in the course of students' gameplay by logging student activities. To support teacher facilitation, and enrich teacher-student interactions, the game also includes lessons plans, teacher and student dashboards, and student data reporting.

Embedding Assessment: Understanding Middle School Students' Knowledge of Physics Concepts

Valerie Shute, the Mack and Effie Campbell Tyner Endowed Professor in Education at Florida State University, is studying the impact of video games on learning, with a focus on building a greater understanding of the future of embedded assessment.

One study conducted by Shute and her colleagues of middle school students focused on the acquisition and embedded assessment of physics concepts by having students play the relatively simple video game, Newton's Playground. Players guide a ball to a balloon across a set of increasingly challenging two-dimensional environments involving the placement and manipulation of ramps, pendulums, levers, and springboards. After taking a traditional pre-test and answering a background questionnaire to assess prior knowledge, students played the game during six class periods—about four hours in total—and concluded their participation by completing a traditional post-test.

Newton's Playground generates detailed log files as students play, capturing data such as time spent on the level, number of restarts of the level, total number of objects used in a solution attempt, whether the solution ultimately worked, and the trajectory of the ball. Each of these data points provides information that the game uses to make inferences about how well each student is doing in the game and to gauge the student's current understanding of the physics concepts being taught.

On the basis of analyses of the pre- and post-test data, game log files, and the background questionnaire, Shute and her colleagues demonstrated the following:

- Students playing the game improved their conceptual physics understanding.
- Students who were more engaged in playing the game learned more than those who were less engaged.
- The assessments embedded in the video game could be used to substitute for the traditional assessments commonly used in today's classrooms.

Shute's work underscores the potential for embedded assessment to play an increasingly important role in helping students to gain and demonstrate mastery of important knowledge, skills, and abilities.[21]

Assess for Ongoing Learning

Technology provides students with multiple pathways to create assessable work throughout the year. To demonstrate their understanding, students can create multimedia productions, construct websites to organize and analyze information, and design interactive presentations to serve as products for assessment. These pathways allow teachers to understand how students access and understand information across given categories. For students who need individual accommodations, advances in technology allow for dynamic and personalized presentation and assessment using alternative representations of the same concept or skill. For example, alternative text can be provided for images through the work of the Diagram Center to make graphics accessible to learners with print disabilities.

Moving forward, increasingly sophisticated technology-driven assessments will enable more powerful personalized learning, likely accelerating the shift from time-based learning to competency-based learning.

The Future of Technology-Based Assessment

Although the process is often challenging, in many places, transitioning to technology-based assessment is well under way. Such assessments will continue to improve across time in the following ways.

Continuous Improvement of Assessments

Traditional paper-and-pencil tests, and even some first-generation technology-based assessments, usually are reviewed and updated only on a designated schedule, often driven by printing and distribution cycles rather than when test items need to be updated. Online delivery of assessments allows for continuous improvement of test items.

Integrated Learning and Assessment Systems

Technology has the potential to move assessment from disjointed separate measures of student progress to an integrated system of assessments and personalized instruction to meet the needs of the learner. Technology can integrate more fully student classroom experiences, homework assignments, and formative and summative assessments, all of which are tied closely to academic standards. Online learning platforms can display effects of missing assignments, progress toward goals, and channels for communication with mentors and teachers.

We also should expect to see integrated systems that make the learning process more seamless for students and educators. As students progress along personalized learning pathways, they will be assessed when they are ready to demonstrate mastery over particular skills and content rather than when the calendar indicates there is a testing date. At the same time, we have a responsibility to ensure that all students are held to high standards and offered excellent educational experiences. Ensuring equity while also providing accelerated personalization is the one of the greatest challenges and opportunities moving forward for technology in assessment.

Using Data Effectively and Appropriately

To realize the vision of sharing data across student information systems, we need to address several challenges. On the technical front, formidable barriers to the development of multi-level assessment systems are created by having several student data systems running side-by-side, coupled with disparate data formats and the lack of interoperability across systems. Student and program data today are collected at various levels and in various amounts to address different needs in the educational system. State data systems generally provide macro solutions, institution-level performance management systems offer micro solutions, and student data generated by embedded assessments create nano solutions. Providing meaningful, actionable information that is collected across all of these systems will require agreement on the technical format for sharing data while attending to student privacy and security.

To assist with overcoming these challenges, the National Center for Education Statistics at the U.S. Department of Education has been leading the Common Education Data Standards (CEDS) Initiative, a national, collaborative effort to develop voluntary, common data standards. The CEDS Initiative's objective is to help state and local education agencies and higher education organizations work together to identify a minimal set of key data elements common across organizations and come to agreement on definitions, business rules, and technical specifications to improve the comparability of and ability to share those elements. (Note: Version 5 was released in January 2015.)

For more information on protecting student data and privacy, see Section 5: Infrastructure.

Learning Dashboards That Enable Visualizations

Although systems that support real-time feedback can increase educator and learner understanding of progress toward learning goals, the feedback is even more valuable if it is available in one easily accessible place. To achieve this, we need to connect information about learning that happens across digital tools and platforms.

Learning dashboards integrate information from assessments, learning tools, educator observations, and other sources to provide compelling, comprehensive visual representations of student progress in real time. A learner's attendance data, feedback from instructors, summative evaluation data, and other useful information all can be made available in formats specific to different stakeholders. Learning dashboards can present this data in easy-to-understand graphic interfaces.

These dashboards also can offer recommendations about resources to help students continue their learning progression as well as help identify students who may be at risk of going off track or even dropping out of school. Across larger education systems, these dashboards can help educators to track learner performance across time as well as monitor groups of students to identify shifts in equity, opportunity, and achievement gaps. Although teacher dashboards are becoming commonplace, student and family dashboards can offer promising opportunities to help students take control of their own learning.

Putting Learning on Display: Summit Public Schools' Student Dashboards Personalize Learning

Each morning, students at Summit Public Schools connect to their Personalized Learning Plans by using their devices. Here, students find both their short-term and long-term project views, the materials they need to complete their projects, and just-in-time formative feedback to improve their individual learning, all in one location. Using a color-coded system, each project is linked explicitly with the associated content knowledge standards, and students can see the progress they have made toward those standards as well as areas in which they need more practice.

This automated feedback and work management system gives students easy access and greater control over their learning and frees educators to spend more time teaching and less time on administrative and organizational tasks. "It was really difficult to track where my students were on their progress towards meeting a learning objective and giving them timely feedback," says Elizabeth Doggett, a teacher at Summit Public Schools. "Often I would take student work home over the weekend, but by the time I got through giving them all feedback, it would be too late for them to make meaningful changes."[22]

With the Personalized Learning Plan system, students have the formative feedback they need in real time, and their educators, such as Doggett, are able to plan and execute differentiated instruction more efficiently and effectively so that all of her students can succeed. Students also are benefiting individually from the student-facing side of the Personalized Learning Plan. Educators have taken notice of how these plans promote student agency and motivation. "Students should be able to

> access what they need at the moment they need it, and we provide the resources so that they can do that," says Jon Deane, the former chief information officer of Summit Public Schools.[23]
>
> Doggett sums up the effect of implementing the Personalized Learning Plan, saying, "It makes the students' lives so much easier. It makes me a better teacher, and it makes them more successful students."[24]

Set of Shared Skill Standards

As we shift toward personalized learning, there is increased need for a shared set of common skill standards. The development of micro-credentials is one approach to address this need by creating a shared language and system for communicating success in developing these competencies.

Micro-credentials, often referred to as *badges*, focus on mastery of a singular competency and are more focused and granular than diplomas, degrees, or certificates. The earning and awarding of micro-credentials typically is supported by a technology-based system that enables students and evaluators to be located anywhere and for these activities to take place everywhere and all the time. Micro-credentials also allow for the portability of evidence of mastery. Information about the student's work that earned a badge can be embedded in the metadata, as can the standards the work reflects and information about the awarder of the badge. As with other data systems, a key goal for the next generation of micro-credentialing platforms is interoperability with other educational information systems.[18]

Recognizing Digital Literacy Skills: Assigning Micro-Credentials

LearningTimes, in partnership with the New York Department of Education Office of Postsecondary Readiness, has developed DIG/IT, a digital learning course that introduces students in transfer schools (second-chance high schools) to digital literacy skills while they develop their plans for college, careers, and life after high school. DIG/IT is an open standards-based system designed specifically for badge-empowered social learning that uses challenge-based quests and badges to recognize competencies and positive behaviors in four areas: digital citizenship, college and career explorations, financial literacy and arts, culture and games. At the end of the course, students design a learning experience for a family member or another important person in their lives.

Future Ready Learning 77

> Upon completing a series of related quests, students earn badges acknowledging tangible new skills they have acquired. They also earn reward badges for contributions to the online and classroom community. As they gather enough rewards, they "level up" and continue to earn rewards for participating in the community and for helping others.
>
> DIG/IT is currently in use in 36 New York City transfer schools. The initial pilot has had promising results, including positive teacher and student feedback and reportedly higher levels of student engagement in school. Student attendance in the DIG/ IT- based course has been higher than in courses not using the approach. The DIG/ IT program will be rolled out to approximately 50 transfer schools over the next two years, reaching more than 5,000 students.
>
> Since DIG/IT's development, LearningTimes has spun off Credly to focus on earning, managing, and analyzing digital credentials and badges in an open and portable way. Credly hosts more than 6,000 organizations and their respective micro-credential initiatives. BadgeOS, the open source environment for setting up progressive credentialing programs, has been installed more than 30,000 times by organizations around the world and supports millions of learners.

Educators also can benefit from earning micro-credentials because they can gain recognition for new discrete skills they learn throughout their careers. The nonprofit, Digital Promise, has developed an educator micro-credentialing system, noting that educator micro-credentials can identify, capture, recognize, and share the practices of our best educators. Proponents view micro-credentials as a promising emerging professional development strategy.

RECOMMENDATIONS

- **Revise practices, policies, and regulations to ensure privacy and information protection while enabling a model of assessment that includes ongoing gathering and sharing of data for continuous improvement of learning and teaching.**
  This will require not only greater systems interoperability standards but also increased capacity on the part of educators and administrators to understand the types of systems they want to establish within schools and colleges. In addition, they will need to have an

understanding of the standards of interoperability they should demand from vendors. A key component of this increased capacity should ensure educational leaders have a firm understanding of privacy and security concerns, how those concerns are addressed within the school or system, and clear communication of policies and procedures with all stakeholders. Achievement of this recommendation would benefit from the involvement and guidance of organizations, such as CoSN, ISTE, and the State Educational Technology Directors Association (SETDA), that have developed specialized expertise in these areas.

- **States, districts, and others should design, develop, and implement learning dashboards, response systems, and communication pathways that give students, educators, families, and other stakeholders timely and actionable feedback about student learning to improve achievement and instructional practices.**
  The next generation of such tools should integrate across platforms and tools seamlessly, be designed with a mobile-first mindset, and be guided by UD and UDL principles to ensure accessibility by all stakeholders. Although current products and dashboards include basic functionality and features that improve on those of their predecessors, future iterations should be built on a premise of feedback and conversation, allowing learners and families to discuss learning outcomes and evidence and increasing agency and ownership across stakeholder groups.

- **Create and validate an integrated system for designing and implementing valid, reliable, and cost-effective assessments of complex aspects of 21st century expertise and competencies across academic disciplines.**
  Interoperable formative assessment formats offered by major testing consortia for use by educators throughout the year are an important first step. However, work remains to ensure more educators have access to high-quality formative assessment tools and to develop additional capacities to assess both cognitive and non-cognitive skills better. Moving forward, increasing educator capacity for the design and deployment of valid and reliable formative assessments will require the concerted efforts of current assessment developers, teacher preparation programs, school systems, and researchers. Furthermore, colleges and universities will benefit from system-wide reviews of assessment practices and from ensuring all faculty have deep

understandings of key principles and practices surrounding the design and implementation of effective learning assessments.

- **Research and development should be conducted that explore how embedded assessment technologies such as simulations, collaboration environments, virtual worlds, games, and cognitive tutors can be used to engage and motivate learners while assessing complex skills.** Although some of this research is in its early stages, the way forward will require close collaboration among organizations—such as GlassLab, Games for Change, and iCivics; colleges, universities, informal learning spaces, and schools; philanthropic organizations; and research institutions—that have a deep understanding of how game mechanics increase learner motivation. This collaboration can lead to the development of more effective and engaging experiences to support learning.

5. INFRASTRUCTURE

Enabling Access and Effective Use

GOAL: All students and educators will have access to a robust and comprehensive infrastructure when and where they need it for learning.

Preparing students to be successful for the future requires a robust and flexible learning infrastructure capable of supporting new types of engagement and providing ubiquitous access to the technology tools that allow students to create, design, and explore. The essential components of an infrastructure capable of supporting transformational learning experiences include the following:

- **Ubiquitous connectivity.** Persistent access to high-speed Internet in and out of school
- **Powerful learning devices.** Access to mobile devices that connect learners and educators to the vast resources of the Internet and facilitate communication and collaboration

- **High-quality digital learning content.** Digital learning content and tools that can be used to design and deliver engaging and relevant learning experiences
- **Responsible Use Policies (RUPs).** Guidelines to safeguard students and ensure that the infrastructure is used to support learning Building a robust infrastructure for learning begins with an understanding of the goals and desired outcomes that support engaging and empowering learning experiences. When based on learning goals, technology infrastructure decisions become clear.

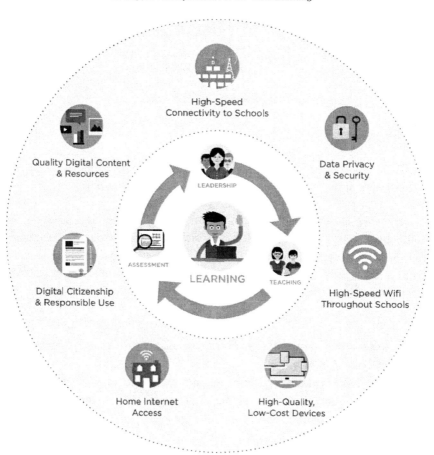

INFRASTRUCTURE
To Support Everywhere, All the Time Learning

Future Ready Learning

Setting Future Goals: Guidance On Assessing Your Current Situation

These questions address many of the important considerations for districts as they begin the development of a comprehensive plan for learning with technology. More detailed information and guidance can be found in the U.S. Department of Education's Future Ready Schools: Building Technology Infrastructure for Learning.

- What is your vision for learning that the technology infrastructure will be supporting?
- What digital learning content, tools, and resources will be supported?
- How many and what types of devices will be supported?
- What kind of professional development will teachers need to become proficient with digital learning?
- What is your current network capacity?
- What is the current state of your physical infrastructure?
- What resources are available to fund this transition?

Developing a Multi-Year Approach: Baltimore County Public School District's (BCPS) Comprehensive Plan for Learning with Technology

To achieve its goal of ensuring that every school has an equitable, effective, digital learning environment and that all students and teachers have the personal technology they need to participate fully in connected learning, BCPS has developed and is implementing the Students and Teachers Accessing Tomorrow (S.T.A.T.) initiative.

S.T.A.T. is a multi-year plan for the transformation of BCPS that includes the following eight conversions:

1. Curriculum. BCPS teachers are creating a digitally enhanced curriculum that redefines how to deliver instruction in a learner-centered, blended learning environment while raising expectations and that places greater emphasis on critical thinking and analytical skills.
2. Instruction. All BCPS teachers will facilitate learning that includes the use of technology where appropriate. BCPS One, a fully integrated technology platform that brings together all of the

district's programs and initiatives, offers a single interface for students and teachers to access blended curriculum content, including digital resources for teaching and learning.

3. Assessment. BCPS One will give teachers the ability to access and administer curriculum-aligned formative and summative assessments easily, as well as access a system-wide grade book, with real-time access for students and parents.

4. Organizational Development. Intensive job-embedded professional learning opportunities continue in the initiative's 10 pilot Lighthouse Schools, which serve as model demonstration sites with a Teacher Leader Corp turning their classrooms into learning labs.

5. Infrastructure. BCPS currently is updating its infrastructure to support S.T.A.T. by issuing mobile devices to instructional staff and students and by updating networks to ensure all schools are fully wireless. In addition, BCPS has partnered with the Baltimore County Public Library system to enable students to access the BCPS network in any county library.

6. Policy. Current BCPS policies are under review and revision to reflect a systematic shift in language that emphasizes empowering students and staff over mandating rules.

7. Budget. The significant changes necessary within BCPS to engage a growing and diverse student population and prepare students for college, career, and life will require substantial financial investment.

8. Communication. BCPS uses several communication outlets to provide information regarding S.T.A.T., including district and school websites, newsletters, social media, BCPS-TV, and Parent University.

In February 2015, the Johns Hopkins Center for Research and Reform in Education released a 2014 mid-year evaluation of the S.T.A.T. initiative's impact on the 10 pilot Lighthouse Schools.[5] Although the report contains early baseline data, findings suggest that these schools are beginning to reflect the goals of S.T.A.T.

> **Planning for the Fast Track: Technology Implementation In Vancouver Public Schools**
>
> In 2013, voters in the Vancouver Public School District, which serves more than 23,000 students, passed a $24 million technology levy after a community outreach and awareness campaign under the leadership of Superintendent Steve Webb. The levy eased one of the greatest challenges of a digital learning implementation—how to pay for it. It also put pressure on the district to develop and execute a plan that would have an impact quickly.
>
> As one teacher put it, the district rapidly went from "totally analog, creating notes pages for students on overhead projector transparencies, to laptops for all teachers to a technology deployment that today equips every student and teacher with a tablet."
>
> Central to the implementation were the values of equity and excellence. From the outset, the district viewed technology as a means to close achievement gaps between high-need, underserved student populations and historically higher performing students.
>
> Equipping every student with a tablet was motivated by student learning needs. Crucial to the implementation plan are a number of pilot programs, focused on serving the unique needs of different populations, currently under way in selected schools. For example, English language learners received devices and other digital tools equipped with translation and language development software.
>
> To extend learning beyond the confines of the school day, and to bridge the digital divide in communities and homes across Vancouver, the district also is outfitting school buses with wireless Internet and creating hot spots at community centers and other anchor community locations such as neighborhood churches.

Ubiquitous Connectivity

Reliable connectivity, like water and electricity, is foundational to creating an effective learning environment. Students and teachers cannot take advantage of the opportunities to connect and engage globally or leverage high-quality learning resources without consistent and reliable access to the Internet. In addition, the U.S. Department of Education's Office for Civil

Rights issued a Dear Colleague letter in October 2014 that included access to technology as an important component of equity of access within U.S. schools.

Connectivity at School

President Obama's ConnectED initiative set a goal for 99 percent of students in the country to have Internet access at a minimum of 100 megabits per second per 1,000 students, with a target speed of one gigabit per second by 2018. Efforts by federal, state, and local institutions in recent years have made huge strides toward this goal. The modernization of the E-rate program in 2014 provided billions of additional dollars to help districts improve the speed of and access to Internet connectivity.

Although unprecedented resources are available to reach this goal, still significant work remains for many schools and districts. Organizations that are part of the Future Ready network, including EducationSuperHighway and CoSN, are committed to supporting schools throughout this transition.

Connectivity at Home

Learning does not stop at the end of the school day, and access to digital learning resources should not either. According to a report from the Council of Economic Advisers, approximately 55 percent of low-income children under the age of 10 in the United States lack Internet access at home.[1]

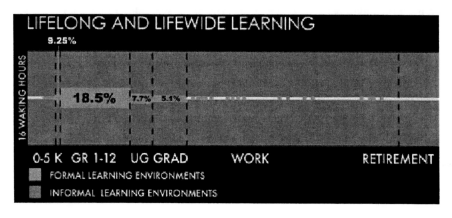

The LIFE Center's Lifelong and Lifewide Diagram by LIFE Center is licensed under a Creative Commons Attribution-NonCommercial-NoDerivs 3.0. (LIFE Center: Stevens, R. Bransford, J. and Stevens, A., 2005).

These statistics along with consideration of the amount of time spent out of school have given rise to concerns about a "homework gap" between students whose Internet connections at home are slow or non-existent—a problem disproportionately common in rural and underserved communities—and those who have home connections with adequate speed. They also give credence to the view that connectivity at home for students is an essential component of a 21st century education—not something merely nice to have—if we are to avoid exacerbating pre-existing inequities in unconnected homes.[2]

Connecthome

ConnectHome is a U.S. Department of Housing and Urban Development program focused on increasing access to high-speed Internet for low-income households. The pilot program launched in 27 cities and one tribal nation in the summer of 2015, initially reaching more than 275,000 low-income households and nearly 200,000 children. As part of the program, Internet service providers, nonprofits, and the private sector will offer broadband access, technical training, digital literacy programs, and devices for residents in assisted housing units.[3] For more information, visit http://connecthome. hud.gov/.

Educational leaders should work to ensure learners have access to connectivity and devices when they leave school grounds so that they are not limited in their ability to experience high-quality connected learning fully. To support schools in this effort, organizations such as EveryoneOn focus on providing highly subsidized Internet access to low-income households. In addition, the U.S. Department of Housing and Urban Development launched ConnectHome in 2015 to focus on bringing high-speed Internet to low-income communities so everyone can participate in our increasingly connected society.

Bringing Connectivity to the Poorest Communities: Coachella Valley, California

When Coachella Valley Unified School District made the decision to implement a plan to transform learning through technology, the plan's architects quickly realized that round-the-clock access to high-speed Internet was essential to create connected learning opportunities in and outside of school. However, because of broad socio-economic diversity in the district, equity of access was a challenge.

86 Office of Educational Technology

Geographically, the district draws from Riverside County, California, and serves the city of Coachella, the community of Thermal, portions of the city of Indio, and Salton City in Imperial County, educating more than 18,000 students across 25 schools. The local cable company refused to run fiber through Native American reservations in the area or through a local mobile home park, leaving some of the district's highest need students on the outside looking in when the school day ended.

To answer the challenge, the district equipped 100 of its school buses with wireless Internet routers with rooftop solar panels to supply power. This enabled students to connect to the Internet on the way to and from school and while traveling to sporting events and extracurricular activities. In addition, at night the Wi-Fi–equipped fleet parked in some of the poorest areas of the district, making high-speed Internet available to students virtually anytime and anywhere.

The initiative was not without challenges. Leadership needed buy-in from the community and the teachers' union, whose members draw salary and benefits from the same general fund. District leaders obtained community buy-in through high-touch outreach that included committee meetings and focus groups as well as speaking directly with or sending e-mail to individual community members. Superintendent Darryl Adams focused on building a bridge between the vision of success that everyone deeply desired for the district's students and the concrete means to realize that vision.

Buoyed by the success of this initiative, Coachella Valley now has a long-term plan for the district to become its own Internet service provider, breaking its dependence on commercial telecom companies.

Bringing Broadband to New Communities: Oklahoma Choctaw Nation Tribal Area Creates Public-Private Collaboration

Because of the high cost of installing and maintaining the infrastructure required for high-speed connectivity, many sparsely populated areas of the country lack access to the Internet, widening the digital divide for people living in rural areas. The Choctaw Nation Tribal Area has demonstrated how—through a combination of grants, loans, and donations—private industries can bring critical access to these underserved communities.

In 2009–10, Pine Telephone, the service provider offering voice, video, cell, long- distance, and high-speed broadband in southeastern Oklahoma applied for and received four American Recovery and Reinvestment awards totaling $56 million to build the infrastructure to provide Internet access to the 10 unserved counties encompassed by the Choctaw Nation.[6]

Prior to this investment, the Choctaw Nation Tribal Area lacked access to reliable broadband service. The low population density (8.3 to 19.7 people per square mile), the high poverty rate (25 percent of the population below the poverty line), and the rugged terrain made the economics of broadband infrastructure very challenging. Initial capital costs to deploy broadband meant that broadband service was limited to commercially viable areas.[7]

Today, more than 1,700 customers have access to high-speed connectivity over both fiber and wireless networks, as does every school in the Pine Telephone service area.

One district, Broken Bow School District, has been able to use digital devices, online lesson plans, and supplemental online programming.

Family engagement in the Broken Bow School District has improved because parents have online access to records of attendance, assignments, and test scores. The connectivity also allows the Choctaw Nation to multicast educational videos and share messages from tribal leadership from a central location. For example, the School of Choctaw Language now offers distance learning courses to approximately 14 Head Starts and 32 high schools within the Choctaw Nation, in addition to several universities.[8]

Taking Service Everywhere: Texas Library Goes All Digital

The librarians at BiblioTech, an all-digital public library in San Antonio, Texas, are interested in how they can leverage their digital status to serve local communities better where a deep divide exists between those who have access to the Internet and those who do not.

Accredited as a state library in Texas, BiblioTech operates under the belief that, "[If] a digital library can go anywhere, it should go everywhere."[9] In an area where 78 percent of library patrons' homes are without Internet access, the library has distributed 10 eReading devices to five schools within the local school district with the greatest need. Schools quickly recognized the value of these resources and matched or exceeded the number of eReaders in circulation as part of their school library collections.

Within the walls of BiblioTech's physical spaces, users will find eReaders for loan, computers for research, reading and story time for younger readers, and community education courses through partnerships with other local organizations. Because all of the content is stored on the eReading devices the library has for circulation, librarians now spend their time assisting patrons with accessing information, resources, and content.

In addition, because BiblioTech branches require only 2,100 square feet of space, the library is able to co-locate within local public housing developments to put resources and connectivity within reach of patrons who might otherwise be cut off from its collections. Opened in September 2013, BiblioTech has an outreach team that is working to make community presentations in every school in the 14 local districts.

Ensuring Access in All Spaces: Indiana Gives Incarcerated Juveniles Internet for Learning

Incarcerated youth attend schools typically not equipped with access to the Internet, making it difficult for teachers to use digital learning materials. Similarly, students are unable to access the vast array of digital learning experiences and resources that are increasingly available to other students.

Attempts to address this problem by providing teacher-only access to Internet-enabled interactive whiteboards served only as a halfway measure in that many Internet sites still were blocked from Internet Protocol addresses emanating from juvenile correctional facilities.

In June 2014, the U.S. Department of Education and the U.S. Department of Justice issued a letter to state departments of education and state juvenile justice agencies stating that incarcerated youth need to have the same educational opportunities as those of their non-system-involved peers.[10]

As a result, Indiana approached American Prison Data Systems, a public benefits corporation based in New York City that offers a private network, to determine whether the technology solution it offered through its secure wireless tablets would work inside Indiana's juvenile correctional system. Digital content is delivered via a special secure wireless connection. Students do not reach out and access content from the Internet; instead, approved content is delivered to the student via the secure connection.

> In collaboration with Oakland City University, the Indiana Department of Correction implemented a pilot project using American Prison Data Systems secure wireless tablets at the Madison Juvenile Correctional Facility located in Madison, Indiana. Each girl in the facility receives a tablet for use during and after school hours. This pilot project also involved 10 entertainment tablets, which were loaded with movies, games, and music and used as incentives for youth who met their behavior goals.
>
> The project began in late September 2014, with positive preliminary results, including a reduction in the number of negative incidences occurring in the living units, a reduction in grievances and acting-out behaviors as a result of students being able to send easily monitored messages to adults, significant interest in accessing content via tablets, and a reduction in idle time among the girls.

Powerful Learning Devices

Any effort to leverage the power of mobile learning devices and resources is dependent on access to high-speed connectivity. Selecting appropriate devices depends in large measure largely on the age of the students, their individual learning needs and the types of learning activities that will be ongoing in the classroom or after school program. The U.S. Department of Education's Office of Educational Technology (OET) published *Future Ready Schools: Building Technology Infrastructure for Learning* in November 2014 to help schools and districts consider device purchases as well as other infrastructure concerns when building technology systems to support learning.

Beware of Bring Your Own Device (BYOD) or Bring Your Own Tech (BYOT)

Many institutions have BYOD or BYOT policies that permit students to use their own mobile devices at school. Although it is certainly reasonable to allow students to learn and communicate using their own devices, serious concerns arise if schools use BYOD as their primary method for ensuring students have devices, including the following:

Economic disparity. The ability to access digital learning resources is distributed disproportionately to students whose families can afford the devices. This can widen the very gaps that technology is capable of closing. This situation also may raise legal concerns because schools are expected to provide a free education for all students.

Instructional burden. It can be very difficult for teachers to manage learning experiences and activities when they have to support multiple platforms and device types, and some activities may be incompatible with some devices. In this situation, teachers may revert to activities of the lowest common denominator that work on older and less robust devices at the expense of a more effective learning experience.

Privacy and security. Student-owned devices may not have appropriate safeguards in place for storing their learning data. In addition, personal devices likely will not have the security features required to provide valid assessment.

High-Quality Digital Learning Content

Schools and colleges need to ensure students have access to a variety of high-quality digital learning materials and resources to support their learning. The ability to curate and share digital learning content is an important component of a robust infrastructure for learning.

Openly Licensed Educational Resources

One of the most effective ways to provide high-quality digital learning materials at scale is through the use of openly licensed educational resources. These resources may be used, modified, and shared without paying any licensing fees or requesting permission. Open licenses for this purpose have been created by organizations such as Creative Commons for learning resources. For software, a number of open license types are available, such as the GNU General Public License and others recognized by the Open Source Initiative or the Free Software Foundation. This is significant considering that the United States currently spends approximately $8 billion each year purchasing commercial learning resources.[4] Replacing just one textbook for one subject can free up tens of thousands of dollars for other purposes.

There are advantages other than just cost savings. Openly licensed materials can be more accurate than traditional textbooks because they can be updated continually as content changes. Openly licensed materials also allow teachers to exercise their own creativity and expertise so they can tailor learning materials to meet the needs of their students.

States including California, Illinois, Utah, and Washington have established programs to help teachers access, curate, refine, and share openly licensed learning resources. In addition, the U.S. Department of Education's Federal Funding for Technology Dear Colleague letter states that Title II funds can be used to prepare teachers to create, use, and share openly licensed digital learning resources.

Platforms and organizations such as the K–12 OER Collaborative, Illinois Shared Learning Environment, and Net Texts are designed specifically for teachers to locate open content and adapt it, as needed, for their students.

Making Open Mean Everyone: University of Mary Washington DS106

An open, online course on digital storytelling, ds106 moves beyond the capabilities of most MOOCs into a learning experience that happens on multiple platforms and across multiple mediums. The course is offered as part of the computer science catalog at the University of Mary Washington—but ds106 is open to anyone, anywhere, at any time.

Participants in ds106 co-learn and co-create to build their own digital story while engaging in dialogue about the ways we communicate with each other through video, audio, social media, and artwork. The course is described as "part storytelling workshop, part technology training, and most importantly, part critical interrogation of the digital landscape that is ever increasingly mediating how we communicate with one another."[11]

Across 15 weeks, ds106 participants complete a number of assignments across platforms (Twitter, YouTube, Instagram, WordPress, and so on), creating their own domain, Web presence, and digital story, as well as exploring the role of digital media in online communication. Materials and learning are tailored completely to student interest and passion. If a section of the course is uninteresting, students can drop in and drop out at any time, allowing ds106 participants to forge their own learning pathway.

To date, students have created a collection of more than 800 assignments, hosted on their own sites and also collected in a searchable assignment bank on the ds106 website. Students can browse or search the assignment bank, add their own creations, or chose to remix an existing creation through a tool called the Remix Machine.

Responsible Use Policies (RUP)

Districts with Internet connectivity and device access also should have policies in place to promote responsible use and protect student privacy. A RUP is a written agreement among parents, students, and school personnel that outlines the terms of responsible use and consequences for misuse. Effective RUPs create an opportunity to teach students, while in school, to become responsible digital citizens, which will help them thrive in a connected world.

RUPs traditionally cover topics such as expectations for how students will interact with one another in digital spaces, what resources students may or may not access with district-provided devices and over a school network, as well as standards for academic integrity when using technology for learning. These policies also can outline school and system agreements as to the use of student data and information. Typically, parents acknowledge that their child agrees to basic care and responsibility guidelines, and students sign a contract agreeing to follow rules governing use of the Internet and online conduct.

RUPs should be written in plain language that is easily accessible to students, parents, and district personnel. Technology also can assist in the easy translation of these policies into other languages, providing a bridge to communication that otherwise might leave some families disconnected. If policies and procedures for the use of devices are too strict, they often have unintended negative consequences, such as preventing access to legitimate educational resources. For additional information on questions to consider when drafting a RUP, see the the U.S. Department of Education's Policies for Users of Student Data: A Checklist or the CoSN publication Rethinking Acceptable Use Policies to Enable Learning: A Guide for School Districts.

Policies and procedures for device management, teaching responsible use, and safeguarding student privacy should be in place and understood by all members of the community prior to providing Internet access or devices. Future Ready Schools: Building Technology Infrastructure for Learning, offers extensive guidance on how to prepare students to use the Internet, a school-provided or personal device at school, or a school-provided device at home appropriately.

In addition to Internet access and device use, with the growing popularity of social media in learning, districts also should consider policies and guidelines for their safe and productive use in schools.

Protections for Student Data and Privacy

The use of student data is crucial for personalized learning and continuous improvement (see Section 4: Assessment). Acting as the stewards of student data presents educators with several responsibilities. School officials, families, and software developers have to be mindful of how data privacy, confidentiality, and security practices affect students. Schools and districts have an obligation to tell students and families what kind of student data the school or third parties (e.g., online educational service providers) are collecting and how the data can be used. As they plan, schools and other educational institutions should be certain that policies are in place regarding who has access to student data and that students and families understand their rights and responsibilities concerning data collection.

These policies should include not only formal adoption processes for online educational services but also informal adoptions such as the downloading of an application to a mobile device and agreeing to clickwraps. A user encounters a clickwrap when asked to click on a button to accept the provider's terms of service before using an app or software. With clickwrap agreements, the act of accepting the terms of service enters the developer and the user (in this case, the school or district) into a contractual relationship akin to signing a contract. The U.S. Department of Education offers schools and families examples, training, and other assistance in navigating privacy concerns through the Privacy Technical Assistance Center. This information includes Protecting Student Privacy While Using Online Educational Services: Requirements and Best Practices, Protecting Student Privacy While Using Online Educational Services: Model Terms of Service, and Checklist for Developing School District Privacy Programs.

Key Federal Laws Protecting Student Data and Privacy

The Family Educational Rights and Privacy Act (FERPA) (20 U.S.C. § 1232g; 34 CFR Part 99) is a federal law that affords parents the right to inspect and review their children's education records, the right to seek to have the education records amended, and the right to have some control over the disclosure of personally identifiable information from the education records. When a student turns 18 or enters a post-secondary education institution at any age, the rights under FERPA transfer to the student. Students to whom FERPA rights have transferred are termed eligible students.

FERPA generally requires that parents or eligible students provide prior written consent before schools can share personally identifiable information from a student's education records, unless an exception applies. For example, when schools and districts use online educational services, they must ensure that FERPA requirements are met. Typically, the FERPA school official exception to consent will apply to schools' and districts' use of online educational services. The U.S. Department of Education issued best practice guidance to address questions related to student privacy and the use of online educational technology in the classroom, available at http://ptac.ed.gov/ document/protecting-student-privacy-while-using-online-educational-services.

The Protection of Pupil Rights Amendment (PPRA) (20 U.S.C. § 1232h; 34 CFR Part 98) governs the administration to students of a survey, analysis, or evaluation that reveals information concerning one or more of eight protected areas, including, but not limited to, sexual behaviors and attitudes and illegal, anti-social, self-incriminating, and demeaning behavior. PPRA also concerns marketing surveys and other areas of student privacy, parental access to information, and the administration of certain physical examinations to minors.

For more information about FERPA and PPRA, visit http://familypolicy.ed.gov/. General questions about FERPA or PPRA may be submitted to the Family Policy Compliance Office by using the Contact Us tab on that website or directly at http://familypolicy.ed.gov/ content/questionscomments.

The Children's Online Privacy Protection Act (COPPA) (15 U.S.C. § 6501–6505) governs online collection of personal information from children under age 13. For example, before a developer can collect any information from a student under 13, verifiable parental consent is required. The FCC, which enforces COPPA, has said that school officials can act in the capacity of a parent to provide consent to sign students up for online educational programs at school. The general guidance is that software companies are allowed to track students within their program, but COPPA prevents them from tracking those students across the Internet.

The Children's Internet Protection Act (CIPA) (47 U.S.C. § 254) imposes several requirements on schools or libraries that receive E-rate discounts for Internet access. Schools and libraries must certify that they have an Internet safety policy that includes technology protection measures. These protection measures must block or filter Internet access to pictures that are obscene, pornographic, or harmful to minors, and schools also must monitor the online activities of minors. Because most schools receive E-rate funds, they are required to educate their students about appropriate online behavior, including on social networking websites and in chat rooms, and to build cyberbullying awareness. Particularly if a digital learning resource requires networking among students, schools must comply with CIPA.

> IDEA also provides confidentiality protections and often additionally will protect information for students with disabilities.

Device and Network Management

Many schools underestimate the importance of a plan for staffing and resources for ongoing monitoring, management, and maintenance of network infrastructure. We must ensure that student data are maintained in secure systems that meet all applicable federal and state requirements concerning the protection of personally identifiable information. Key elements of an infrastructure plan should include the following:

- Network management and monitoring
- User help desk and technical support
- Maintenance and upgrade of devices and equipment
- Insurance for devices
- Estimates of future demand and network capacity planning
- Licensing fees for digital learning content
- Security filtering
- Network redundancy
- Use of open standards to ensure interoperability with other learning networks

Interoperability. As teachers and students go online for more of their teaching and learning needs, the number of systems they rely on increases. This makes it very difficult for teachers and students to see a comprehensive picture of their learning progress or to know where students are struggling so that teachers can give them effective support. There are some approaches in place to address these challenges. For example, the Guide to EdTech Procurement from Digital Learning Now! recommends leveraging industry standards for single sign-on and data interoperability.

Single sign-on. Apps and tools can be built to enable single sign-on— allowing teachers and students to log in to all their applications with a single password. A teacher teaching six classes of students a day with multiple apps and tools needs a way to manage learning content, attendance, student progress, and grades. Students and teachers having to keep track of a different user name and password to log in to each system wastes time and creates

96 Office of Educational Technology

frustration. In addition, if all the different learning systems do not recognize who a student is, they cannot help schools create a complete picture of that student's learning. For all these reasons, solutions involving single sign-on are needed for teachers and students to access all their applications through a single log-in credential. Many districts are even moving from preferring single sign-on to requiring it.

Interoperable systems. No one app or tool can provide all the functionality that every teacher, student, or parent may need. Enabling teachers and students to use more than one app seamlessly goes beyond just having a common log-in. Basic information, such as student schedules or courses completed, may need to be shared from one system to another to provide the best learning experience. For example, if a student demonstrates the mastery of a new concept in an online learning platform, that might be reflected in an app that the teacher or families use to track student progress.

One common format for Web services in education is the Learning Tools Interoperability standard. The IMS Global Learning Consortium developed this standard, and information about the specification can be found on its website. This standard allows learning management systems to exchange data with other learning tools and applications approved for use by the school so that students can have a seamless learning experience even if they are using apps created by different developers.

Data interoperability and standards. Regardless of whether you enable data sharing through an existing or custom application program interface or through a data export option, in order to be useful, the data need to be in a common format. For example, when transferring student data between systems, should a system indicate gender as *M* or *F* or as *male* or *female*? Should the name of the field be *student name* or *first name*? These are essential items to define if we are going to allow students to move seamlessly between learning apps. Fortunately, data interoperability frameworks have been established to ensure data are presented in usable formats. In additional to the CEDS mentioned earlier, the following are examples of existing frameworks, resources, and organizational alliances that address the issue of data interoperability:

- The Schools Interoperability Framework (SIF) is an open data sharing specification that includes an Extensible Markup Language (XML) for modeling educational data and service-oriented architecture for sharing the data between institutions.

- The Interoperability Standards for Education: Working Together to Strategically Connect the K–12 Enterprise, developed by CoSN, is a primer for education leaders to better understand issues related to building technology infrastructures that support learning.
- The Postsecondary Electronic Standards Council is a nonprofit umbrella organization that promotes the implementation and usage of data exchange standards.
- The Ed-Fi Alliance supports the creation of common data standards for communication among educational tools. Ed-Fi focuses on providing educators with dashboard starter kits showing real-time data displays.

Recommendations

- **Ensure students and educators have broadband access to the Internet and adequate wire-Less connectivity, with a special focus on equity of access outside of school.**
  Although connectivity itself does not ensure transformational use of technology to enable learning, lack of connectivity almost certainly precludes it. Working with federal programs such as E-rate through the FCC, as well as with nonprofit partners such as CoSN, EducationSuperHighway, EveryoneOn, and others, states, districts, and post-secondary institutions should make sure technology-enabled learning is available for all students, everywhere, all the time.
- **Ensure that every student and educator has at Least one Internet access device and appropriate software and resources for research, communication, multimedia content creation, and collaboration for use in and out of school.**
  Only when learners have the tools necessary to complete these activities are they able to realize the potential of education technologies fully. States and districts should make sure such device purchases are funded sustainably with a plan for device refresh.
- **Support the development and use of openly licensed educational materials to promote innovative and creative opportunities for all learners and accelerate the development and adoption of new open technology–based learning tools and courses.**

Similar to those leading state and local efforts under way in California, Illinois, and Washington state, administrators and policymakers at all levels and in formal and informal spaces should consider the diversified learning paths and potential cost savings inherent in the use of such openly licensed resources.

- **Draft sustainability plans for infrastructure concerns that include upgrades of wired and wireless access as well as device refresh plans and sustainable funding sources while ensuring the safety and protection of student data.**
As state and local education institutions work to bridge the existing digital divide, they concurrently should be drafting plans for the upgrade of infrastructure necessary to meet the needs of increased user demand as well as speeds necessary for the use of evolving technologies. These plans should include specific systems and strategies for protecting student data, be drafted with cross-stakeholder groups, and include special consideration of funding sustainability and possible partners.

- **Create a comprehensive map and database of connectivity, device access, use of openly licensed educational resources, and their uses across the country.**
To understand the digital divide better and progress toward bridging it, researchers, state and local officials, and district administrators should work in concert with one another to test connectivity speeds in schools and homes and to identify the kinds of devices to which educators and students have access and the ratios of devices to users within education institutions. The building of such a map and database would allow for the visualization of inequities of access and targeted interventions to alleviate them. In addition, the level of engagement with openly licensed learning materials should be made transparent as an indicator of progress toward equitable access and effective allocation of resources.

CONCLUSION

The timing has never been better for using technology to enable and improve learning at all levels, in all places, and for people of all backgrounds. From the modernization of E-rate to the proliferation and adoption of openly licensed educational resources, the key pieces necessary to realize best the transformations made possible by technology in education are in place.

Educators, policymakers, administrators, and teacher preparation and professional development programs now should embed these tools and resources into their practices. Working in collaboration with families, researchers, cultural institutions, and all other stakeholders, these groups can eliminate inefficiencies, reach beyond the walls of traditional classrooms, and form strong partnerships to support everywhere, all-the-time learning.

Although the presence of technology does not ensure equity and accessibility in learning, it has the power to lower barriers to both in ways previously impossible. No matter their perceived abilities or geographic locations, all learners can access resources, experiences, planning tools, and information that can set them on a path to acquiring expertise unimaginable a generation ago.

All of this can work to augment the knowledge, skills, and competencies of educators. Tools and data systems can be integrated seamlessly to provide information on student learning progress beyond the static and dated scores of traditional assessments. Learning dashboards and collaboration and communication tools can help connect teachers and families with instantaneous ease. This all is made more likely with the guidance of strong vision and leadership at all levels from teacher-leaders to school, district, and state administrators. For these roles, too, technology allows greater communication, resource sharing, and improved practice so that the vision is owned by all and dedicated to helping every individual in the system improve learning for students.

It is a time of great possibility and progress for the use of technology to support learning.

Challenges Remain

For all the possibilities of technology-enabled learning, it also creates challenges we will face as we embrace the change necessary to realize its potential. With the proliferation of devices and applications, we should build all educators' understanding of and ability to serve as stewards of student data so that only those with lawful access to the data can access it. We also need to find new and creative ways to solve the problem of connectivity in learners' homes so that the learning made possible in connected schools does not end when students leave for the day.

As we bridge the digital divide in schools and homes across the country, we also should build educator capacity to ask students to take part in new and transformational learning experiences with technology. This will require more than sharing tips in the faculty lounge or after-school professional development for educators. It also will require systemic change on the part of teacher preparation providers so their faculty and programming reflect more closely the standards and settings for which they are preparing teacher candidates.

These partnerships between teacher preparation programs and school districts are emblematic of the types of partnerships we will need to build across all education groups if we hope to increase the use of technology in learning from an add-on to an integral and foundational component of our education system.

We Already Have Begun

As illustrated in the examples throughout this plan, there are schools, organizations, and partnerships across the country already engaged in the important work of shifting practices to serve students better through technology. Indeed, it never has been easier to share innovations and lessons learned and muster the resources necessary to catalyze learning with technology. From the NETP to Connected Educator Month to LearningRegistry.org, from rapid cycle technology evaluations to education innovation clusters: The work of educators and other stakeholders with vision and a commitment to improving learning in America is well under way.

RECOMMENDATIONS

Section 1: Learning

- **States, districts, and post-secondary institutions should develop and implement learning resources that embody the flexibility and power of technology to create equitable and accessible learning ecosystems that make learning possible everywhere and all the time for all students.**

Whether creating learning resources internally, drawing on collaborative networks, or using tradi- tional procurement procedures, institutions should insist on the use of resources and the design of learning experiences that use UD practices to ensure accessibility and increased equity of learning opportunities.

- **States, districts, and post-secondary institutions should develop and implement learning resources that use technology to embody design principles from the learning sciences.**
  Educational systems have access to cutting-edge learning sciences research. To make better use of the existing body of research literature, however, educators and researchers will need to work together to determine the most useful dissemination methods for easy incorporation and synthesis of research findings into teachers' instructional practices.
- **States, districts, and post-secondary institutions should take inventory of and align all learning technology resources to intended educational outcomes. using this inventory, they should document all possible learner pathways to expertise, such as combinations of formal and informal learning, blended learning, and distance learning.**
  Without thoughtful accounting of the available tools and resources within formal and informal learning spaces within a community, matching learners to high-quality pathways to expertise is left to chance. Such an undertaking will require increased capacity within organizations that have never considered such a mapping of educational pathways. To aid in these efforts, networks such as LRNG, the Hive Learning Networks, and education innovation clusters can serve as models for cross-stakeholder collaboration in the interest of best using existing resources to present learners with pathways to learning and expertise.
- **Education stakeholders should develop a born accessible standard of learning resource design to help educators select and evaluate learning resources for accessibility and equity of learning experience.**
  Born accessible is a play on the term born digital and is used to convey the idea that materials that are born digital also can and should be born accessible. If producers adopt current industry standards for producing educational materials, materials will be accessible out of the box. Using the principles and research-base of UD and UDL, this standard would serve as a commonly accepted framework and language around design

for accessibility and offer guidance to vendors and third-party technology developers in interactions with states, districts, and institutions of higher education.

Section 2: Teaching

- **Provide pre-service and in-service educators with professional learning experiences powered by technology to increase their digital literacy and enable them to create compelling learning activities that improve learning and teaching, assessment, and instructional practices.**
  To make this goal a reality, teacher preparation programs, school systems, state and local poli- cymakers, and educators should come together in the interest of designing pre- and in-service professional learning opportunities that are aligned specifically with technology expectations outlined within state standards and that are reflective of the increased connectivity of and access to devices in schools. Technology should not be separate from content area learning but used to transform and expand pre- and in-service learning as an integral part of teacher learning.

- **Use technology to provide all learners with online access to effective teaching and better learning opportunities with options in places where they are not otherwise available.**
  This goal will require leveraging partner organizations and building institutional and teacher capac- ity to take advantage of free and openly licensed educational content such as that indexed on LearningRegistry.org. Adequate connectivity will increase equitable access to resources, instruc- tion, expertise, and learning pathways regardless of learners' geography, socio-economic status, or other factors that historically may have put them at an educational disadvantage.

- **Develop a teaching force skilled in online and blended instruction.**
  Our education system continues to see a marked increase in online learning opportunities and blended learning models in traditional schools. To meet the need this represents better, institu- tions of higher education, school districts, classroom educators, and researchers need to come together to ensure practitioners have access to current information regarding research-supported practices and an

understanding of the best use of emerging online technologies to support learn- ing in online and blended spaces.

- **Develop a common set of technology competency expectations for university professors and candidates exiting teacher preparation programs for teaching in technologically enabled schools and post-secondary education institutions.**
There should be no uncertainty of whether a learner entering a PK–12 classroom or college lecture hall will encounter a teacher or instructor fully capable of taking advantage of technology to transform learning. Accrediting institutions, advocacy organizations, state policymakers, administrators, and educators have to collaborate on a set of clear and common expectations and credentialing regarding educators' abilities to design and implement technology-enabled learning environments effectively.

Section 3: Leadership

- **Establish clear strategic planning connections among all state, district, university, and school levels and how they relate to and are supported by technology to improve learning.**
Although some of these efforts are supported by summits organized at the federal level by Future Ready Schools, state and local authorities are uniquely suited to understand the needs and resources available within their local education ecosystems. Broad, coordinated strategic planning requires a commitment from all parties involved to collaborate consistently across organizational boundaries. These conversations and connections need proactive champions who will invest in working at this level and who can take advantage of existing state and regional conferences to further this work.
- **Set a vision for the use of technology to enable learning such that leaders bring all stakeholder groups to the table, including students, educators, families, technology professionals, community groups, cultural institutions, and other interested parties.**
Although not all parties will be responsible for the execution of a vision for the use of technology to enable learning, by making certain all involved stakeholder groups are part of the vision-setting process, leaders will ensure better community support and the establishment of a plan for learn- ing technology that reflects local needs and goals.

- **Develop funding models and plans for sustainable technology purchases and leverage openly licensed content while paying special attention to eliminating those resources and tasks that can be made obsolete by technology.**
Rather than viewing technology as an add-on component to support learning, leaders should take stock of current systems and processes across learning systems and identify those that can be augmented or replaced by existing technologies. During the planning process, they also should identify systems and processes for which no replacement currently exists within the district, school, or college and set goals for developing more efficient solutions.

- **Develop clear communities of practice for education leaders at all levels that act as a hub for setting vision, understanding research, and sharing practices.**
Building on the model of the education innovation clusters, state, district, university, and com- munity organization leaders should establish cohesive communities of practice—in person and online—to create virtuous cycles for sharing the most recent research and effective practices in the use of educational technology.

Section 4: Assessment

- **Revise practices, policies, and regulations to ensure privacy and information protection while enabling a model of assessment that includes ongoing gathering and sharing of data for con- tinuous improvement of learning and teaching.**
This will require not only greater systems interoperability standards but also increased capacity on the part of educators and administrators to understand the types of systems they want to establish within schools and colleges. In addition, they will need to have an understanding of the standards of interoperability they should demand from vendors. A key component of this increased capacity should ensure educational leaders have a firm understanding of privacy and security concerns, how those concerns are addressed within the school or system, and clear communication of policies and procedures with all stakeholders. Achievement of this recommendation would benefit from the involvement and guidance of organizations, such as CoSN,

ISTE, and the State Educational Technology Directors Association (SETDA), that have developed specialized expertise in these areas.

- **States, districts, and others should design, develop, and implement learning dashboards, response systems, and communication pathways that give students, educators, families, and other stakeholders timely and actionable feedback about student learning to improve achieve- ment and instructional practices.**

The next generation of such tools should integrate across platforms and tools seamlessly, be designed with a mobile-first mindset, and be guided by UD and UDL principles to ensure acces- sibility by all stakeholders. Although current products and dashboards include basic functionality and features that improve on those of their predecessors, future iterations should be built on a premise of feedback and conversation, allowing learners and families to discuss learning out- comes and evidence and increasing agency and ownership across stakeholder groups.

- **Create and validate an integrated system for designing and implementing valid, reliable, and cost-effective assessments of complex aspects of 21st century expertise and competencies across academic disciplines.**

Interoperable formative assessment formats offered by major testing consortia for use by educa- tors throughout the year are an important first step. However, work remains to ensure more educa- tors have access to high-quality formative assessment tools and to develop additional capacities to assess both cognitive and non-cognitive skills better. Moving forward, increasing educator capacity for the design and deployment of valid and reliable formative assessments will require the concerted efforts of current assessment developers, teacher preparation programs, school systems, and researchers. Furthermore, colleges and universities will benefit from system-wide reviews of assessment practices and from ensuring all faculty have deep understandings of key principles and practices surrounding the design and implementation of effective learning assessments.

- **Research and development should be conducted that explore how embedded assessment technologies such as simulations, collaboration environments, virtual worlds, games, and cognitive tutors can be used to engage and motivate learners while assessing complex skills.**

Although some of this research is in its early stages, the way forward will require close collaboration among organizations—such as GlassLab, Games for Change, and iCivics; colleges, universities, infor- mal learning spaces, and schools; philanthropic organizations; and research institutions—that have a deep understanding of how game mechanics increase learner motivation. This collaboration can lead to the development of more effective and engaging experiences to support learning.

Section 5: Infrastructure

- **Ensure students and educators have broadband access to the Internet and adequate wire- Less connectivity, with a special focus on equity of access outside of school.**
  Although connectivity itself does not ensure transformational use of technology to enable learn- ing, lack of connectivity almost certainly precludes it. Working with federal programs such as E-rate through the FCC, as well as with nonprofit partners such as CoSN, EducationSuperHighway, EveryoneOn, and others, states, districts, and post-secondary institutions should make sure tech- nology-enabled learning is available for all students, everywhere, all the time.

- **Ensure that every student and educator has at Least one Internet access device and appro- priate software and resources for research, communication, multimedia content creation, and collaboration for use in and out of school.**
  Only when learners have the tools necessary to complete these activities are they able to realize the potential of education technologies fully. States and districts should make sure such device purchases are funded sustainably with a plan for device refresh.

- **Support the development and use of openly licensed educational materials to promote innovative and creative opportunities for all learners and accelerate the development and adoption of new open technology–based learning tools and courses.**
  Similar to those leading state and local efforts under way in California, Illinois, and Washington state, administrators and policymakers at all levels and in formal and informal spaces should consider the diversified learning paths and potential cost savings inherent in the use of such openly licensed resources.

- **Draft sustainability plans for infrastructure concerns that include upgrades of wired and wire-less access as well as device refresh plans and sustainable funding sources while ensuring the safety and protection of student data.**
- As state and local education institutions work to bridge the existing digital divide, they concur- rently should be drafting plans for the upgrade of infrastructure necessary to meet the needs of increased user demand as well as speeds necessary for the use of evolving technologies. These plans should include specific systems and strategies for protecting student data, be drafted with cross-stakeholder groups, and include special consideration of funding sustainability and possible partners.
- **Create a comprehensive map and database of connectivity, device access, use of openly licensed educational resources, and their uses across the country.**
- To understand the digital divide better and progress toward bridging it, researchers, state and local officials, and district administrators should work in concert with one another to test connectivity speeds in schools and homes and to identify the kinds of devices to which educators and students have access and the ratios of devices to users within education institutions. The building of such a map and database would allow for the visualization of inequities of access and targeted interventions to alleviate them. In addition, the level of engagement with openly licensed learning materials should be made transparent as an indicator of progress toward equitable access and effective allocation of resources.

APPENDIX A - FUTURE READY RESOURCES

Alberta Education. (2013). *Learning and technology policy framework 2013.* Edmonton, AB, Canada: Alberta Education, School Technology Branch. Retrieved from http://www.education. alberta.ca/media/7792655/learning-and-technology-policy-framework-web.pdf

Alliance for Excellent Education. (2012). *The digital learning imperative: How technology and teaching meet today's education challenges.* Retrieved from http://all4ed.org/wp-content/uploads/2012/01/Digital LearningImperative.pdf

American Association of School Administrators. (2010). *2011 district excellence award for digital learning*. Retrieved from http://www.aasa.org/uploadedFiles/Programs_and_Events/Awards_ and_Scholarships/Technology_Award/2011_Technology_Award/2011_Te chnology_Award2011_ AASA_LS_App_procedure_082410.pdf

Amirian, S. (2007). Digital backpacks: Facilitating faculty implementation of technologies for teaching and learning. *Computers in the Schools, 24*(1/2), 5–14.

Anderson, R. E. and Dexter, S. L. (2000). School technology leadership: Incidence and impact. Irvine: University of California, Center for Research on Information Technology and Organizations. Retrieved from http://escholarship.org/uc/item/76s142fc#page-7

Anderson, R. E. and Dexter, S. L. (2005). School technology leadership: An empirical investigation of prevalence and effect. *Educational Administration Quarterly, 41*(1), 49–82.

Anderson, T. and Elloumi, F. (Eds.). (2004). *The theory and practice of online learning*. Athabasca, AB, Canada: Athabasca University Press.

Annenberg Institute for School Reform. (2004). *Professional learning communities: Professional development strategies that improve instruction*. Providence, RI: Author. Retrieved from http:// www.annenberginstitute.org/pdf/proflearning.pdf

Argueta, R., Huff, J., Tingen, J. and Corn, J. O. (2011). *Laptop initiatives: Summary of research across seven states* (Friday Institute White Paper No. 4). Raleigh: North Carolina State University, the William & Ida Friday Institute for Educational Innovation. Retrieved from https://www.fi.ncsu.edu/wp-content/uploads/2013/05/laptop-initiatives-summary-of-research-across-seven-states.pdf

Armstrong, M. and Earle, L. (2012). *Sustained blended professional development in the 21st century*. Retrieved from http://etec.ctlt.ubc.ca/ 510wiki/Sustained_Blended_Professional_Developmentjn_the_21st_Cent ury

Attwell, G. (2007). Personal learning environments—The future of elearning? *eLearning Papers, 2*(1), 1–8.

Barnett, H. (2002). How to guarantee a learning return on your technology investment. *eSchool News*, 1–5.

Bauer, J. and Kenton, J. (2005). Toward technology integration in the schools: Why it isn't happening. *Journal of Technology and Teacher Education, 13*(4), 519–546.

Bolam, R., McMahon, A., Stoll, L., Thomas, S. and Wallace, M. (2005). *Creating and sustaining effective professional learning communities* (Research Report No. 637). Bristol, England: University of Bristol. Retrieved from http://dera.ioe.ac.uk/5622/1/RR637.pdf

Buckingham, D. (2007). Digital media literacies: Rethinking media education in the age of the Internet. *Research in Comparative and International Education, 2*(1), 43–55.

Burden, K., Hopkins, P., Male, T., Martin, S. and Trala, C. (2012). *iPad Scotland evaluation*. Hull, England: University of Hull. Retrieved from http://www.janhylen.se/wp-content/ uploads/2013/01/Skottland.pdf

Cavanaugh, C., Dawson, K. and Ritzhaupt, A. (2011). An evaluation of the conditions, processes, and consequences of laptop computing in K–12 classrooms. *Journal of Educational Computing Research, 45*(3), 359–378.

Clifford, M., Behrstock-Sherratt, E. and Fetters, J. (2012). *The ripple effect: A synthesis of research on principal influence to inform performance evaluation design.* Washington, DC: American Institutes for Research. Retrieved from http://www.air.org/sites/default/files/downloads/ report/ 1707_The_Ripple_Effect_d8_Online_0.pdf

Clifford, M., Fetters, J. and Yoder, N. (2014). *The five essential practices of school leadership: A framework for assessing practice.* Washington, DC: American Institutes for Research. Retrieved from http://tle.vide.vi/ data/userfiles/14-2159_AIR_5_Essential%20Practices% 20USVI%20 FINAL.pdf

Clifford, M. and Ross, S. (2011). *Designing principal evaluation systems: Research to guide decision-making.* Washington, DC: National Association of Elementary School Principals. Retrieved from https://www.naesp.org/sites/default/files/PrincipalEvaluation_ExecutiveSu mmary.pdf

Coggshall, J. G., Rasmussen, C., Colton, A., Milton, J. and Jacques, C. (2012). *Generating teaching effectiveness: The role of job-embedded professional learning in teacher evaluation.* Washington, DC: National Comprehensive Center for Teacher Quality. Retrieved from http://www.gtlcenter. org/sites/default/files/docs/GeneratingTeachingEffectiveness.pdf

Consortium for School Networking. (2012). *Framework of essential skills of the K–12 CTO.* Washington, DC: Author. Retrieved from http://www.cosn.org/sites/default/files/Framework_1218_2013_Public. pdf?sid=4509

110 Office of Educational Technology

Consortium for School Networking. (2013). *Administrator's guide to mobile learning*. Washington, DC: Author. Retrieved from https://sites.google.com/site/cosnlmlresources/

Consortium for School Networking. (2014a). *The empowered superintendent: Professional learning module 1—Five imperatives for technology leadership*. Washington, DC: Author. Retrieved from http://cosn.org/sites/default/files/pdf/CoSN%20Empowered%20Superintendent%20Module%201%20FINAL.pdf

Consortium for School Networking. (2014b). *The empowered superintendent: Self-assessment for superintendents*. Washington, DC: Author. Retrieved from http://cosn.org/sites/default/files/pdf/CoSN%20Superintendent%20Self-Assessment%20FINAL.pdf

Consortium for School Networking. (2014c). *Rethinking educational equity in a digital era: Forging a strong partnership between district Title I and technology leaders*. Washington, DC: Author. Retrieved from http://www.cosn.org/sites/default/files/pdf/Rethinking%20Educational%20 Equity%20in%20a%20Digital%20Era,%20June%202014.pdf

Consortium for School Networking. (2015). *NMC horizon report: 2015 K–12 edition*. Washington, DC: Author. Retrieved from http://www.nmc.org/publication/ nmc-horizon-report-2015-k-12-edition/

Council of Chief State School Officers. (2008). *Educational leadership policy standards: ISLLC 2008*. Washington, DC: Author. Retrieved from http://www.ccsso.org/Documents/2008/Educational_Leadership_Policy_Standards_2008.pdf

Croft, A., Coggshall, J. G., Dolan, M. and Powers, E. (with Killion, J.). (2010). *Job-embedded professional development: What it is, who is responsible, and how to get it done well*. Washington, DC: National Comprehensive Center for Teacher Quality. Retrieved from http://www.gtlcenter.org/sites/default/files/docs/JEPD%20Issue%20Brief.pdf

Darling-Hammond, L., Wei, R. C., Andree, A., Richardson, N. and Orphanos, S. (2009). *Professional learning in the learning profession: A status report on teacher development in the United States and abroad*. Oxford, OH: National Staff Development Council and the School Redesign Network at Stanford University. Retrieved from http://www.learningforward.org/docs/pdf/nsdcstudy2009.pdf

Dawson, K. (2012). Using action research projects to examine teacher technology integration practices. *Journal of Digital Learning in Teacher Education, 28*(3), 117–124.

Dawson, K., Cavanaugh, C. and Ritzhaupt, A. D. (2008). Florida's EETT Leveraging Laptops Initiative and its impact on teaching practices. *Journal of Research on Technology in Education, 41*(2), 143–159.

Dede, C. (1998). The scaling-up process for technology-based educational innovations. In C. Dede (Ed.), *Learning with technology 1998: ASCD yearbook* (pp. 199–215). Alexandria, VA: ASCD.

Dede, C., Breit, L., Ketelhut, D. J., McCloskey, E. and Whitehouse, P. (2005). *An overview of current findings from empirical research on online teacher professional development.* Cambridge, MA: Harvard University Press. Retrieved from http://citeseerx.ist.psu.edu/viewdoc/ download?doi= 10.1.1.117.1285&rep=rep1&type=pdf

Derntl, M. and Motschnig-Pitrik, R. (2005). The role of structure, patterns, and people in blended learning. *The Internet and higher education, 8*(2), 111–130.

Devono, F. and Price, T. (2012). How principals and teachers perceived their superintendents' leadership in developing and supporting effective learning environments as measured by the superintendent efficacy questionnaire. *National Forum of Educational Administration and Supervision Journal, 29*(4), 1–14.

Digital Promise. (n.d.). *Educator micro-credentials.* Retrieved from http://www.digitalpromise.org/ initiatives/educator-micro-credentials

District Reform Support Network. (2015). *Blended learning readiness and progress rubric.* Raleigh, NC: Friday Institute for Educational Innovation. Retrieved from https://rttd.grads360. org/#communities/pdc/documents/ 7209

Duty, L. and Kern, T. (2014). *So you think you want to innovate? Emerging lessons and a new tool for state and district leaders working to build a culture of innovation.* Retrieved from http:// learningaccelerator.org/ media/29004d8f/Assessing%20Culture%20of%20Innovation_2Rev-TLA_j0.9_final.pdf

Education Reform Initiative (ERI) & Research Triangle Institute (RTI) International. (2013). *Turkey's FATIH project: A plan to conquer the digital divide, or a technological leap of faith?* Istanbul, Turkey: ERI, and Research Triangle Park, NC: RTI International. Retrieved from http://erg.sabanciuniv.edu/sites/erg.sabanciuniv.edu/files/Fatih.rapor_.EN G_.son_.pdf

Ertmer, P. (1999). Addressing first- and second-order barriers to change: Strategies for technology integration. *Educational Technology, Research and Development, 47*(4), 47–61.

112 Office of Educational Technology

Evans, M. (2012). *A guide to personalizing learning: Suggestions for the Race to the Top–District competition.* San Mateo, CA: Innosight Institute. Retrieved from http://www.christenseninstitute.org/wp-content/uploads/2013/04/A-guide-to-personalizing-learning.pdf

Flipped Learning Network. (2014). *What is flipped learning?* Retrieved from http://flippedlearning.org/cms/lib07/VA01923112/Centricity/Domain/46/FLIP_handout_FNL_Web.pdf

Forner, M., Bierlein-Palmer, L. and Reeves, P. (2012). Leadership practices of effective rural superintendents: Connections to Waters and Marzano's leadership correlates. *Journal of Research in Rural Education, 27*(8). Retrieved from http://jrre.vmhost.psu.edu/wp-content/uploads/2014/02/27-8.pdf

Fox, C., Waters, J., Fletcher, G. and Levin, D. (2012). *The broadband imperative: Recommendations to address K–12 education infrastructure needs.* Washington, DC: State Educational Technology Directors Association. Retrieved from http://www.setda.org/wp-content/uploads/2013/09/The_Broadband_Imperative.pdf

Freeland, J. and Hernandez, A. (with Samouha, A.). (2014). *Schools and software: What's now and what's next?* San Mateo, CA: Clayton Christensen Institute. Retrieved from http://www.christenseninstitute.org/wp-content/uploads/2014/06/Schools-and-Software.pdf

Fullan, M. and Donnelly, K. (2013). *Alive in the swamp: Assessing digital innovations in education.* London, England: Nesta. Retrieved from http://www.nesta.org.uk/sites/default/files/alive_in_ the_swamp.pdf

Garet, M. S., Porter, A. C., Desimone, L., Birman, B. F. and Yoon, K. S. (2001). What makes professional development effective? Results from a national sample of teachers. *American Educational Research Journal, 38*(4), 915–945.

Gray, T. and Silver-Pacuilla, H. (2011). *Breakthrough teaching and learning: How educational and assistive technologies are driving innovation.* New York: Springer.

Greenhow, C., Robelia, B. and Hughes, J. E. (2009). Learning, teaching, and scholarship in a digital age: Web 2.0 and classroom research—What path should we take "now"? *Educational Researcher, 38*(4), 246–259.

Grismore, B. A. (2012). *Mini technology manual for schools: An introduction to technology integration.* Retrieved from ERIC database. (ED533378)

Guskey, T. R. (2000). *Evaluating professional development.* Thousand Oaks, CA: Corwin. Hallinger, P. and Heck, R. (1998). Exploring the principal's contribution to school effectiveness: 1980–1995. *School Effectiveness and School Improvement, 9*(2), 157–191.

Hamdan, N., McKnight, P., McKnight, K. and Arfstrom, K. (2013). *The flipped learning model: A white paper based on the literature review titled "A review of flipped learning."* Retrieved from http://flippedlearning.org/cms/lib07/VA01923112/Centricity/Domain/41/WhitePaper_FlippedLearning.pdf

Hanover Research Council. (2009). *Best practices in online teaching strategies.* Washington, DC: Author. Retrieved from http://www.uwec.edu/AcadAff/resources/edtech/upload/BestPractices-in-Online-Teaching-Strategies-Membership.pdf

Horn, M. B., Gu, A. and Evans, M. (2014). *Knocking down barriers: How California superintendents are implementing blended learning.* San Mateo, CA: Clayton Christensen Institute. Retrieved from http://www.christenseninstitute.org/wp-content/uploads/2014/08/Knocking-downbarriers.pdf

Hsu, P. and Sharma, P. (2008). A case study of enabling factors in the technology integration change process. *Educational Technology & Society, 11*(4), 213–228.

Iiyoshi, T., Hannafin, M. J. and Wang, F. (2005). Cognitive tools and student-centered learning: Rethinking tools, functions and applications. *Educational Media International, 42*(4), 281–296.

iNACOL. (2011). *National standards for quality online courses.* Vienna, VA: International Association for K–12 Online Learning. Retrieved from http://www.inacol.org/cms/wp-content/uploads/2013/02/iNACOL_CourseStandards_2011.pdf

International Society for Technology in Education. (2008). *ISTE standards: Teachers.* Washington, DC: Author. Retrieved from http://www.iste.org/docs/pdfs/20-14_ISTE_Standards-T_PDF.pdf

International Society for Technology in Education. (2009a). *Essential conditions: Necessary conditions to effectively leverage technology for learning.* Arlington, VA: Author. Retrieved from http:// www.iste.org/docs/pdfs/netsessentialconditions.pdf

International Society for Technology in Education. (2009b). *ISTE standards: Administrators (ISTE standards•A).* Washington, DC: Author. Retrieved from http://www.iste.org/docs/pdfs/20- 14_ISTE_Standards-A_PDF.pdf

International Society for Technology in Education. (2011). *ISTE standards: Coaches.* Arlington, VA: Author. Retrieved from http://www.iste.org/docs/pdfs/20-14_ISTE_Standards-C_PDF.pdf

Ivanova, M. and Popova, A. (2009). An exploration of formal and informal learning flows in LMS 2.0: Case study Edu 2.0. *International Joint Conference on Web Intelligence and Intelligent Agent Technologies, 3,* 227–230. Washington, DC: IEEE Computer Society.

John Edward Porter Professional Development Center at Learning Point Associates. (2004). School survey for professional development tool: A measure of capacity. *Journal of Staff Development, 25*(1), 23–25.

Johnson, P. E. and Chrispeels, J. H. (2010). Linking the central office and its schools for reform. *Educational Administration Quarterly, 46*(5), 738–755.

Joint Information Systems Committee. (2004). *Effective practice with e-learning: A good practice guide in designing for learning.* Bristol, England: Author.

LaFee, S. (2013, March). Flipped learning. *School Administrator, 3*(70), 19–25.

Lai, K. W., Pratt, K., Anderson, M. and Stigter, J. (2006). *Literature review and synthesis: Online communities of practice.* Wellington, New Zealand: Ministry of Education. Retrieved from http://www.educationcounts.govt.nz/__data/assets/pdf_file/0019/7480/lrs-online-com.pdf

Laine, S. (with Behrstock-Sherratt, E. and Lasagna, M.). (2011). *Improving teacher quality: A guide for education leaders.* San Francisco, CA: Jossey-Bass.

Lankshear, C. and Knobel, M. (2011). *New literacies: Everyday practices and social learning.* New York, NY: McGraw-Hill.

Learning Accelerator. (n.d.). *District stakeholder blended learning readiness assessments.* Retrieved from http://learningaccelerator.org/media/91350018/BL%20District%20Assessment-FIN.pdf Learning Forward. (n.d.). *Standards for professional learning.* Retrieved from http://learning for-ward.org/standards-for-professional-learning

Leithwood, K., Louis, K. S., Anderson, S. and Wahlstrom, K. (2004). *How leadership influences student learning.* New York, NY: The Wallace Foundation.

Lombardi, M. M. (2007). *Authentic learning for the 21st century: An overview.* Louisville, CO: EDUCAUSE. Retrieved from http://net.educause.edu/ir/library/pdf/ELI3009.pdf

Lu, R. and Overbaugh, R. (2009). School environment and technology implementation in K–12 classrooms. *Computers in the Schools, 26*(2), 89–106.

Marzano, R., Waters, T. and McNulty, B. (2005). *School leadership that works: From research to results.* Alexandria, VA: ASCD.

McConnell, T. J., Parker, J. M., Eberhardt, J., Koehler, M. J. and Lundeberg, M. A. (2013). Virtual professional learning communities: Teachers' perceptions of virtual versus face-to-face professional development. *Journal of Science Education and Technology, 22*(3), 267–277.

Mid-continent Research for Education and Learning. (2000). *Principles in action: Stories of award-winning professional development* [Video]. Aurora, CO: Author.

Money matters: Budgets, finances, and resources for tech programs. (2008). *Technology and Learning, 28*(12), 2. Retrieved from https://www.questia.com/magazine/1G1-183422475/money-matters-budgets-finances-and-resources-for Moore, J. E. and Barab, S. A. (2002). The inquiry learning forum: A community of practice approach to online professional development. *Technology Trends, 46*(3), 44–49.

National Association of Secondary School Principals. (n.d.a). *Breaking ranks: The comprehensive framework for school improvement—Executive summary.* Reston, VA: Author. Retrieved from http://www.nassp.org/Content/158/BRFrameworkExecSummary.pdf

National Association of Secondary School Principals. (n.d.b). *Breaking ranks: A field guide for leading change—Executive summary.* Reston, VA: Retrieved from http://www.nassp.org/Content/158/BR3Change_Exec Summ_web.pdf

National Council of Teachers of English. (2008). *NCTE framework for 21st century curriculum and assessment.* Retrieved from http://www.ncte.org/governance/21stcenturyframework

National Education Association. (2012). *Preparing 21st century students for a global society: An educator's guide to the "four Cs."* Washington, DC: Author. Retrieved from http://www.nea.org/ assets/docs/A-Guide-to-Four-Cs.pdf

National Policy Board for Educational Administration. (2011). *Educational leadership program recognition standards: District level.* Austin, TX: Author. Retrieved from http://www.ncate.org/ LinkClick.aspx?fileticket= tFmaPVlwMMo%3D&tabid=676

National PTA. (n.d.). *National standards for family-school partnerships.* Alexandria, VA: Author. Retrieved from http://www.pta.org/files/National_Standards.pdf

Next Generation Learning Challenges. (n.d.). *Personalized learning.* Retrieved from http://nextgenlearning.org/topics/personalized-learning

North Carolina State University, The William & Ida Friday Institute for Educational Innovation. (n.d.a). *1:1 administrator survey*. Retrieved from https://eval.fi.ncsu.edu/wp-content/uploads/2013/12/1-1-Administrator-Survey_12-2013.pdf

North Carolina State University, The William & Ida Friday Institute for Educational Innovation. (n.d.b). *1:1 implementation rubric*. Raleigh, NC: Author. Retrieved from https://eval.fi.ncsu.edu/ wp-content/uploads/2013/06/1to1implementationrubric.pdf

North Carolina State University, The William & Ida Friday Institute for Educational Innovation. (n.d.c). *Profile for administrators (NETS*A)*. Raleigh, NC: Author. Retrieved from https://eval. fi.ncsu.edu/wp-content/uploads/2013/12/NETS-Profile-for-Administrators_12-2013.pdf

North Carolina State University, The William & Ida Friday Institute for Educational Innovation. (n.d.d). *School technology needs assessment*. Raleigh, NC: Author. Retrieved from https://www. fi.ncsu.edu/wp-content/uploads/2013/05/School-Technology-Needs-Assesment-STNA.pdf

North Carolina State University, The William & Ida Friday Institute for Educational Innovation. (2015). *North Carolina digital learning plan*. Raleigh, NC: Author. Retrieved from http:// ncdlplan.fincsu.wpengine. com/wp-content/uploads/sites/10/2015/09/NC-Digital-LearningDetailed-Plan-9-14-15.pdf

Nussbaum-Beach, S. and Hall, L. R. (2012). *The connected educator: Learning and leading in a digital age*. Bloomington, IN: Solution Tree.

O'Dwyer, L. M., Masters, J., Dash, S., De Kramer, R. M., Humez, A. and Russell, M. (2010). *e-Learning for educators: Effects of on-line professional development on teachers and their students— Executive summary of four randomized trials*. Chestnut Hill, MA: inTASC.

Owston, R., Wideman, H., Murphy, J. and Lupshenyuk, D. (2008). Blended teacher professional development: A synthesis of three program evaluations. *Internet and Higher Education, 11*, 201–210.

Parsad, B., Lewis, L. and Farris, E. (2001). *Teacher preparation and professional development: 2000* (NCES No. 2001-088). Washington, DC: U.S. Department of Education, Office of Educational Research and Improvement, National Center for Education Statistics. Retrieved from http:// nces.ed.gov/pubs2001/2001088.pdf

Penuel, W. R. (2006). Implementation and effects of one-to-one computing initiatives: A research synthesis. *Journal of Research on Technology in Education, 38*(3), 329–348.

Future Ready Learning 117

Porter, A. C., Garet, M. S., Desimone, L., Yoon, K. S. and Birman, B. F. (2000). *Does professional development change teaching practice? Results from a three-year study*. Washington, DC: U.S. Department of Education. Retrieved from http://files.eric.ed.gov/fulltext/ED455227.pdf

Preece, J. and Shneiderman, B. (2009). The reader-to-leader framework: Motivating technology-mediated social participation. *AIS Transactions on Human-Computer Interaction, 1*(1), 13–32.

Project RED. (n.d.). *Project RED: Findings*. Retrieved from http://www.one-to-oneinstitute.org/ findings

Project RED. (2012). *Project RED readiness tool*. Retrieved from https://docs.google.com/ spreadsheets/d/1A0Ez6KTPmGf5vryM0bEnsshOa5RHz_fbC1GtDd41IPg /edit?usp=sharing

Public Impact. (2013a). *A better blend: A vision for boosting student outcomes with digital learning*. Chapel Hill, NC: Author. Retrieved from http://opportunityculture.org/wp-content/uploads/2013/04/A_Better_ Blend_A_Visionjor_Boosting_Student_Outcomes_with_Digital_ Learning-Publicjmpact.pdf

Public Impact. (2013b). *Redesigning schools: Financial planning for secondary-level time-technology swap and multi-classroom leadership*. Chapel Hill, NC: Retrieved from http://opportunityculture. org/wp-content/uploads/2013/10/Financial_Planning_Secondary_Level_Time-Tech_Swap_MCLPublicjmpact.pdf

Rasmussen, C., Hopkins, S. and Fitzpatrick, M. (2004). Our work done well is like the perfect pitch. *Journal of Staff Development, 25*(1), 16–25.

Reeves, T. D. and Pedulla, J. J. (2011). Predictors of teacher satisfaction with online professional development: Evidence from the USA's e-Learning for Educators Initiative. *Professional Development in Education, 37*(4), 591–611.

Rogers Family Foundation. (2014). *Blended learning in Oakland: Initiative update, part 3*. Oakland, CA: Author. Retrieved from http://rogers foundation.org/system/resources/0000/0052/Oakland_Blended_Learning_ Case_Study_Part_3.pdf

Senge, P. (2000). *Schools that learn: A fifth discipline fieldbook for educators, parents, and everyone who cares about education*. New York, NY: Doubleday.

Shapley, K. S., Sheehan, D., Maloney, C. and Caranikas-Walker, F. (2010). Evaluating the implementation fidelity of technology immersion and its relationship with student achievement. *Journal of Technology, Learning, and Assessment, 9*(4), 5–68.

Stansbury, M. (2008). Schools need help with tech support. *eSchool News.* Retrieved from http:// www.eschoolnews.com/2008/01/09/schools-need-help-with-tech-support/

Staples, A., Pugach, M. C. and Himes, D. (2005). Rethinking the technology integration challenge: Cases from three urban elementary schools. *Journal of Research on Technology in Education, 37*(3), 285–311.

Steiner, L. (2004). *Designing effective professional development experiences: What do we know?* Naperville, IL: Learning Point Associates.

Stronge, J. H., Richard, H. B. and Catano, N. (2008). *Qualities of effective principals.* Alexandria, VA: ASCD.

Thigpen, K. (2014). *Creating anytime, anywhere learning for all students: Key elements of a comprehensive digital infrastructure.* Washington, DC: Alliance for Excellent Education. Retrieved from http://all4ed.org/reports-factsheets/creating-anytime-anywhere-learning-for-all-students-key-elements-of-a-comprehensive-digital-infrastructure/

Thomas, L. and Knezek, D. (2008). Information, communication, and educational technology standards for students, teachers, and school leaders. In J. Voogt & G. Knezek (Eds.), *International handbook of information technology in primary and secondary education* (Vol. 20, pp. 333–348). New York, NY: Springer.

Vescio, V., Ross, D. and Adams, A. (2008). A review of research on the impact of professional learning communities on teacher practice and student learning. *Teaching and Teacher Education, 24*(1), 80–91.

Wang, S.-K., Hsu, H.-Y., Campbell, T., Coster, D. C. and Longhurst, M. (2014). An investigation of middle school science teachers and students use of technology inside and outside of classrooms: Considering whether digital natives are more technology savvy than their teachers. *Education Technology Research and Development, 62*(6), 637–662.

Waters, J. T. and Marzano, R. J. (2006). *School district leadership that works: The effect of superintendent leadership on student achievement* (Working Paper). Denver, CO: Mid-continent Research for Education and Learning. Retrieved from http://www.ctc.ca.gov/educator-prep/ ASC/4005RR_Superintendent_Leadership.pdf

Waters, J. T., Marzano, R. J. and McNulty, B. (2003). *Balanced leadership: What 30 years of research tells us about the effect of leadership on student achievement* (Working Paper). Denver, CO: Mid-continent Research for

Education and Learning. Retrieved from http://www.ctc.ca.gov/educator-prep/ASC/5031RR_BalancedLeadership.pdf

Waugh, R. and Godfrey, J. (1993). Teacher receptivity to system-wide change in the implementation stage. *British Educational Research Journal, 19*(5), 565–578.

Wenger, E., Trayner, B. and de Laat, M. (2011). *Promoting and assessing value creation in communities and networks: A conceptual framework.* Heerlen, The Netherlands: Open University, Ruud de Moor Centrum.

Wolf, M. A. (2010). *Innovate to educate: System [re]design for personalized learning—A report from the 2010 symposium.* Washington, DC: Software & Information Industry Association. Retrieved from http://www.ccsso.org/Documents/2010%20Symposium%20on%20Personalized%20Learning.pdf

Yoon, K. S., Duncan, T., Lee, S. W.-Y., Scarloss, B. and Shapley, K. L. (2007). *Reviewing the evidence on how teacher professional development affects student achievement* (Issues & Answers Report, REL 2007–No. 033). Washington, DC: U.S. Department of Education, Institute of Education Sciences, National Center for Education Evaluation and Regional Assistance. Retrieved from http://ies.ed.gov/ncee/edlabs/regions/southwest/pdf/REL_2007033.pdf

APPENDIX B - ACKNOWLEDGMENTS

Project Team

This plan was developed under the guidance of **Richard Culatta, Joseph South, Katrina Stevens, Zac Chase,** and **Joan Lee** of the U.S. Department of Education, OET. Within the OET, technical assistance was provided by **Ernest Ezeugo, Daniel Kao, Ryan Lee, Laura McAllister,** and **Seth Wilbur.** Additional support was provided by **Heidi Silver-Pacuilla** of the U.S. Department of Education Office of Career, Technical, and Adult Education.

Tracy Gray of AIR led a team of experts in the development of the 2016 NETP. Valuable support was provided by **Alise Brann, Marshal Conley, Arayle Freels, Jillian Reynolds,** and **Kristin Ruedel.** Additional contributions were made by **Bani Dheer, Larry Friedman, Jessica Heppen, Michael McGarrah, Caroline Martin, Snehal Pathak,** and **Cheryl Pruce. Karen Cator** and **Doug Levin** served as independent consultants.

Office of Educational Technology

Susan Thomas served as the principal writer for the NETP. Graphics were developed by **O2 Lab** in Washington, D.C.

Technical Working Group

In addition, we extend our thanks to a Technical Working Group (TWG) of leading educators, technology innovators, and researchers who reviewed drafts of the guide and provided invaluable feedback, writing, and examples from their experiences.

James Basham Associate Professor, University of Kansas

Cathy Casserly Vice President, Learning Networks, EdCast Inc.

Vint Cerf Vice President & Chief Internet Evangelist, Google

Dallas Dance Superintendent, Baltimore County Public Schools

Melissa Gresalfi Assistant Professor, Learning Sciences, Vanderbilt University

Harrison Keller Vice Provost for Higher Education Policy & Research & Executive Director of the Center for Teaching and Learning, University of Texas at Austin

Michael Levine Founding Director, Joan Ganz Cooney Center, Sesame Workshop

Jeremy Macdonald Director, Technology and Innovation, Redmond School District, Oregon **Jennie Magiera** Chief Technology Officer, Des Plaines Public School District 62, Illinois

Beth Simone Noveck Professor and Director, The Govlab, New York University

Kylie Peppler Associate Professor, Learning Sciences, Indiana University at Bloomington

Candace Thille Senior Research Fellow, Office of the Vice Provost for Online Learning & Assistant Professor, Stanford University

Yong Zhao Presidential Chair & Director, Institute for Global & Online Education, University of Oregon

We extend our appreciation to the many individuals who participated in the numerous discussions, focus groups, presentations, webinars, public forums, and Web-based comment events that were held throughout the plan development process. A broad cross section of stakeholders contributed their input through the following activities. Our appreciation also goes to those who organized outreach efforts that helped gather valuable insights from across the field.

Interviews

Public Policymakers

Claudine Brown Assistant Secretary for Education & Access, Smithsonian Institution

Nadya Chinoy Dabby Assistant Deputy Secretary, U.S. Department of Education, Office of Innovation and Improvement

Seth Galanter Deputy Assistant Secretary, U.S. Department of Education, Office for Civil Rights

Dipayan Ghosh National Economic Council, White House Office of Science and Technology Policy

Roosevelt Johnson Deputy Associate Administrator, NASA, Office of Education

Patrick Martin Instructional Systems Specialist for Educational Technology, U.S. Department of Defense, Education Activity

Ruth Neild Director, U.S. Department of Education, Institute of Education Sciences

Jim Shelton Deputy Secretary, U.S. Department of Education

Adrian Talley Principal Deputy Director & Associate Director for Education, U.S. Department of Defense, Education Activity

Bob Wise Director, Alliance for Education

Michael Yudin Acting Assistant Secretary, U.S. Department of Education, Office of Special Education & Rehabilitative Services

Leaders of National Organizations

Karen Cator President & Chief Executive Officer, Digital Promise

Gail Connelly Executive Director, National Association of Elementary School Principals

Betsy Corcoran Chief Executive Officer & Co-founder, EdSurge

Dan Domenech Executive Director, American Association of School Administrators

Elyse Eidman-Aadahl Executive Director, National Writing Project

Scott Ellis Chief Executive Officer, Learning Accelerator

Ann Flynn Director of Education Technology, National School Boards Association

Stephanie Hirsch Executive Director, Learning Forward

Margaret Honey Project Director, New York Hall of Science

Michael Horn Co-founder & Executive Director for Education, Clayton Christensen Institute

122 Office of Educational Technology

Keith Krueger Chief Executive Officer, Consortium for School Networking
Doug Levin Executive Director, State Educational Technology Directors Association
Brian Lewis Chief Executive Officer, International Society for Technology in Education
Evan Marwell Chief Executive Officer and Founder, EducationSuperHighway
Barbara Means Director, Technology in Learning, SRI International
Chris Minnich Executive Director, Council of Chief State School Officers
Diana Oblinger Chief Executive Officer, EDUCAUSE
Shelley Pasnik Director and Vice President, Center for Children and Technology
Susan Patrick President and Chief Executive Officer, iNACOL
Shawn Rubin Director, Technology Integration, Highlander Institute

Outreach Events

SETDA October 29, 2014
iNACOL Conference November 4, 2014
Higher Education Experts November 9, 2014
ConnectED to the Future Superintendent Summit November 18, 2014
Open Education Experts November 20, 2014
ISTE Conference December 5, 2014
Silicon Valley—Innovators February 24, 2015
Silicon Valley—Developers and Investors February 24, 2015
PDX—Portland State University Conference February 25, 2015

Target Virtual Outreach

Classroom Teachers February 9, 2015
Assessment Experts February 11, 2015
Adult Education Experts February 18, 2015
Librarians February 18, 2015
Teacher Preparation Experts February 18, 2015
District Administrators February 19, 2015
Informal Learning Experts February 20, 2015
Researchers February 20, 2015

External Reviewers

Frederick Brown Deputy Executive Director, Learning Forward
Stevie Chepko Council for the Accreditation of Educator Preparation
Elyse Eidman-Aadahl Executive Director, National Writing Project
Keith Krueger Chief Executive Officer, Consortium for School Networking
Evan Marwell Chief Executive Officer, EducationSuperHighway
Diana Oblinger President Emeritus, EDUCAUSE
Desiree Pointer-Mace Associate Professor and Associate Dean for Graduate
Programs in the School of Education, Alvemo College

APPENDIX C - THE DEVELOPMENT OF THE 2016 NETP

The 2016 NETP builds on the foundation of the 2010 Plan, *Transforming American Education: Learning Powered by Technology.* The 2016 NETP explores the exciting advances, opportunities, and research that illustrate how teaching and learning can be enhanced with the innovative use of technology and openly licensed content and resources. The 2016 NETP offers a vision of how technology can transform formal and informal learning, the critical elements such as qualified teachers and staff, high-quality curriculum and resources, strong leadership, robust infrastructure, and aligned assessments.

The development of the 2016 NETP began with a series of meetings with the TWG, which consisted of 13 leading educators, technology innovators, and researchers. The first meeting was a one-day gathering to develop the vision and overarching themes. On the basis of expertise and interest, each of the TWG members was assigned to a sub-group to focus on one of the five key topic areas: Learning, Teaching, Leadership, Assessment, and Infrastructure. TWG members provided feedback that informed the development of the 2016 NETP outline and working drafts, including the identification of relevant research and exemplary programs. The TWG reviewed two drafts and offered their comments and recommendations, which were incorporated into the final document. In addition, a group of national content experts and members of key stakeholder groups reviewed and provided feedback on an early draft, which was also incorporated into the document.

The 2016 NETP also was informed by a series of interviews conducted by the AIR team with 31 leaders from the U.S. Department of Education; the White House Office of Science and Technology Policy; and other government agencies, technology innovators, and nonprofit organizations. These

124 Office of Educational Technology

interviews provided valuable insight into the priorities and practices being implemented to further the goals of ensuring equity and accessibility to high-quality instruction enabled by technology for all students.

In addition, the AIR team convened a series of nine face-to-face and eight virtual focus groups to gather further insights and recommendations for the 2016 NETP. The participants represented a broad cross section of key stakeholders, including practitioners, state and local administrators, technology innovators, experts, and developers. The focus groups also provided the opportunity for participants to identify exemplars of the innovative use of technology in formal and informal educational settings.

Throughout the development process for the 2016 NETP, attention was focused on the compilation and review of proposed examples to illustrate the innovative use of technology across the five areas of Learning, Teaching, Leadership, Assessment, and Infrastructure. Suggestions were collected from the TWG members, interviewees, focus group participants, and AIR and OET staff. In addition, the AIR team conducted a review of the literature, a survey of national education technology initiatives (for example, Future Ready, CoSN, ISTE, and Digital Promise), and Internet searches to identify these exemplary programs and initiatives. More than 235 examples were identified during the course of the project. In an effort to identify those examples that best aligned with the 2016 NETP, the AIR and OET teams used the following screening criteria to make the final selection: quality of the user experience, evidence of success, and clear use of technology (where appropriate). A total of 53 examples are included in the 2016 NETP to deepen an understanding of the innovative use of technology to enhance teaching and learning in formal and informal settings.

End Notes for Introduction

[1] U.S. Department of Education. (2013). *U.S. Department of Education strategic plan for fiscal years 2014–2018*. Washington, DC: Author. Retrieved from http://www2.ed.gov/about/reports/strat/plan2014-18/strategic-plan.pdf.

[2] Assistive Technology Industry Association. *What is assistive technology? How is it funded?* Retrieved from http:// www.atia.org/i4a/pages/index.cfm?pageid=3859.

[3] American Association of School Administrators, Consortium for School Networking, and National School Boards Association. *Leading the digital leap*. Retrieved from leaddigitalleap.org.

[4] McConnaughey, J., Nila, C. A. and Sloan, T. (1995). *Falling through the net: A survey of the "have nots" in rural and urban America*. Washington, DC: National Telecommunications and Information Administration, United States Department of Commerce.

Future Ready Learning 125

[5] Culp, K. M., Honey, M. and Mandinach, E. (2005). A retrospective on twenty years of education technology policy. *Journal of Educational Computing Research, 32*(3), 279–307.

[6] Warschauer, M. (2012). The digital divide and social inclusion. *Americas Quarterly, 6*(2), 131–135.

[7] Fishman, B., Dede, C. and Means, B. (in press). Teaching and technology: New tools for new times. In D. Gitomer & C. Bell (Eds.), *Handbook of Research on Teaching* (5th ed.).

[8] Valadez, J. R. and Durán, R. P. (2007). Redefining the digital divide: Beyond access to computers and the Internet. *The High School Journal, 90*(3), 31–44.

[9] Borghans, L., Duckworth, A. L., Heckman, J. J. and ter Weel, B. (2008). The economics and psychology of personality traits. *Journal of Human Resources, 43*(4), 972–1059.

[10] Durlak, J. A., Weissberg, R. P., Dymnicki, A. B., Taylor, R. D. and Schellinger, K. B. (2011). The impact of enhancing students' social and emotional learning: A meta-analysis of school-based universal interventions. *Child Development, 82*(1), 405–432.

[11] Spitzer, B. and Aronson, J. (2015). Minding and mending the gap: Social psychological interventions to reduce educational disparities. *British Journal of Educational Psychology, 85*(1), 1–18.

End Notes for Learning—Engaging and Empowering Learning Through Technology

[1] Bransford, J. D., Brown, A. L. and Cocking, R. R. (2000). *How people learn: Brain, mind, experience, and school* (p. 133). Washington, DC: National Academy Press. Retrieved from http://www.nap.edu/catalog/9853/ how-people-learn-brain-mind-experience-and-school-expanded-edition.

[2] Lave, J. and Wenger, E. (1991). *Situated learning: Legitimate peripheral participation.* Cambridge, England: Cambridge University Press.

[3] Molnar, M. (2014). Richard Culatta: Five ways technology can close equity gaps. *Education Week.* Retrieved from http://blogs.edweek.org/edweek/marketplacek12/2014/11/richard culatta five ways technology can close equity gaps.html.

[4] Culatta, R. (2015, March 3). *Technology as a tool for equity* [Video file]. Retrieved from http://www.youtube.com/ watch?v=6m-eMFz0iZI.

[5] Partnership for 21st Century Learning. (2013). *Framework for 21st century learning.* Retrieved from http://www. p21.org/our-work/p21-framework.

[6] Bandura, A. (2001). Social cognitive theory: An agentic perspective. *Annual Review of Psychology, 52*(1), 1–26.

[7] Durlak, J. A., Weissberg, R. P., Dymnicki, A. B., Taylor, R. D. and Schellinger, K. B. (2011). The impact of enhancing students' social and emotional learning: A meta-analysis of school-based universal interventions. *Child Development, 82*(1), 405–432.

[8] Durlak, J. A., Weissberg, R. P. and Pachan, M. (2010). A meta-analysis of after-school programs that seek to promote personal and social skills in children and adolescents. *American Journal of Community Psychology, 45*(3-4), 294–309.

[9] Farrington, C. A., Roderick, M., Allensworth, E., Nagaoka, J., Keyes, T. S., Johnson, D. W. and Beechum, N. O. (2012). *Teaching adolescents to become learners: The role of noncognitive factors in shaping school performance: A critical literature review.* Chicago, IL: University of Chicago Consortium on Chicago School Research.

[10] Johnson, L., Adams Becker, S., Estrada, V. and Freeman, A. (2014). *NMC horizon report: 2014 K-12 edition*. Austin, TX: The New Media Consortium.

[11] Smith, G. E. and Throne, S. (2007). *Differentiating instruction with technology in K-5 classrooms*. Washington, DC: International Society for Technology in Education.

[12] Ito, M., Gutiérrez, K., Livingstone, S., Penuel, B., Rhodes, J., Salen, K....Watkins, C. S. (2013). *Connected learning: An agenda for research and design*. Irvine, CA: Digital Media and Learning Research Hub.

[13] Office of Educational Technology. (2015). *Ed tech developer's guide*. Washington, DC: U.S. Department of Education. Retrieved from http://tech.ed.gov/developers-guide/.

[14] The Center for Innovative Research in Cyber Learning. (2014). *NSF cyberlearning program*. Retrieved from http:// circlcenter.org/projects/nsf-cyber-projects/.

[15] Culp, K. M., Honey, M. and Mandinach, E. (2005). A retrospective on twenty years of education technology policy. *Journal of Educational Computing Research, 32*(3), 279–307.

[16] Fishman, B., Dede, C. and Means, B. (in press). Teaching and technology: New tools for new times. In D. Gitomer & C. Bell (Eds.), *Handbook of Research on Teaching* (5th ed.).

[17] Purcell, K., Heaps, A., Buchanan, J. and Friedrich, L. (2013). *How teachers are using technology at home and in their classrooms*. Washington, DC: Pew Research Center's Internet & American Life Project.

[18] Valadez, J. R. and Durán, R. P. (2007). Redefining the digital divide: Beyond access to computers and the Internet. *The High School Journal, 90*(3), 31–44.

[19] Warschauer, M. and Matuchniak, T. (2010). New technology and digital worlds: Analyzing evidence of equity in access, use, and outcomes. *Review of Research in Education, 34*(1), 179–225.

[20] Warschauer, M. (2003). Demystifying the digital divide. *Scientific American, 289*(2), 42–47.

[21] Attewell, P. (2001). Comment: The first and second digital divides. *Sociology of Education, 74*(3), 252–259.

[22] Campos-Castillo, C. and Ewoodzie, K. (2014). Relational trustworthiness: How status affects intra-organizational inequality in job autonomy. *Social Science Research, 44,* 60–74.

[23] Darling-Hammond, L., Wilhoit, G. and Pittenger, L. (2014). Accountability for college and career readiness: Developing a new paradigm. *Education Policy Analysis Archives, 22*(86), 1–38.

[24] Gee, J. P. (2009). Deep learning properties of good digital games: How far can they go? In U. Ritterfeld, M. Cody, & P. Vorderer (Eds.), *Serious Games: Mechanisms and Effects* (pp. 67–82). New York, NY: Routledge.

[25] Rose, D. H. and Meyer, A. (2002). *Teaching every student in the digital age: Universal design for learning*. Alexandria, VA: Association for Supervision and Curriculum Development.

[26] Gray, T. and Silver-Pacuilla, H. (2011). *Breakthrough teaching and learning: How educational and assistive technologies are driving innovation*. New York, NY: Springer.

[27] Meyer, A., Rose, D. H. and Gordon, D. (2014). *Universal design for learning: Theory and practice*. Wakefield, MA: CAST Professional Publishing.

[28] Reardon, C. (2015). More than toys—Gamer affirmative therapy. *Social Work Today, 15*(3), 10. Retrieved from http://www.socialworktoday.com/archive/051815p10.shtml.

[29] 3C Institute. (2015). *Serious games*. Retrieved from https://www.3cisd.com/what-we-do/serious-games.

[30] Mindset Works. (2012). The Experiences. Retrieved from https://www.mindsetworks.com/webnav/experiences.aspx.

[31] Ibid.

Future Ready Learning

[32] Governor's Budget FY2012. (2011). *Eliminating the Achievement Gap*. Retrieved from http://www.mass.gov/bb/ h1/fy12h1/exec 12/hbudbrief2.htm.

[33] The Joan Ganz Cooney Center. (2014). *Family time with apps: A guide to using apps with your kids*. Retrieved from http://www.joanganzcooneycenter.org/publication/family-time-with-apps/.

[34] Black Girls Code: Imagine, Build, Create. (2013). *Programs/events*. Retrieved from http://www.blackgirlscode.com/programsevents.html.

[35] Black Girls Code: Imagine, Build, Create. (2013). *Programs/events*. Retrieved from http://www.blackgirlscode.com/programsevents.html.

[36] Tupa, M. (2014). Black Girls Code teaches girls digital technology skills. Retrieved from https://oaklandnorth.net/2014/11/11/black-girls-code-teaches-girls-digital-technology-skills/.

End Notes for Teaching—Teaching with Technology

[1] McCaffrey, D. F., Lockwood, J. R., Koretz, D. M. and Hamilton, L. S. (2003). *Evaluating value-added models for teacher accountability*. Santa Monica, CA: RAND. Retrieved from http://www.rand.org/pubs/monographs/2004/ RAND MG158.pdf.

[2] Rivkin, S. G., Hanushek, E. A. and Kain, J. F. (2005). Teachers, schools, and academic achievement. *Econometrica, 73*(2), 417–458. Retrieved from http://www.econ.ucsb.edu/~jon/Econ230C/HanushekRivkin.pdf.

[3] Rowan, B., Correnti, R. and Miller, R. (2002). What large-scale survey research tells us about teacher effects on student achievement: Insights from the Prospects Study of Elementary Schools. *Teachers College Record, 104*(8), 1525–1567.

[4] Nye, B., Konstantopoulos, S. and Hedges, L. V. (2004). How large are teacher effects? *Educational Evaluation and Policy Analysis, 26*(3), 237–257.

[5] Chetty, R., Friedman, J. N. and Rockoff, J. E. (2011). *The long-term impacts of teachers: Teacher value-added and student outcomes in adulthood* (Working Paper 17699). Cambridge, MA: National Bureau of Economic Research. Retrieved from http://www.uaedreform.org/wp-content/uploads/2013/08/Chetty-2011-NBER-Long-term-impact-of-teacher-value-added.pdf.

[6] PBS LearningMedia. (2013). *Teacher technology usage*. Arlington, VA: PBS LearningMedia. Retrieved from http://www.edweek.org/media/teachertechusagesurveyresults.pdf.

[7] Bill & Melinda Gates Foundation. (2012). *Innovation in education: Technology & effective teaching in the U.S.* Seattle, WA: Author.

[8] Dewey, J. (1937). *Experience and education*. New York, NY: Simon and Schuster.

[9] Hannafin, M. J. and Land, S. M. (1997). The foundations and assumptions of technology-enhanced student-centered learning environments. *Instructional Science, 25*(3), 167–202.

[10] Sandholtz, J. H., Ringstaff, C. and Dwyer, D. C. (1997). *Teaching with technology: Creating student-centered classrooms*. New York, NY: Teachers College Press.

[11] Herrington, J., Reeves, T. C. and Oliver, R. (2014). Authentic learning environments. In J. M. Spector, M. D. Merrill, J. Elen, & M. J. Bishop (Eds.), *Handbook of research on educational communications and technology* (pp. 401–412). New York, NY: Springer.

[12] Utah State University. (2005). *National Library of Virtual Manipulatives*. Retrieved from http://nlvm.usu.edu/en/ nav/vlibrary.html.

128 Office of Educational Technology

[13] Ching, D., Santo, R., Hoadley, C. and Peppler, K. (2015). *On-ramps, lane changes, detours and destinations: Building connected learning pathways in Hive NYC through brokering future learning opportunities.* New York, NY: Hive Research Lab.

[14] Kafai, Y. B., Desai, S., Peppler, K. A., Chiu, G. M. and Moya, J. (2008). Mentoring partnerships in a community technology centre: A constructionist approach for fostering equitable service learning. *Mentoring & Tutoring: Partnership in Learning, 16*(2), 191–205.

[15] Kafai, Y. B., Desai, S., Peppler, K. A., Chiu, G. M. and Moya, J. (2008). Mentoring partnerships in a community technology centre: A constructionist approach for fostering equitable service learning. *Mentoring & Tutoring: Partnership in Learning, 16*(2), 191–205.

[16] Darling-Hammond, L. and Rothman, R. (2015). *Teaching in the flat world: Learning from high-performing systems.* New York, NY: Teachers College Press.

[17] iEARN. (2005). About. Retrieved from http://www.iearn.org/about.

[18] Garcia, Antero, ed., 2014. Teaching in the Connected Learning Classroom. Irvine, CA: Digital Media and Learning Research Hub.

[19] Ibid.

[20] Ibid.

[21] iEARN. (2005). About. Retrieved from http://www.iearn.org/about.

[22] ISTE. (2013). *Standards for teachers.* Retrieved from http://www.iste.org/standards/standards-for-teachers.

[23] TPACK.org. (2002). *Quick links.* Retrieved from http://www.tpack.org/.

End Notes for Leadership—Creating a Culture and Conditions for Innovation and Change

[1] Lemke, C., Coughlin, E., Garcia, L., Reifsneider, D. and Baas, J. (2009). *Leadership for Web 2.0 in education: Promise and reality.* Culver City, CA: Metiri Group.

[2] Consortium for School Networking. *CoSN's 2015 annual E-rate and infrastructure survey.* (2015). Retrieved from http://cosn.org/sites/default/files/pdf/CoSN 3rd Annual Survey Oct15 FINALV2.pdf.

[3] The full list of resources and literature reviewed in developing the Future Ready leaders rubric is included in Appendix A.

[4] Consortium for School Networking. *CoSN's 2015 annual E-rate and infrastructure survey.* (2015). Retrieved from http://cosn.org/sites/default/files/pdf/CoSN 3rd Annual Survey Oct15 FINALV2.pdf.

[5] Sheninger, E. (2014). *Digital leadership: Changing paradigms for changing times.* Thousand Oaks, CA: Corwin Press.

[6] John Carver. (2015). 2020 Howard-Winn Admin Update. Retrieved from http://2020hwinnadminupdates.blogspot.com/2015/10/jcc-october-16-2015.html? sm au =iVVZSvStrsDP4TqR.

End Notes for Assessment—Measuring for Learning

[1] Gohl, E. M., Gohl, D. and Wolf, M. A. (2009). Assessments and technology: A powerful combination for improving teaching and learning. In L. M. Pinkus (Ed.), *Meaningful*

measurement: The role of assessments in improving high school education in the twenty-first century (pp. 183–197). Washington, DC: Alliance for Excellent Education.

[2] Reeves, D. (2007). *Ahead of the curve: The power of assessment to transform teaching and learning.* Bloomington, IN: Solution Tree Press.

[3] U.S. Department of Education. (2010). *Beyond the bubble tests: The next generation of assessments—Secretary Arne Duncan's remarks to state leaders at Achieve's American Diploma Project leadership team meeting.* Retrieved from http://www.ed.gov/news/ speeches/beyond-bubble-tests-next-generation-assessments-secretary-arne-duncans-remarks-state-leaders-achieves-american-diploma-project-leadership-team-meeting.

[4] Chappuis, J., Chappuis, S. and Stiggins, R. (2009). Formative assessment and assessment for learning. In L. M. Pinkus (Ed.), *Meaningful measurement: The role of assessments in improving high school education in the twenty-first century* (pp. 55–77). Washington, DC: Alliance for Excellent Education.

[5] Chappuis, S. and Chappuis, J. (2008). The best value in formative assessment. *Educational Leadership, 65*(4), 14–19.

[6] Stiggins, R. and DuFour, R. (2009). Maximizing the power of formative assessments. *Phi Delta Kappan, 90*(9), 640–644.

[7] Bill & Melinda Gates Foundation. (2015). *Teachers know best: Making data work for teachers and students.* Retrieved from https://s3.amazonaws.com/edtech-production/reports/Gates-TeachersKnowBestMakingDataWork.pdf.

[8] Darling-Hammond, L. (2010). Teacher education and the American future. *Journal of Teacher Education, 61*(1-2), 35–47.

[9] Data Quality Campaign. (2014). *Data for action 2014.* Retrieved from http://dataqualitycampaign.org/wp-content/uploads/files/DataForAction2014.pdf.

[10] Data Quality Campaign. (2014). Teacher data literacy: It's about time. Retrieved from http://www.dataqualitycampaign.org/wp-content/uploads/files/DQC-Data%20Literacy%20Brief.pdf.

[11] Darling-Hammond, L. and Adamson, F. (2010). *Beyond basic skills: The role of performance assessment in achieving 21st century standards of learning.* Stanford, CA: Stanford Center for Opportunity Policy in Education. Retrieved from https://scale.stanford.edu/ system/files/beyond-basic-skills-role-performance-assessment-achieving-21st-century-standards-learning.pdf.

[12] Pellegrino, J. W. and Hilton, M. L. (Eds.). (2012). *Education for life and work: Developing transferable knowledge and skills in the 21st century.* Washington, DC: National Research Council of the National Academies.

[13] Shute, V. J., Ventura, M. and Kim, Y. J. (2013). Assessment and learning of qualitative physics in Newton's Playground. *The Journal of Educational Research, 106*(6), 423–430.

[14] Gee, J. P. (2003). What video games have to teach us about learning and literacy. *Computers in Entertainment, 1*(1), 20–20.

[15] Toppo, G. (2015). *The game believes in you: How digital play can make our kids smarter.* New York, NY: Palgrave Macmillan Trade.

[16] Fishman, B., Riconscente, M., Snider, R., Tsai, T. and Plass, J. (2014). *Empowering educators: Supporting student progress in the classroom with digital games.* Ann Arbor, MI: University of Michigan. Retrieved from http://gamesandlearning.umich.edu/wp-content/uploads/2014/11/A-GAMES-Part-I A-National-Survey.pdf.

[17] Owen, V. E., Ramirez, D., Salmon, A. and Halverson, R. (2014, April). *Capturing learner trajectories in educational games through ADAGE (Assessment Data Aggregator for Game Environments): A click-stream data framework for assessment of learning in play.*

Presentation given at the annual meeting of the American Educational Research Association, Philadelphia, PA.

[18] HASTAC. (2014). *Open badges case study*. Retrieved from http://www.reconnectlearning.org/ wp-content/ uploads/2014/01/UC-Davis case study final.pdf.

[19] Mindset Works. (2010). *Brainology Transforming Students' Motivation to Learn*. Retrieved from https://www. mindsetworks.com/websitemedia/info/brainology intro pres.pdf.

[20] Dweck, C. and Rule, M. (2013, September). *Mindsets: Helping students to fulfill their potential*. Presentation given at the Smith College Lecture Series, North Hampton, MA.

[21] Shute, V. J., Ventura, M. and Kim, Y. J. (2013). Assessment and learning of qualitative physics in Newton's Playground. *The Journal of Educational Research, 106*(6), 423–430.

[22] Bill & Melinda Gates Foundation. (2015). *Reaching the summit of data-driven instruction*. Retrieved from http:// collegeready.gatesfoundation.org/2015/06/summit-of-data-driven-instruction/.

[23] Ibid.

[24] Ibid.

End Notes for Infrastructure—Enabling Access and Effective Use

[1] Council of Economic Advisers Issue Brief. (2015). *Mapping the digital divide*. Retrieved from https://www.whitehouse.gov/sites/default/files/wh digital divide issue brief.pdf.

[2] Digital Inclusion Survey. (2013). *Digital inclusion survey 2013*. Retrieved from http://digitalinclusion.umd.edu/.

[3] The White House Office of the Press Secretary. (2015). *FACT SHEET: ConnectHome: Coming together to ensure digital opportunity for all Americans*. Retrieved from https://www.whitehouse.gov/the-press-office/2015/07/15/ fact-sheet-connecthome-coming-together-ensure-digital-opportunity-all.

[4] Association of American Publishers. (2015). *Instructional materials funding facts*. Retrieved from http://publishers. org/our-markets/prek-12-learning/instructional-materials-funding-facts.

[5] Morrison, J. R., Ross, S. M. and Reid, A. J. (2015). *Report for Baltimore County Public Schools: Students and teachers accessing tomorrow—Mid-year evaluation report*. Baltimore: Center for Research and Reform in Education (CREE), Johns Hopkins University. Retrieved from https://www.boarddocs.com/mabe/bcps/Board.nsf/files/9UB87F-639DC1/$file/BCPSMidYearReportFINAL2.26.pdf.

[6] United States Department of Agriculture Rural Development. (2015). *USDA, Pine Telephone bring broadband Internet to areas of southeast Oklahoma, Choctaw Nation for first time*. Retrieved from http://www.rd.usda.gov/ newsroom/news-release/usda-pine-telephone-bring-broadband-internet-areas-southeast-oklahoma-choctaw.

[7] The White House. *ConnectED: President Obama's plan for connecting all schools to the digital age*. Retrieved from https://www.whitehouse.gov/sites/default/files/docs/connected fact sheet.pdf.

[8] The White House Executive Office of the President. (2015). *Community-based broadband solutions: The benefits of competition and choice for community development and*

Future Ready Learning 131

highspeed Internet access. Retrieved from https://www. whitehouse.gov/sites/default/files/ docs/community-based broadband report by executive office of the president.pdf.

[9] Bob Warburton. (2014). *Second BiblioTech Coming to Bexar County Housing Development.* Retrieved from http://lj.libraryjournal.com/2014/12/industry-news/ second-bibliotech-coming-to-bexar-county-housing-development/#.

[10] U.S. Department of Education. (2014). *Key policy letters signed by the education secretary or deputy secretary.* Retrieved from http://www2.ed.gov/policy/elsec/guid/secletter/ 140609.html.

[11] DS106. *About dc106.* Retrieved from http://ds106.us/about/.

In: Technology in Education
Editor: Austin Carlson

ISBN: 978-1-53610-234-5
© 2016 Nova Science Publishers, Inc.

Chapter 2

FUTURE READY SCHOOLS: BUILDING TECHNOLOGY INFRASTRUCTURE FOR LEARNING[*]

Office of Educational Technology

INTRODUCTION: THE PROMISE OF UBIQUITOUS CONNECTED LEARNING

The U.S. Department of Education's National Educational Technology Plan (NETP) presents a model of learning powered by technology to help the nation's schools provide all students with engaging and powerful learning content, resources, and experiences. The plan calls for revolutionary transformation rather than evolutionary tinkering.

"Technology is at the core of virtually every aspect of our daily lives and work, and we must leverage it to provide engaging and powerful learning experiences and content, as well as resources and assessments that measure student achievement in more complete, authentic, and meaningful ways."

National Education Technology Plan, p. ix

---

[*] This is an edited, reformatted and augmented version of a document issued by the U.S. Department of Education, Office of Educational Technology, November 2014.

Outside of school, many students enjoy technologies that give them 24/7 access to information and resources and that enable them to find, curate, and create content and connect with people all over the world to share ideas, collaborate, and learn new things. For the vision established by the NETP to be fully realized, access to web-based tools and resources needs to be both instantaneous and ubiquitous inside as well as outside school. To provide students with the education they need to thrive in a globally connected world, we must find ways to design, fund, acquire, and maintain the infrastructure that will make connectivity a reality for every teacher and student in every classroom.

This guide provides practical, actionable information intended to help district leaders (superintendents, principals, and teachers leaders) navigate the many decisions required to deliver cutting-edge connectivity to students. It presents a variety of options for district leaders to consider when making technology infrastructure decisions, recognizing that circumstances and context vary greatly from district to district.

The Need for Speed

"We are denying our teachers and students the tools they need to be successful. That is educationally unsound and morally unacceptable."

Secretary Duncan, June 17, 2013

Concerted efforts by federal, state, and local institutions over the last decade have brought some level of Internet connectivity to nearly all the nation's schools and libraries. However, this connectivity often has gone only as far as the school office or computer lab, where it can be inconsistent at times and staff are unsure how to address routine disruptions in service. In addition, while the speed of the connections in many schools was acceptable for the tools and abilities of yesterday's technologies, it is nowhere near adequate for today's classrooms and falls short of providing our schools, classrooms, and teachers with the digital connectivity and tools necessary to supply our students with a world-class education. The bandwidth required for today's student to upload high-definition multimedia content, participate in an online video conference, and curate an electronic portfolio of learning far exceeds what was required to give students access to early online tools such as email and static reference materials. For students to access cutting-edge digital learning tools, schools will need to upgrade their technical infrastructure to extend high-speed Internet access to every classroom and instructional space.

Definition

Broadband refers to high-speed Internet access that is always on and faster than traditional dial-up access. Broadband provides higher-speed data transmission, as it allows more content to be carried through the "pipe." Although there is not a particular speed that defines them, broadband connections in schools enable students to engage in rich digital learning experiences such as streaming videos, gaming, and interactive services. To better understand the nation's broadband coverage, visit the FCC's National Broadband Map.

Access to high-speed Internet in schools is a pressing social issue as well. When Internet connections in schools are too slow—a problem disproportionately common in rural and underresourced communities—students miss the benefits of educational technologies entirely. Gaps in access

136 Office of Educational Technology

to broadband tools and content exacerbate other, preexisting inequities in underconnected schools and unconnected homes.

Outmoded Internet access also raises productivity and efficiency concerns that have financial implications for districts and schools. Teachers without high-speed Internet cannot join streaming global professional conferences, share video of their practice with online peer-coaching groups, or respond via multimedia screen capture to student work in a timely and efficient way during school hours. Often, they must stay late or work from home, where they have access to a faster Internet connection.

> "[I]n a country where we expect free Wi-Fi with our coffee, why shouldn't we have it in our schools? Why wouldn't we have it available for our children's education?"

> President Obama, June 6, 2013

Nearly half of respondents to a survey of schools and districts by the Federal Communications Commission (FCC) in 2010 reported lower speed connectivity than the average American home.[2] Eighty percent of respondents to a 2011 FCC survey said their broadband connections did not fully meet their needs,[3] and more than half of teachers surveyed reported that slow or unreliable Internet access prevents effective use of technology in their classrooms.[2]

Definitions

Bandwidth is the amount of data that passes through a network as measured in bits per second (bps).

Kbps is short for kilobits per second. A kilobit is a data transfer rate of 1,000 bits per second. A fax machine takes about 12 seconds to send a page at 30 Kbps.

Mbps is short for megabits per second. A megabit is a data transfer rate of 1,000,000 bits per second. The State Educational Technology Directors Association (SETDA) recommends schools have a minimum of 1 Mbps per student.[1] Mbps of connectivity would enable a single student to stream a 10-minute high-definition video.

Gbps is short for gigabits per second. A gigabit is a data transfer rate of 1,000,000,000 bits per second. This is the ConnectED goal for a school to achieve by 2018. At this speed, 1,000 students could stream a 10-minute high-definition video in real time.

Future Ready Schools 137

Recognizing the growing opportunities and need for student and teacher access to high-speed Internet, President Obama launched the ConnectED Initiative, setting a goal of connecting 99% of students to the Internet in their schools and libraries at speeds of no less than 100 megabits per second (Mbps) per 1000 students and a target speed of 1 gigabit per second (Gbps) by 2018.[4]

A second component of the ConnectED Initiative calls on the private sector to provide digital learning devices as well as content and resources for teachers and students that are price-competitive with print-based learning tools such as textbooks and provide cutting-edge access to digital tools.

Equally important is the investment in high-quality professional development so teachers enter classrooms ready to use the new tools to support personalized learning for students.[5]

Through the ConnectED Initiative, significant progress has been made toward increasing school-based access to broadband:

- more than $2 billion in private-sector commitments to deliver technologies to classrooms, including mobile devices, free software, teacher professional development, and home wireless connectivity;
- an additional $2 billion from the FCC in E-rate funding to connect 20 million more students to next-generation high-speed broadband and wireless; and
- clarification that supporting the transition to digital learning is an allowable use of billions of dollars of U.S. Department of Education grant funds through the Office of Educational Technology's Dear Colleague Letter.

What this guide won't do for you...

This guide focuses on the steps and decisions you need to make in implementing the technological infrastructure to support a comprehensive educational technology plan. This guide does not address the other key steps in such a plan—determining how students will use technology to advance learning goals, how to provide teachers with the training necessary to use these tools, and what content and instructional methods to use. Establish your vision for how technology will be used to transform learning before using this guide. For more information about crafting a comprehensive district educational technology plan, you should consult other resources, starting with the NETP.

Technological infrastructure is just one element of educational transformation. Its use should be guided by clear goals and effective planning, which require that stakeholders in the system act together and plan beyond technology alone. Therefore, this guide also provides considerations for digital learning resources and staff professional development and addresses other implementation issues such as device selection, responsible use policies, privacy, and security associated with creating effective connected schools.

1. GETTING STARTED

In This Section

- Planning and leadership demands associated with technical upgrades
- Key questions for assessing conditions in schools and districts
- Setting technical goals for the future

Technology-supported learning across the country is enabling students to create multimedia, to collaborate with experts and learners across the world, and to employ tools to access deeper, more personalized learning, which, in turn, helps them become more college- and career-ready. Teachers, parents, and students are looking for schools to provide high-quality, sustainable, dependable learning tools and cutting-edge connectivity.

Put Learning First

Examples abound of ill-fated "technology first" investments in schools. Instead of a single wide-scale rollout, consider small pilots and phased implementation approaches, which enable you to adjust even the best-laid plans to meet unexpected needs. Check with hardware and software providers as they may offer an opportunity to pilot a solution at little or no cost before making a larger financial commitment. As you refine your pilot, begin to plan how you will move it to scale. Begin to ask which components will need to be reconsidered when applied to entire schools or districts as compared to a select group of users.

Future Ready Schools 139

While getting connected devices in the hands of students and teachers is important, it takes more than that to shift practices within classrooms, schools and districts and therefore outcomes.

Most important to this transition is a clear vision of the actions and attributes of learning and teaching you hope for as you move toward universal highspeed broadband access. This vision will provide you and your district with a compass by which you can steer the process outlined in this guide. This section explores some important elements of the process.

Look to Those Who've Come Before You

Considering the efforts of those who have come before you can prevent missteps and lead to a more efficient use of time and money. More experienced districts such as those referenced in this guide can share best practices and lessons learned, which can be valuable for planning and monitoring.

You can also find guidance from state and national agencies and nonprofit organizations such as:

- Alliance for Excellent Education
- CoSN
- Digital Promise
- Education Superhighway
- ISTE
- National Clearinghouse for Educational Facilities
- Project RED
- SETDA

Check your state department of education website for further guidance. For example, the New Jersey Department of Education has a Facilities Guide for Technology available online. Many districts post technology plans online that can serve as examples, like Pleasanton Unified School District in California and Santa Rosa County District Schools in Florida.

In successful implementations, superintendents lead the transition to connected learning (where students and teachers have access to people and resources to improve learning whenever they need it) and they ensure districts build high-level leadership teams (or call on existing ones) to develop a

140 Office of Educational Technology

districtwide vision for how technology supports educational goals and garner staff and community support. In addition to leadership and support from a superintendent, a CTO or CIO offers deep technology expertise, and a chief financial officer actively pursues funding options and opportunities. Superintendents may also rely on recommendations from knowledgeable members of the community and colleagues in other districts.

Hire the Best

If you are looking to hire a district technology lead/chief technology officer (CTO) or chief information officer (CIO), the Consortium for School Networking (CoSN) has a description of recommended skills for a K–12 CTO at http://www.cosn.org/Framework.

After identifying a strong planning team, the next step is to assess the capacity of current network infrastructure and devices, gauge current levels of usage, and estimate the demands needed in the future. This assessment will help you determine which parts of the current infrastructure need to be replaced, upgraded, or supplemented.

The following seven questions can guide an evaluation of district Internet needs and capacity.

1. What Is the Vision for Learning That Technology Will Be Supporting?

Bandwidth requirements depend on the role technology plays in supporting teaching, learning, and assessment within districts and schools. It's easy to be drawn in by flashy promotional materials and offers of discounts. Without first knowing what learning opportunities you want the devices and connectivity to enable, you'll never know if they were successful. Before making decisions about technology, schools and districts need to articulate how students will use technology to learn. Learning objectives should drive the technology implementation and not the other way around.

Future Ready Schools 141

The benefits of putting Learning first

In an effort to address long-standing academic issues, **Revere High School** in Revere School District in Massachusetts, implemented a school-wide blended learning model. Students, parents, and school staff post lectures, videos, and assignments online so the entire school community has access to needed information. Educators were provided with virtual tools to collaborate with school leaders on a regular basis, thereby receiving more immediate feedback, as well as access to online teaching resources that support professional development needs. The high school's student achievement results have been impressive, particularly compared to peer schools, including winning the 2014 High School Gold Award from the National Center for Urban School Transformation.[67] A robust investment in supporting teachers and leaders with technology-enabled tools can transform instruction and generate dramatic improvement in student outcomes.

As you begin to talk with students and instructional leaders, ask how they envision students using devices inside and outside the classroom. If part of the instructional plan is for students to use devices at home, then it is also important to have a realistic picture of how many students have reliable home Internet access. Surveying families through an initial home access inventory will reveal what percentage of students have access to broadband Internet at home and guide what you need to do to bring connectivity to all students.

Engage the Community

Community and stakeholder ownership is key to the success of any major school initiative. Involve stakeholders across all stages of planning and implementation by establishing transparent policies and procedures. Communicate these policies with stakeholders and, when possible, remain flexible and responsive to the needs of individual schools to implement their own practices (while defining and communicating the consequences of doing so).

As you better understand connectivity in your district, consider convening families and community leaders for discussions of digital equity. New plans

142　　　　　　　　　　Office of Educational Technology

for technology use and infrastructure within schools can provide the perfect opportunity to engage the larger community in conversations about what it means to be a connected community. *See page 52 for additional information about ensuring home access.*

2. What Digital Tools Will Be Needed?

Get a baseline usage estimate by talking with students, teachers, and school administrators about how they currently use learning technologies. Augment these informal conversations by holding listening sessions or organizing standing advisory groups to ensure clear channels of communication. Outside your district, seek guidance from state assessment officials regarding projected testing demands on technology resources.

Consider how high-speed Internet access and new devices will create opportunities for new kinds of digital learning content and resources schools might not currently be using because of bandwidth limitations. Tasks like audio/video production and videoconferencing require large amounts of bandwidth, especially if used simultaneously by many students. Keep in mind other possible demands on your technology infrastructure such as administrative software, security, web hosting, and other applications that align with administrative needs and communications in schools. Plan to support resource uses as they are as well as how your district or school will adapt to unforeseeable technology demands down the road. *See Factors to Consider When Selecting Devices on page 44 for more information on digital learning resources.*

3. What Kind of Professional Development Will Teachers and Administrators Need?

Districts can distribute devices and links to learning resources, but administrators and teachers might not use them unless they understand how they support their work. This will take time and training. Because educators differ in technology expertise and pedagogical knowledge, professional development should be designed to meet the needs of teachers at all levels – from the most traditional teachers to the earliest adopters of blended learning practices. This may mean different training for different administrators and teachers, combined with in-school and online professional learning communities. Consider ISTE's standards for administrators, teachers, and instructional coaches when designing your professional development expectations.

You will need to provide a significant amount of professional development to ensure that the transition is successful and lasting. While not the focus of this guide, ongoing, fully-funded professional development regarding use and research-supported practices for technology in learning and teaching is extremely important to any effort. See the U.S. Department of Education's *Future Ready Schools: Empowering Educators through Professional Learning* (tech.ed.gov/futureready/professional-learning) for more information on professional development planning using the many existing online communities and resources. In addition, opportunities such as Connected Educator Month can help teachers begin to join and create online communities and networks of practice.

4. How Much Bandwidth Will Be Needed?

Your current Internet provider should be able to provide you with usage data for your school network (how much bandwidth is currently being used, at what time, etc.). If your school runs its own network, you will have network monitoring tools that provide a more comprehensive and accurate assessment of current bandwidth. It is a good idea to verify those data by running a web-based speed test such as those listed below. For districts without a current Internet infrastructure, set a target for connectivity speeds such as the ConnectED Initiative's target speed of 1 gigabit per second (Gbps) per 1000 students by 2018.

- **SchoolSpeedTest.org** calculates a network's usable speed—the amount of bandwidth while the network is in use.
- The **Smarter Balanced diagnostic tool** from the Smarter Balanced Assessment Consortium tests whether schools have sufficient bandwidth and browser capabilities to run the Smarter Balanced computer-adaptive tests. If your school is participating in the consortium, ensure you meet all the assessment requirements. Districts that are taking the PARCC or other online assessments should have capacity planning tools on their respective websites.

Professional Learning Pathways

The San Diego County Office of Education's Professional Learning Center (PLC) provides county educators opportunities to learn more about instructional technologies through face-to-face workshops, blended courses, online courses, and a fully online Master's in Education Leadership with an emphasis in technology. All the blended and online professional development courses have university credit options provided through a partnership with San Diego State University. When planning professional development in conjunction with your educational technology resources, consider offering a variety of choices to enable teachers to personalize their learning as well.

While speed tests are helpful in determining available bandwidth, they do not pinpoint which part of a network needs to be improved to increase its speed. In addition, precisely measuring connection speeds is difficult because actual speeds will vary based on such factors as the number of simultaneous users and software accessing the network. You get more exact data with a network monitoring service, which provides end-to-end monitoring of a network in varying conditions over time. Many different paths exist for getting highspeed connectivity to your schools. *See Section 2 on page 17 for more information on planning high-speed broadband pathways to your schools.*

Future Ready Schools 145

Know Your Network

If choosing an independent vendor to manage your network, consider requesting network monitoring as part of your agreed-upon services. If you maintain your own network, you most likely are able to do network monitoring in house.

---

5. What Will the Needs of Your in-School Network Be?

Some school buildings, especially older ones, may require special considerations as you build or improve your network to include high-speed connections. The best way to determine your schools' physical readiness is to have your technology support team or certified consultant conduct a network assessment. During this process, the team will note mechanical, electrical, and environmental conditions that will need to be addressed as you upgrade your network. For example, is existing network cabling sufficient or will new cable need to be installed? How many wireless access points does your school have now, if any, and where are they located? Beyond the network assessment, you may also want to consider other physical infrastructure questions such as whether each classroom has enough electrical outlets for charging devices. *See Planning Your Network on page 35 for more information on these and other network infrastructure questions.*

Remember Personal Devices

Under a BYOD (bring your own device) policy, students may be permitted to bring their own laptop, tablet, smartphone, or other Internet-enabled device to school. When planning how much bandwidth your school will need, don't forget to account for these personal devices. High school students are most likely to own mobile devices (80%), but 65% of students in grades 6–8 are also smartphone users.[8] A majority of teachers (52%), parents (57%), and district administrators (52%) now use a personal mobile device such as a smartphone.[9] For most schools, the way that students and staff access the school Wi-Fi network with personal devices should differ from how they access the network with school-issued devices. *For more information on network planning, see page 35. For more about BYOD policies, see page 48.*

146 Office of Educational Technology

6. How Many and What Type of Devices Are Needed?

Once a clear vision for the role of technology in learning and teaching has been established, two factors will help you determine and plan for how many devices your network can support. One factor is how many devices students and teachers can connect to the school network. When determining the number of devices, differentiate between devices owned by the school district and those that are personally owned by students and staff. A second factor is peak demand—the time(s) of day when the most devices are accessing the network simultaneously. This is often first thing in the morning or at the start of every class period. See *Getting High-Speed Internet to Schools on page 17 for additional information on estimating bandwidth needs.*

Assess Physical Needs Early

Upgrading your physical infrastructure can be expensive and time consuming, so it is best to determine whether this is necessary at your school and develop a plan to tackle the problem early.

You also need to know what types of devices are currently owned and in use by the school—desktops, laptops, tablets, and/or smartphones—and when they will reach end of life. Even when you expand the actual broadband capacity in your school, older devices with slower processors might not be able to benefit from faster speeds and will need to be upgraded or replaced. *See page 48 for additional information on purchasing devices.*

7. What Resources Are Available to Fund the Transition?

One of the most important resources available for the transition to sustainable broadband connectivity in schools is the Schools and Libraries Universal Service Support Program, also known as the E-rate program. The FCC's E-rate program provides discounts of up to 90% to help elementary and secondary schools and eligible libraries connect to the Internet and maintain internal connections. The highest discounts are provided to high-poverty schools and libraries, and rural schools and libraries can also apply for higher discount rates.

In recent years, E-rate funding requests have far exceeded available funding. On July 23, 2014, in response to the President's ConnectED Initiative, the FCC released the E-rate Modernization Order targeting funding to Wi-Fi networks in schools and libraries across the United States while ensuring support continues to be available for broadband connectivity to schools and libraries.

In addition to E-rate, some federal education grants may be applied to supporting the transition to digital learning. There are also some innovative cost-saving models worth considering. Some schools have partnered with other area educational institutions or even their town or city to pool bandwidth needs and create local or municipal networks that save all parties money. Each section of this Guide points to funding resources and suggestions specific to its topic. For a comprehensive list of connectivity funding resources, please see tech.ed.gov/funding/.

The next two sections discuss considerations in upgrading Internet connections to the school and within a school, respectively.

2. GETTING HIGH-SPEED INTERNET TO SCHOOLS

In This Section

- Understanding types of available connectivity
- Four paths for connecting districts and schools
- Cost drivers and funding sources to consider
- Special considerations for rural areas

The U.S. Department of Education recommends a minimum connectivity speed of 100 Mbps and a target speed of 1 Gbps per 1000 students for schools by 2018.[9] This translates to a per-student target of at least 1 Mbps to meet the 2018 ConnectED Initiative goal.[10,11] This section gives an overview of the technical details associated with getting high-speed Internet to your school. It first reviews the wired and wireless types of connectivity and then outlines how those connectivity types are most commonly used to create high-speed pathways for schools. This section is designed to help you understand the most common models for connecting schools and districts to broadband so you can ask informed questions and identify which options are right for your district.

148 Office of Educational Technology

Definitions

Backbone describes the major network connections across the country. Think of them as the major highways of the Internet.

Middle mile Refers to the part of a telecommunications network that connects the Internet backbone and regional Internet service provider or district.

Last mile refers to the connection between the regional Internet service provider and individual school buildings.

Types of Internet Connections

Wired Connections

Wired technologies are faster and more reliable than wireless technologies for getting high-speed Internet to your district or school because they experience fewer threats to signal quality such as weather and geographic interference. The most common wired technologies are fiber-optic cable (known as fiber) and Data Over Cable Service (known as cable or DOCSIS).

The easiest way to take advantage of either of these options is to use wires that have already been installed. Although cable wiring is likely to be the most prevalent in your area and is less likely to require installation, fiber can be faster and more reliable and is often less expensive over a period of time, as its high capacity often means a lower price per megabyte. Installing fiber requires specialized training and equipment and often requires underground trenching or stringing the fiber from telephone poles to connect the Internet service provider (ISP) to the district.

Some areas are experimenting with ways to reduce fiber installation costs. A California executive order permits ISPs to install fiber at cost as part of any public works project that already requires an open trench in which fiber could be also laid. The cost to install fiber is substantially lower when the trench has already been dug or when fiber has been strung aerially for the majority of distance and trenched from the poles to schools.[12]

New installation techniques are also being piloted to reduce the cost of laying fiber. During microtrenching, fiber is laid into a slot less than 1 inch wide and about a foot deep.[13]

Future Ready Schools

> **Definitions**
>
> **Fiber-optic cable (fiber)** consists of a thin cylinder of glass encased in a protective cover. It uses light rather than electrical pulses to transmit data. Each strand of the cable can pass a signal in only one direction, so fiber-optic cable must have at least two strands: one for sending and one for receiving data. Unlike Data Over Cable Service, fiber-optic cables are not subject to interference, which greatly increases the transmission distance. Fiber speeds are currently limited by the abilities of the equipment on either end of the connection. Some fiber connections allow for speeds up to 100 Gbps.
>
> **Internet Over Cable Service (cable)** is Internet provided via cable TV networks. Currently, cable can enable download speeds in excess of 300 Mbps, depending on local infrastructure. The cable industry is working to increase downloading speeds up to 10 Gbps in the coming years.

Consult closely with ISPs and check with utility and municipal institutions to understand all possible wired access and installation options in your area. When comparing the cost cable and fiber, consider the "total cost of ownership" (see below), and check with your local ISP because rates and availability vary by region.

Internet over Fiber

Fiber is the fastest and most reliable connection to the Internet. Most customers, including schools, do not own their own fiber (similar to telephone or electric lines) because owning it requires purchasing the property rights along the trench where the fiber is installed, which tends to make it cost prohibitive. Two frequently used options for getting fiber Internet access are leasing or obtaining a right of use contract.[14,15]

An indefeasible right of use contract (IRU) generally provides complete use of a fiber line without any limitations for a long period of time. IRUs are often negotiated on terms similar to mortgages (e.g., 15–30 years) with a single payment up front. IRUs typically come from utility companies, telecoms, or railroads that maintain and service dark fiber. This means that fiber obtained through an IRU does not come with any of the network equipment required to activate it, and substantial up-front costs to "light" the fiber must be factored in. However, IRUs can result in significantly reduced long-term costs relative to leasing.

150 Office of Educational Technology

With leased fiber, the owner retains the fiber and provides the district with the ability to use a certain amount of capacity based on the lease agreement. Similar to an IRU, unused dark fiber can be leased, requiring the district to provide the network equipment to activate the fiber. However, there are also options to lease fiber at a higher cost that already includes all the required equipment. Leases are usually shorter contracts of up to 1–5 years with monthly payments to the service provider. Districts can choose to use less than the full capacity of the fiber up front and pay for additional capacity later if it becomes necessary.

Check Total Cost of Ownership

When comparing prices of network connections, make sure to compare the **price per megabyte**, not just up-front costs. To calculate price per megabyte, add all capital expenses and recurring costs and divide by the number of megabytes received. For example, a 100- MB connection may cost $100 per month, or $1 per megabyte. A 10-GB connection may cost $500 per month—a substantially higher monthly bill but resulting in a cost of only $0.50 per megabyte. Keep in mind, however, that not every school needs a 10-GB connection. If a school is only using 1 GB but is paying for a 10-GB connection, it would be overbuying for its needs.

Definitions

Dark fiber is fiber optic cable that has already been laid, generally underground, but does not have the networking equipment on each end to connect to the Internet.

Indefeasible right of use (IRU) is a contract to use someone's dark fiber for a long period at a low cost. A district that acquires fiber through an IRU is responsible for providing the equipment to connect (or light) the fiber.

Leased fiber is a contract between an ISP and a district whereby the ISP agrees to deliver Internet services using fiber owned by public telephone network or other provider. The connection fee is a fixed monthly rate determined by the distance and speed provided. Leased fiber can either be dark (as in an IRU) or include all the required network equipment.

Either through an IRU or a lease, dark fiber can provide almost limitless future capacity at a marginal cost because the expense in increasing bandwidth

Future Ready Schools 151

generally comes from the network equipment that is connected to the fiber, not the fiber itself.

Connecting via Fiber through Creative Approaches

In 2011, **Chesterfield County Public Schools** in Virginia had a network that was slow and unreliable, especially for remotely located schools, which prevented many teachers from using digital media with their students. As part of an ambitious district strategic plan to support blended learning, the district technology team designed and implemented a complete leased fiber network. The lease required the vendor to provide equitable bandwidth to all schools and administrative buildings. Because the new fiber network was more expensive than the previous approach, Chesterfield Schools needed more funding than its existing E-rate discounts. The district decided to prioritize bandwidth over other technology expenses like accidental damage warranties on staff and student computers or support on old hardware. In addition, the district reduced print textbook purchases to fund the new digital content strategy. The staff agreed that the end result—a scalable and reliable network that supported blended learning in every classroom—was worth it.

Butte School District in Montana initiated a public-private partnership in 2013 with a fiber provider and the Montana Economic Revitalization and Development Institute to build a new network connecting the district office with all district schools.[16,17] Originally, the district's remote location meant schools were forced to use outdated telephone lines for their primary connection to the Internet. A slight improvement was made when Butte was able to upgrade to a shared fiber network providing a 10-Mbps connection. Unfortunately, 10-Mbps was still too slow for simultaneous online learning and assessment, leading to the creation of the public-private partnership. The district has an IRU with the telecommunications provider that built the network.[18] Now all nine Butte schools have access to a 2-Gbps fiber connection fast enough to videoconference between classrooms, enable teachers to complete online professional development, and give every student simultaneous high-speed Internet access.

Internet over Cable

Internet service provided over cable has the benefit of using the more prevalent existing cable infrastructure, which can reduce the initial cost of installation. However, if your district requires more bandwidth than the existing cable infrastructure can provide, options for increasing bandwidth may be limited.

Check with your provider to get a clear understanding of current capacity and potential expansion of bandwidth. Make sure whatever bandwidth level you negotiate is provided as a guaranteed minimum, and not just an "average" or "best-efforts" level.

Check Cable Capacity

Check with your cable provider for details on the maximum capacity available at your location. If it is not sufficient for a primary connection, cable still may be a cost-effective backup solution.

When negotiating agreements for cable connectivity, include terms setting clear understandings of how changes in bandwidth pricing will affect your district. One such option is a multiyear lease with the ability to renegotiate bandwidth and price structure annually.

Wireless

In some areas such as rural regions that span great distances, neither fiber nor cable service is available. In those situations, your district will need a wireless solution such as fixed wireless, mobile broadband, or a satellite Internet connection.

Fixed Wireless

Fixed wireless options (sometimes called WiMAX) often require erecting towers and installing wireless transmission/receiver platforms to carry the signal from place to place (thus the term *fixed* wireless). Each requires a clear line of sight between the tower and the school (or directly between two schools if there is line of sight between them). Generally, wireless options provide a lower speed at a higher price per megabyte than wired options, and not all options will be available in your region. Fixed wireless is generally much faster to set up than fiber or cable, especially where district-owned buildings are in line of sight to each other. Fixed wireless connections are subject to a small amount of latency, similar to being on a phone call with a bit

Future Ready Schools 153

of a delay. This may create challenges for students who are using videoconferencing or other real-time interactions.

> ### Leverage ConnectED Partners
>
> Many private ConnectED Initiative partners are offering schools mobile connectivity services as part of their commitments. These connections can follow students home, providing access outside school.

Mobile Broadband

Mobile data services, like those that provide the data service on smartphones, may be available under limited circumstances where schools may have rights to a wireless spectrum based on existing educational spectrum licenses from the FCC. These licenses were historically issued by the FCC to educational agencies around the country under the Educational Broadcast Spectrum program. While the FCC is not currently granting any new licenses, the Commission is developing a new mechanism for education organizations to apply for this type of connectivity where it is available. As with fixed wireless, mobile wireless users will experience a small amount of latency.

Satellite Internet

Satellite service is a type of wireless connection for schools where cable or fiber is not available. Satellite Internet requires a good line of sight from the school to the correct orbiting satellite. When terrain or frequent bad weather makes other wireless solutions impossible, satellite may be the only feasible option. Of all the wireless options, satellite tends to be the most expensive per megabit per second. It also typically includes monthly usage caps and limited maximum download and upload speeds. Satellite connections are subject to significant latency due to the distance the signal must travel to connect to the satellite. This means that satellite connections may not allow for real-time services such as videoconferencing.

If multiple wireless options are available in your area, know that each comes with its own trade-off between speed, stability, and cost. Because wireless connections are subject to more environmental interferences than wired connections, service can be disrupted in areas with rough terrain or in bad weather.

Given the various capabilities and restrictions of fixed wireless and satellite technologies, be sure to compare services before deciding on a

154 Office of Educational Technology

provider by determining price per megabyte, latency, environmental issues, and any bandwidth usage limits.

Definitions

Fixed wireless can currently provide speeds up to 1 Gbps, is suitable for portable mobile broadband connectivity and cellular backbone as an alternative to cable, and can deliver data, Voice over Internet Protocol (VoIP), and Internet Protocol Television (IPTV). WiMAX comes in two forms: mobile and fixed. Mobile connects buildings to user devices, and fixed connects buildings together. When considering WiMAX, look for industry certification regarding WiMAX standards to ensure interoperability with other certified products.

Mobile broadband is wireless Internet access from cell towers via a mobile phone, tablet, or portable modem. Mobile broadband (also called 4G or LTE) can provide high-speed connections up to 1 Gbps for downloading and uploading over the same network infrastructure wireless carriers.

Satellite Internet can provide fixed, portable, and mobile Internet access with data rates of up to 1 Gbps downloading and up to 10 Mbps uploading. Satellite broadband is among the most expensive forms of wireless Internet access, but it can provide connectivity in the most remote areas where no other connectivity options exist. Best performance requires a clear line of sight between the satellite and the antenna at the connecting building.

Approaches for Connecting Schools

Once you understand the types of Internet connections available, you are prepared to consider the best approach for getting that access to your district. Possible pathways are described below, along with associated pros and cons of each, to help you decide which path is right for you.

In your approach for connecting your school, you can plan for additional speed and reliability through multiple connections or by contracting with multiple Internet service providers (ISP). This can keep your network functioning in the event that any one ISP experiences an outage or a connecting line is cut. Multiple connections can also allow for connectivity

Future Ready Schools 155

speeds beyond your baseline goal and increase the area within which students and teachers can connect to your network.

Path 1: Schools Connect Through the District to Research & Education Networks

Research and education networks, called R&E networks or RENs, are high-speed wired networks independent of the commercial Internet. They are run by state or regional consortia and were originally developed to meet the needs of academic and research communities.

RENs vary in their funding and operating models but generally offer the same benefit to their members: low-cost connectivity achieved by aggregating demand. RENs are typically funded by a combination of government and member fees.[19] Thirty-one states offer their RENs to K–12 districts and schools.[20] These are usually fiber connections, although schools in rural areas may also connect wirelessly.

Definitions

A **Wide Area Network (WAN)** provides the connection *between* the district office and all the schools and sites within a district. A WAN may also connect to other educational institutions (such as universities and libraries) if your district is part of a regional education network.

A **Local Area Network (LAN)** is the network *within* a school or district building through which computers and devices connect to the Internet. LANs, in contrast to WANs, service much smaller geographic areas.

All state RENs are supported by either a national consortium or regional RENs. This structure allows REN members to save money by pooling bandwidth across more users. Another advantage to RENs is the ability to access content stored within the network at a lower cost because users do not need to access the Internet outside the REN. For example, if an online video collection is housed at a university that is part of the REN, the schools can download those materials without having to pay for access to the Internet. This provides a cost-effective solution for normal usage while giving members the ability to occasionally spike Internet usage for short periods, such as for assessments and software updates.

> **Find RENs**
>
> Not all districts are located near a REN connection point. To find out if a REN is located nearby, go to this website: http://www.internet2.edu.

If a REN is available in your region, compare the speed and cost of it with those of the other paths described below.

Illustrated below are schools connecting through the district to a REN. Note that the REN uses multiple ISP connections to pool bandwidth for members and provide redundancy should an ISP experience an outage.

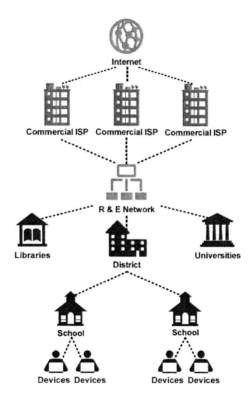

> **Where this path makes sense:**
>
> If your district or school is in an area where you have access to a state-operated network, this may be the most cost-effective way to connect to high-speed Internet.

Pros

- Can be cost-effective because RENs can negotiate lower costs by purchasing Internet access on behalf of all institutions in the REN.
- If your REN has the ability, additional capacity can be added for short periods of time when usage is expected to spike (such as during assessments).
- With fiber RENs, increasing bandwidth can be accomplished at a fraction of the cost of the initial setup.
- Hardware and services such as firewalls, security, and content filtering can be centralized at the district level, which simplifies management and avoids increased costs from multiple purchases.
- Greater reliability exists on RENs because they use multiple Internet service providers at the same time to manage information loads.
- Content providers may house content within the network so the need to pay for bandwidth to access content outside the network is reduced.

Research & Education Networks in Action

The **North Carolina Research and Education Network** (NCREN), one of the first statewide RENs in the country, provides high-speed Internet to all K–12 districts as well as higher education campuses and academic research institutions across North Carolina.[23] Whereas NCREN was primarily funded by in-state resources, the state took advantage of two Broadband Technology Opportunities Program grants through the Recovery Act and Race to the Top to expand its network and cloud infrastructure.[24]

Network Nebraska provides 232 districts and more than 350,000 K–20 students with Internet access that supports a statewide videoconferencing service and e-learning courses. The network purchasing consortium aggregates and shares bandwidth demands for groups of districts so that they can peak demand when needed without paying extra costs. For example, one group of 92 districts in the northeast part of the state cooperatively purchases Internet capacity of 3 Gbps per month.[22] Network Nebraska has been able to provide 94% of Nebraska school districts with high-speed Internet connectivity.[22] Network Nebraska cooperatively purchases its core routers with the University of Nebraska and leverages state master contracts for its last mile connections (the segments that connect the network backbone to the school). This aggregated demand lowers the cost of connecting schools.

> The **Utah Education Network** (UEN) is a statewide, publicly funded partnership between the state's education institutions and local telecommunications providers that connects all of Utah's K–12 schools, colleges, and libraries to the Internet. UEN also offers its members Internet filtering, network support, and a learning management system.[21] The foundation of the UEN is a high-capacity fiber backbone. Smaller fiber segments connect the core backbone to WANs, which in turn connect the state's colleges and universities to the Internet. Ninety percent of the state's K–12 districts connect either directly to that backbone or indirectly through the colleges and universities. Most public high schools and middle schools connect at 100 Mbps, with some connecting at speeds up to 1 Gbps.[21]

Cons

- Up-front costs for building a connection from a district to the REN can be high.
- A high-speed WAN connecting the district and schools must already exist (or be constructed) for this approach to work.
- A high-speed LAN must exist for distributing the Internet access from the WAN throughout the school.
- Because of funding models for consortia, costs may vary with usage rates, which can make projecting long-term cost difficult.
- Accessing content outside the REN (on the Internet) can have restrictions in addition to a metered cost beyond recurring membership fees.

Path 2: Schools Connect Through District to Commercial ISP

On the second path, your district buys bandwidth from a commercial ISP. The ISP creates a high-speed backbone to a centralized district connection. This type of connection is called the middle mile. Schools connect to the Internet through the district WAN. This is similar to RENs, but instead of being part of a consortium of other state institutions, districts connect directly to a commercial ISP. Districts can contract with their ISP or another entity to build the infrastructure for their schools' WAN if they do not have the internal capacity.

Illustrated below is the path of schools connecting through the district to a commercial ISP.

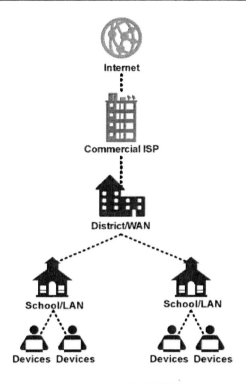

Where this path makes sense:

If your school is in a medium to large district where the district can exercise bulk purchasing power—and a local REN does not exist or offer the most cost-effective connectivity—this may be the most cost-effective option for you.

Pros

- This can be cost-effective because districts can negotiate lower costs by purchasing Internet access on behalf of all schools in the district.
- If your ISP has the ability, additional capacity can be added for short periods of time when usage is expected to spike (such as during assessments).
- By pooling capacity, large schools benefit by sharing the cost of anticipated usage spikes while smaller schools are able to take advantage of the cheaper rate offered with high-volume purchasing.

160 Office of Educational Technology

- Hardware and services such as firewalls, security, and content filtering can be centralized at the district level, which simplifies management and avoids increased costs from multiple purchases.
- The ISP may subsidize the cost of establishing the infrastructure to the district with a longer contract.

A District's Direct Path to Its ISP

Forsyth County School District, north of Atlanta, Georgia, serves approximately 42,400 students and is growing at a rate of 1,600 students per year. The district has 35 physical schools and an online school for grades 6–12. The district and schools are connected through a redundant fiber network, with a managed 1 GB connection through one ISP and an additional leased fiber connection that the district manages. In addition to the approximately 500MB connection provided by the state, the district contracts for Internet access from two separate ISPs for an aggregated 2.5 GB of total bandwidth.

Forsyth's approach has the advantage of multiple ISPs, which allows rerouting of Internet traffic should one ISP experience an outage. Because network management is centralized at the district level, fewer firewall and filter appliances are required. Purchasing bandwidth at the district level enabled the district to negotiate more competitive pricing than purchasing Internet access individually for each school. By incorporating redundant connections from school sites to the data center and maintaining redundant connections to the Internet from the district office, the district is well protected from Internet outages interfering with lessons.

Cons

- Up-front costs for building a connection from a district to the ISP network can be high.
- A high-speed WAN connecting the district and schools must already exist (or be constructed) for this approach to work.
- A district must contract with multiple ISPs in order to have redundant secondary or tertiary Internet connections should one experience an outage due to malfunction or a severed cable.
- A high-speed LAN must exist for distributing the Internet access from the WAN throughout the school.

Future Ready Schools 161

- This approach lacks the purchasing power and possibly the redundancy of a larger REN.

Path 3: Schools Connect Directly to Commercial ISP

In the third path, schools connect directly to the ISP for broadband access rather than through a district connection. The ISP manages and maintains the connection right to the school. This can be a more expensive path to connectivity because it has limited opportunities to take advantage of economies of scale.

The district is still responsible for providing a LAN for distributing connectivity to classrooms and throughout the building as in the other paths, but it does not have to worry about creating a connection to the district or to the ISP.

Definition
Virtual private network (VPN) encryption software enables computers to connect with each other across a public network as if they were connected to a private, secure network.

Illustrated below is the path of schools connecting directly to a commercial ISP.

Where this path makes sense:
If your school lacks the purchasing power of a big district and the ability to operate its own WAN, and if a local REN does not exist or offer the most cost-effective connectivity, this path could be right for you. For schools in geographically remote locations, this may be the only option.

Pros

- Schools can negotiate variable usage agreements to accommodate spikes in demand.
- Districts are not responsible for maintaining a district network because the ISP connects directly to the school.

162 Office of Educational Technology

- Direct ISP-to-site connections mean that an interruption in connectivity for one school or district building does not result in an interruption for the entire district.
- The ISP may subsidize the cost of establishing the infrastructure to the district with a longer contract.

Cons

- Up-front costs for building a connection from the schools to the ISP network can be high.
- A high-speed LAN must exist for distributing the Internet access throughout the school.
- The district must contract with multiple ISPs in order to have redundancy.
- This path lacks the purchasing power of either RENs or district-purchased Internet access.
- This path has no redundancy should the ISP experience a network outage.
- Without a central district network, this path lacks the capacity to store heavily used content internally.

Path 4: Devices Connect Directly to Commercial ISP

In the fourth path, a district leases mobile broadband wireless services from an ISP, which then provides high-speed Internet access directly to student devices. The key advantage to this approach is that it does not require students to be connected to a school network and can function anywhere that cellular service is available. Although this approach can be used independently of the other three paths, it is typically used to augment a school or district network to provide connectivity when students are not in a school building. In this approach, devices do not connect to the Internet through a school network (LAN), so content filtering or security settings would have to be implemented by the ISP.

Not all devices are compatible with mobile broadband, so it is important to check on device options when considering this approach. Often, service providers will offer discounts on device purchases when you are purchasing data plans.

The major downside of this path is that it can be extremely expensive at large scale and does not offer the connectivity speeds required by some learning resources. It is the newest of the four paths for connecting to the Internet and thus is still evolving.

Until speeds and costs improve, this path can be used as a supplement at schools that have a wireless connection within the school (using one of the other paths) to provide students with equitable connectivity outside school.

> **Provide Home Access Equity**
>
> Schools that encourage off-campus use of school-owned mobile devices should explore Path 4 when students' home Internet connections are not available or sufficient.

It is possible, as technology and capacity increase over time, that this approach will become more economical.

The illustration below shows this path in use, providing a connection directly to student devices when outside of school and students connecting to school-provided wireless when inside school.

> **Where this path makes sense:**
>
> If your school lacks the purchasing power of a big district and the ability to operate its own WAN, and if a local REN does not exist or offer the most cost-effective connectivity, this path could be right for you. For schools in geographically remote locations, this may be the only option.

Pros

- Internet connectivity can be provided to students off campus.
- Districts are not responsible for maintaining a district or school network because the ISP connects directly to the devices.
- There are no upfront construction costs.
- The ISP may subsidize the cost of devices for the district with a longer contract.

> **Connecting Student Devices Using Mobile Cellular Broadband**
>
> Located in the Sierra Nevada mountain range, **Lake Tahoe Unified School District** (LTUSD) is a rural district of six schools, with 60% of students qualifying for free or reduced-price lunch. Lake Tahoe wanted to provide connectivity to students at home, as well as at school, so the mobile broadband solution was appealing. LTUSD partnered with a commercial 3G mobile broadband provider and device vendor to supply netbooks to 3,000 students in grades 3–12.[25] Each computer is equipped with Wi-Fi and a 3G wireless modem. LTUSD provides in-school and home Internet connectivity by permitting students to connect to Wi-Fi and 3G networks managed by the mobile broadband provider.
>
> The district wanted to deploy the devices without overburdening its small IT staff, so the mobile broadband provider also is responsible for content filtering in conjunction with district IT staff. These vendor relationships permit LTUSD to provide students with connectivity without having to continuously update IT staff on latest technologies.[25] The district estimates that the implementation plan for all costs, including staff development and operating expenses, will total approximately $600,000 per year.[26] While some of the materials were paid for using bonds, other components of the technology implementation, such as the connection to the ISP, were paid for using general funds, categorical funding, and E-rate.[26]

Future Ready Schools 165

Cons

- This path can cost significantly more than others.
- There is no ability to contract with multiple ISPs to have redundancy.
- This path lacks the purchasing power of either RENs or district-purchased Internet access.
- This approach will work only with devices that support mobile broadband.
- This path does not support Internet telephone service (VoIP). *See Section 3 for additional information on VOIP.*
- The potential for vendor lock-in is high because it is not easy to change mobile broadband providers as technology varies from one provider to another.

Major Cost Drivers

Actual costs will vary widely from district to district based on local circumstances. As you are generating comparisons of the total cost of ownership of the network, the following factors will most likely have the greatest impact:

- How many devices and which digital learning resources your network must support
- The capacity and age of your physical infrastructure, including conduits, cables, and wireless access points
- How much of your existing equipment can be used in your new network
- The distance and geographic difficulty (terrain, weather) of connecting your school buildings to the Internet
- The paths for connecting that are available to you (joining an REN, leasing dark fiber, etc.)
- The level and type of security measures you need to provide.

Two cost drivers many schools underestimate are those for human capital and ongoing network monitoring and maintenance. Human capital costs include the time, personnel, sustained professional development, and expertise to manage the network and provide technical support for teachers, staff, and students. Staff can include consultants to assist with technology planning, set-

166 Office of Educational Technology

up, and testing. When you are calculating the total cost of operating your network, be sure to inquire about which services are included and which the district would need to provide to make sure you are comparing like services.

Ongoing network monitoring and maintenance costs include the following:

- Network management and monitoring
- User help desk/technical support
- Maintenance and upgrade of devices and equipment
- Insurance for devices
- Estimates of future demand
- Licensing fees for digital learning content
- Security filtering
- Network redundancy.

Save Costs and Bandwidth Through Caching

One way to reduce overall bandwidth fees is to relocate content on the Internet into local caching proxies. A **cache** is a special high-speed storage mechanism that can be either a reserved section of main memory or an independent high-speed storage device. High-use content can be accessed from the cache multiple times without going back to the Internet for downloading. This tactic helps reduce costs for schools and can lower delivery costs for content providers. Caching proxies can be located within REN, with private third-party services, or at the district level. You may also consider inquiring about hosting content from frequently used services to lower bandwidth use. Districts can further reduce costs by installing caching proxies within their LANs. Consider a class of 30 students, all of whom need to review the same video lesson. Instead of being downloaded 30 times, the video is downloaded once and redistributed from the local cache to each student's device.

As your district transitions to greater connectivity, some costs can be redirected to help support the new costs. Schools have redirected funding that had been used to pay for textbooks, printers, copiers, and computer labs to help cover the cost of network and mobile devices.

The demand for network speed and capacity will continue to increase over time. Build a network that can be improved rather than one that will require an

Future Ready Schools 167

entirely new network at the end of your contract in order to meet future demands. Consider the absolute maximum speed of your network, the maximum number of devices you can accommodate, and your ability to take advantage of falling bandwidth prices if you enter into a long-term contract.

E-Rate Funding for Internet Connectivity

The Schools and Libraries Universal Service Support Program, often referred to as E-rate, makes telecommunications and information services more affordable for U.S. schools and libraries. Mandated by Congress in 1996 and implemented by the FCC in 1997, the E-rate program provides eligible schools and libraries with discounted telecommunications, telecommunications services, Internet access, and internal connections.

The FCC has modernized the E-rate program—one of the largest financial resources available for schools to transition to broadband. The 2014 E-rate Modernization Order intensified focus on the greatest and most urgent need— closing the Wi-Fi gap—while transitioning support away from legacy technologies to advanced broadband connectivity. The changes to the program are expected to ensure greater access to E-rate support to connect 10 million students a year to 21st century educational tools and target an additional $5 billion for Wi-Fi services over the next 5 years.

The FCC established the following goals as guidance in its modernization efforts:

1. Ensuring affordable access to high-speed broadband sufficient to support digital learning in schools and robust connectivity for all libraries
2. Maximizing the cost-effectiveness of spending for E-rate–supported purchases
3. Making the E-rate application process and other E-rate processes fast, simple, and efficient.[27]

Special Considerations for Rural Areas

Rural areas often have unique challenges to getting high-speed Internet to their schools. Delivering high-speed bandwidth to remote districts and schools may first require improvements to the region's network infrastructure before it

168 Office of Educational Technology

can become available to the district. Connecting remote regions can be challenging because of physical obstacles as well as land-right usage. The Navajo Nation Telecommunications Regulatory Commission noted that the barriers for its tribe in obtaining high-speed Internet include a lack of adequate physical infrastructure, which is difficult to build because of "complications with land status, rights of way and building regulations."[29] These challenges can lead to schools in rural areas paying significantly more per megabyte than suburban and urban schools.[30] Despite these difficulties, rural districts are succeeding in developing innovative approaches to providing teachers and students with the connectivity they need within and beyond schools.

Supplementing E-Rate with State and Local Efforts

The **State of Maine** pays for broadband in schools using a fee of up to 0.7% on telecommunication services, similar to the Federal Universal Service fund, called the Maine Telecommunications Education Access Fund (MTEAF). The Maine Public Utilities Commission collects this fee on phone bills and then disperses it to the statewide broadband network to pay for the non-E-rate portion of the cost of broadband. The MTEAF was the result of legislation passed in 1999 authorizing its creation by the Public Utilities Commission. Other states such as Georgia, Iowa, and North Carolina allow counties to enact similar paths using taxes rather than fees to finance technology for student learning.[28] Typically, the tax is for a limited number of years, after which it must be reapproved by a vote or it will expire.

Many communities have succeeded in creating low-cost fiber systems that benefit schools, local government, businesses, and residents. These involve partnering with municipal governments to engage in community-wide rollout of increased broadband access in schools, libraries, government buildings, and other public places. While these efforts can require years of coordination and planning, the costs are often offset for school districts and other local stakeholders by lower bandwidth cost once the networks come online. Collaborating with municipal governments can reduce the cost to schools and districts of establishing and maintaining broadband connections because they are shared over a wider number of users. Some districts work with housing developments, development groups, and city government to bury fiber optic cable for schools when they are digging trenches for construction.

Mobile Wireless Hotspots Providing Connectivity Outside of School

Sunnyside Unified School District in Tucson, Arizona, is an example of a district pursuing strategies to connect students when they are off campus. Although 86% of students are low income and many lack Internet access at home, the district is one of the few in the United States to move entirely to digital textbooks.[31] To provide access, school buses are equipped with mobile wireless hotspots, enabling students to access the Internet and do homework on the way to and from school.[32] Through a partnership with the Native American Advancement Foundation,[33] the district is increasing mobile learning opportunities for children in remote villages in the nearby Tohono O'odham Indian Reservation. Sunnyside outfitted a used City of Tucson van with the same wireless hotspot equipment that is on the school buses, and the van travels daily to a new village in the reservation to provide access to students. *See Home Access in Section 4 for more information on other strategies districts are using to increase student home access.*

Districts and Municipalities Building Networks Together

For years, **Craven County School District** in rural North Carolina faced difficulties providing the connectivity required to support learning. The district was too far from the state's REN to make that a viable option. Nor could the district afford an upgraded WAN to connect to its schools because of the high cost of wired and wireless options. The existing WAN and 25 Mbps connectivity conditions could not support services such as multimedia streaming, video conferencing, and centralized web servers. In 2005, Craven County Schools began exploring the possibility of constructing its own fiber optic network by learning where fiber already existed in the county and identifying potential partners. The nearby cities of Havelock and New Bern had already constructed municipal fiber optic networks. Craven County Schools initiated a partnership with Havelock and New Bern, Craven Community College, and Craven County Government to build shared infrastructure.

The local board of education told the district that it would fund the project as long as it found a favorable comparison between the total cost of ownership and current leasing costs. The district, of approximately 15,000 students across 695 square miles, was paying nearly $350,000 per year to lease telecommunications services. The partnership achieved substantial savings by working directly with fiber manufacturers, paying $1.2 million for its 76 miles of fiber and accompanying infrastructure. In addition, the groups developed a consortium agreement and a memorandum of understanding to outline responsibilities. The project was completed within 18 months, and the network has been operational since early 2009.[34] Internet connectivity will ultimately be expanded to 100 MB and beyond for the schools.

For Craven County, one of the most important lessons learned was the challenge of communicating between and within different agencies.[35] School officials are still getting calls today on how to get county and municipal governments to talk to one another.[34] Their advice is to start meeting early with city, county, and community college officials. In addition, the group has been well organized and planned for maintenance. Because the district designed and built the network, staff also know how to maintain it, which saves maintenance costs.

3. GETTING HIGH-SPEED INTERNET TROUGHOUT SCHOOLS

In This Section

- Providing wireless access in your schools
- Network planning
- Physical infrastructure considerations
- Network provisioning, configuration, and management
- Managing risks

High-speed Internet in your district becomes useful when it is available in all places where teaching and learning are taking place. This section presents information to help you understand what factors are important and what questions to ask as you design your school networks.

Planning Your Network

While the fastest way to get an Internet connection to schools is typically with a wired connection, wireless access within school buildings is the best

Future Ready Schools 171

way to connect students and staff. Wireless access throughout all learning spaces enables students and staff to have mobility and flexibility when engaging with learning devices, such as tablets, laptops, and smartphones. The first step in creating or upgrading wireless access in your school is to identify who will be using the network and for what purposes. This will help you determine the number of connections you need to support as well as the amount of bandwidth required in each location. Knowing this, you can decide on the physical location for access points throughout your school. To meet demand, it is also important to conduct a network assessment to determine how many access points are needed throughout the school building. If your district lacks the capacity to do this, a professional network designer can help.

Definitions

Wi-Fi is a wireless network connection using one or more of the IEEE 802.11 network specifications that carry a "Wi-Fi CERTIFIED" seal of approval from the Wi-Fi Alliance. "Wi-Fi ac" is the current generation of Wi-Fi certified devices. Devices with a "Wi-Fi CERTIFIED n" designation are from the previous generation (and therefore are usually less expensive—and slower—than ac devices). A Wi-Fi channel is one frequency within the Wi-Fi spectrum. Most Wi-Fi networks have approximately 11–15 channels.

A **wireless access point** (AP) is a device that allows wireless connections to a wired network using Wi-Fi or a related standard wireless network protocol.

Ethernet is a family of networking technologies for LANs. Ethernet standards are most commonly provisioned with twisted-pair and fiber optic cable. When twisted-pair is used, CAT 6a cabling is required to support speeds up to 10 Gbps. For fiber optic cable, there is a range of Ethernet standards to support a variety of distances over 300 feet and speeds in excess of 100 Gbps.

Wireless signals are influenced by environmental factors such as radio frequencies, electrical interference from power sources, and building design and construction, so the placement of access points is important. A network assessment will provide you with recommendations for the location and capacity of access points that need to be installed. Knowing the number of devices that will connect to the network, as well as anticipated use for each location in the school, is necessary to make the determination. When performing the network assessment, it is helpful to test some of the actual devices you are considering using if they are available.

Leverage Outside Organizations for Help

For more specific guidance on conducting a site survey, both CoSN and Education Superhighway have resources on their websites outlining allocation of resources and options for external consultation.

Wireless signals have difficulty passing through concrete walls and are subject to interference from such sources as Bluetooth devices or microwave ovens. Check for interference at different times of day and on different days as part of your network assessment. It may be that interference from devices peaks at a key time during the day, requiring an increase in access points to compensate.

Remember to Count ALL Devices

As **Burlington High School** in Burlington, Massachusetts prepared to provide mobile devices for just over 1,000 students, school staff did their homework in creating a wireless infrastructure. A vendor completed a network assessment to provide the school with the correct number of wireless access points for the 360,000-square-foot campus.

On the first day of school, however, Burlington's CTO came to the quick realization that students' personal devices had not been considered in the network assessment. Burlington was not actually a 1:1 (device-to-student) school, but a 2:1 or even 3:1 school when considering all the personal devices being used on the network. This created limited access to the network and was particularly problematic for classrooms near the cafeteria, where 500 students regularly attempted to access Wi-Fi during lunch from their personal devices. District IT staff were able to make the necessary adjustments to wireless access points to support the actual number of devices. Burlington's experience offers an important lesson: Consider every device that will be using the network, not just the devices provided by the school.

> ## Consider All Physical Aspects of the Network
>
> There are a number of components to consider when planning to create or upgrade your network, including:
>
> - **Electricity**—What elements of the network require external power? How many outlets are required to meet these needs? Will a generator be necessary to support the network in the case of a power outage?
> - **Cabling**—How far from where the network enters your school will the access points be installed?
> - **Access points**—How will your school conduct a proper site survey to determine both the number and types of access points? In general, at least one access point per classroom is a good rule, but precisely how many will depend on the hardware selection. Larger rooms (e.g., cafeteria) will require more access points. Will a consultant assist with this process?

Determine Wiring Needs

Once you have a high-speed Internet connection to the school, it is critical to have internal cabling to distribute the connection to all classrooms and learning spaces such as cafeterias, gymnasiums and other common areas. Even if a high-speed connection exists to the school, students and teachers will be able to take advantage of it only if updated cabling is in place to bring the bandwidth to the wireless access points. Fiber or CAT 6a cabling is recommended for in-school networks. If the signal must travel more than 300 feet, you will need to use fiber or add repeaters to strengthen the signal. Cables designed to be run through drop ceilings (known as plenum cables) are subject to special fire-safety standards for flammability and smoke density. A licensed electrical or telecommunications contractor can advise you on the relevant codes for your location and type of installation.

Consider Phone Requirements (VoIP)

Voice communications should also be considered when planning a network. VoIP technology enables schools to use the same network that provides Internet access to provide phone service. This approach eliminates the cost of maintaining a separate phone system and can reduce the amount of cabling needed throughout the building. When planning your network, additional capacity and cabling should be factored in if you plan to support VoIP.

> ### The Speed of the Entire Network Matters
>
> To get high-speed Internet connectivity from where it enters the building to classrooms, every segment of the network must be able to accommodate high speeds. Even if a school is connected to the Internet via fiber, if the network inside the school is outdated, students will not experience high-speed connectivity in their classrooms. In short, the slowest segment of your network determines the speed of the network downstream from that point. Be sure to check that the equipment connecting each network segment at least meets your minimum speed requirements. Routine inspection and continuous monitoring of the network will help you identify misconfigured and/or failing equipment, inferior or damaged cables, or radio interference that is causing dropped connections. Internal or consulting IT experts can help you define a strategy that best fits your installation.
>
>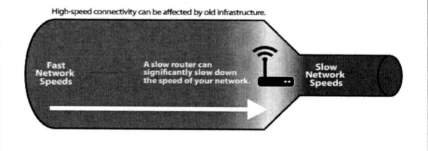
> High-speed connectivity can be affected by old infrastructure.

> ### Register with E911
>
> In order for emergency service providers (such as 911) to determine the location of calls made over VoIP, the address of the phone must be registered manually. Schools must ensure their provider is properly registering the handset's physical location information with the E911 registry if they are using VoIP phones.

Important Questions to Ask

When designing a network for a school, several operational and logistical questions should be asked and answered by the team planning and implementing the network:

- **Intrusion detection** – Are automated alerts in place if software is acting malicious or someone is unlawfully accessing the school network?
- **Security** – Is network equipment safe from theft, vandalism, and physical hacking?
- **Firewalls** – Are you able to restrict what data enter and exit the school network?
- **Load balancing** - Can you ensure that school/district network resources scale to meet student and staff needs?
- **Content filtering** – Are tools in place to restrict access to inappropriate content while still permitting access to all learning tools?
- **Network management** – Will the network be required to initiate wireless software updates to connected devices?
- **Mobility** - Is the network configured so that students can remain connected even if they move to different physical locations in the building?
- **User log-ins** - Will users need to log in to access the network? Does the network hardware support the kinds of log-in services you want to offer?

Compare Costs

Having a comparison against which you can measure your network design and cost can be helpful. Look to the Analysis of Costs to Upgrade and Maintain Robust Local Area Networks for All K-12 Schools by CoSN and Education Superhighway to compare your plan with that of others who have gone before you.

> **Definitions**
>
> **Content filtering** is the ability to screen content traveling over the network in real time and either restrict access to a resource or censor content. For example, schools should filter access to sites known to contain inappropriate content. Schools should perform due diligence to censor/flag potentially restricted content.
>
> A **firewall** is a physical hardware device that acts as a gatekeeper on the network, restricting access into and out of the network based on a predefined policy.
>
> An **intrusion detection system (IDS)** is a service used to identify security threats within a network. These solutions alert the operator to suspicious files, processes, and configurations on a network.
>
> **Load balancing** is the ability to adjust the network to scale access to resources on demand. Load balancing provides equitable access to network resources.
>
> **Log-in services** validate identity so a user can gain access to a computer system or other technology.
>
> **Network management** refers to the activities, methods, procedures, and tools that pertain to the operation, administration, and maintenance of networked systems. This includes the management of access points and other devices that constitute the network.
>
> **Quality of service (QoS)** is used to prioritize certain types of network traffic over other types, such as traffic to online assessments and learning management systems over content sites to ensure students have the best access available to most important content.
>
> **Student mobility** refers to students needing to move without losing connectivity within a wireless network as they relocate each period or block.

Configuring and Managing Your Network

Having a plan for configuring and managing your school network will position you to better respond to issues as they arise. The information presented here can help you consider which options are best for your network and know what features and services to ask for.

Consider purchasing commercial-grade equipment. While small office/home office-grade equipment may be easier to obtain and lower in cost,

Future Ready Schools 177

it may not offer key features that will reduce your overall ownership costs. Features you will probably want in whatever device model you choose include the abilities to update device control programs remotely, update the configuration of devices en masse rather than one by one, connect all devices to a single monitoring system, provide an access point on more than one Wi-Fi channel, provide log-in capability to a central log-in server (make sure the device supports the log-in technology you plan to use), and provide virtual LAN (VLAN) routing on a peruser basis (so students can use the same router as teachers but have access to a different VLAN).

SOHO for Mobile Labs

Compared to commercial-grade equipment, an unmanaged small office/home office (SOHO) wireless access point might be acceptable for a laptop cart, in a mobile lab where equipment is moved around frequently, or for an ad hoc event like providing a temporary wireless bridge for a sporting event. If you use a SOHO in addition to your main network, make sure filtering and security settings are in place to protect users.

A comprehensive network monitoring service should be included in a connectivity plan. While IDSs and network management are part of the solution, a good monitoring system analyzes and discovers such information as:

- Network traffic and saturation – identify parts of the network that are over- or under-utilized
- Time of use - identify peak times or conditions
- System-wide status and capacities - detect when a service (like VoIP) might be failing or when storage needs expansion or archiving
- Unreachable or misconfigured devices - quickly diagnose a problematic network.

Most servers, routers, and wireless access points need to be refreshed every 4 to 6 years. Selecting hardware that can discover its configuration from a central management tool is preferred and will save you time over devices that need to be configured individually. It is also important to ensure that new hardware is compatible with available software before working at full scale.

178 Office of Educational Technology

Trust Experts for Installation

Installing network cable in your school is a technical job that is often subject to local and state electrical building and fire codes. Configuring network hardware for use with wireless access points requires considerable expertise. The installation should be secure from damage and tampering, and the work performed by trusted individuals. Be sure to involve network professionals and school IT decision-makers when making any changes to the network configuration or infrastructure.

Prioritizing Traffic

An important approach to maximizing bandwidth is to prioritize certain types of traffic. For example, downloading videos may be a lower priority at times when bandwidth is needed for testing or other classroom projects. You can also mark specific domains or sites as high- or low-priority traffic depending on instructional value.

In addition to providing access to school-owned devices, you may consider providing access for student and staff personal devices or public guest access for school visitors. Segmenting your network gives students and staff prioritized access separate from public access.

Segment for Security

Segmenting your wireless network can allow different types of access and provide greater security. For example, there may be a BYOD network for students, faculty, or guests to use their personal devices that is separate from the official school wireless network used by school-provided devices.

Some schools segment their network in ascending order of priority: high-priority traffic (e.g., testing), normal classroom traffic, BYOD traffic, and public guest traffic. Providing public guest access will affect the design of your wireless infrastructure because it adds more complexity to the network architecture given the requirement for additional layers of security and authentication.

Future Ready Schools

Segmenting Networks to Align with Learning Priorities

Fairfax County Public Schools (FCPS) in northern Virginia has a dedicated network for BYOD devices. FCPS has over 200 schools and centers serving 185,000 students and more than 30,000 staff, and it provides public Wi-Fi access in all facilities. To support this large number of users, the district configured its network into three segments. Students use the FCPSMobile configuration by authenticating themselves to the network using their student ID and password. Once authenticated, students have access to filtered high-speed Internet, intranet resources, print and file share services, and learning resources. The FCPS staff accesses the secure Fairfax network, which provides additional access to intranet and business systems like the student information system, online testing, human resources, and financial systems. The public FCPS access provides filtered broadband but no access to the FCPS private intranet. By configuring the network into three segments, priorities can be set so that during peak bandwidth traffic times, the highest priority traffic (e.g., student access to learning resources) is given preference over public access. If your school has or is planning a BYOD policy to complement other changes, it may be worth considering configuration of the network and wireless infrastructure to support separate segments of access.

As you monitor peaks, track both upload and download speeds. Students may show a high rate of downloads as they access content and require more upload speed as they stream video tutoring sessions with neighboring schools or videoconference with outside experts for research projects.

The illustration below provides an example of connections that can be used to extend high-speed connectivity throughout a school campus.

Be Mindful of Multiple Peaks

One of the highest traffic peaks typically occurs when students log in at the beginning of each instructional period. Because all students generally do this at approximately the same time during their day or class period, it is the most likely time for peak conditions to occur. However, it may not be the only occurrence, although pace and network use are usually more staggered once students are logged in. Knowing when to expect peaks and the bandwidth required to accommodate them will help you build a network ready for the extremes of use demands rather than the average.

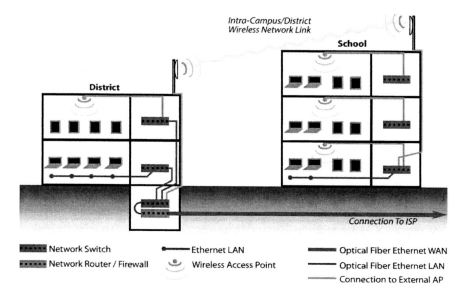

Managing Threats

When installing or upgrading your network, include plans to manage physical and virtual threats such as those outlined here. In many cases, access to networks and the information stored on them can be as enticing to thieves and hackers as the equipment used to create the network.

Building cybersecurity capacity of district personnel is an important line of defense against the inadvertent disclosure of student data such as the attachment of a file that includes protected information. Helping everyone in your district understand basic cybersecurity practices will reduce risky behavior where data are concerned.

Unauthorized users could try to gain access to steal school or district property (licensed software and other paid resources), personal information (student/staff grades, records, contact information, medical information), or operate malicious services (illegal file sharing, game servers, etc.). Authenticating users before permitting network access can help reduce this threat.

No matter how strong the safeguards, no network is impenetrable. Develop and share your plan for responding to a data breach so that you and your district can best ameliorate any inadvertent or malicious disclosure of private data. See PTAC's Data Security and Management Training: Best

Future Ready Schools 181

Practice Considerations and Data Breach Response Checklist for guidance in protecting against and dealing with unintended and malicious data disclosures.

A single virus or malware infection can render an entire network inoperable within a few minutes. Virus and malware scanning and removal software at the central network level and on all learning devices reduces risk from these threats.

Equipment rooms should be secured with access limited to authorized personnel. Network equipment not in a locked facility, such as wireless and rooftop-mounted APs, should be protected by commonly available housing and protective cabling to discourage tampering. School IT staff can consult with an IT security specialist to audit and make recommendations specific to your needs.

Include Teachers in Filtering

Content filters are not perfect, and Internet content changes frequently. Ensure that your content-filtering process can be quickly modified. Creating and managing content filters often require human intervention. Be sure to have instructional staff participate or run this process. Sometimes, schools delegate content filtering to IT staff who have little experience with instruction, which can create problems for staff and students. When instructional staff members discover inappropriate content is accessible via the school network, a streamlined process should exist for reporting, evaluating, and implementing temporary or permanent blocks for the content. A temporary block may be needed when a usually useful site becomes compromised and displays inappropriate content.

For school IT staff, ensuring students are protected from harm and have sufficient trouble-free access to network resources to meet learning objectives is paramount. VLANs with authentication based on user type rather than location can provide more seamless access for students as they move through schools. When combined with a content filter, firewalls are effective at preventing access to inappropriate content and websites, and many include QoS features. *See Section 5 for more guidance on privacy and protection considerations.*

4. GETTING DEVICES TO STUDENTS AN TEACHERS

In This Section
- Importance of devices in modern education environments
- Considerations when selecting devices
- BYOD programs
- Funding strategies
- Device maintenance and management
- Home access
- Rollout models

The educational benefits of increased connectivity are realized only when Internet-enabled devices are available to teachers and students. Devices that must be shared by many students or accessed only in designated computer labs limit the ability of students to engage in ongoing collaboration and of teachers to use high-quality digital learning materials. Students who do not have their own devices may not have access to the same level of personalized learning that enables students to learn through practices best suited to their needs and related to their interests and experiences. They also may not learn as productively as those in an environment where all students have access to devices whenever they need them.[36] Moreover, many states have college- and career-ready standards, which require students to possess certain technological competencies to prepare them to thrive in a connected world.

More school districts are adopting web-based productivity tools and digital content for teaching and learning. These shifts to web-based materials and tools can decrease paper usage, make teacher time more efficient, and enable students and teachers to access learning materials at any time of day.

Factors to Consider When Selecting Devices

Learning objectives and your vision for technology-enabled teaching and learning should be the primary driving factors in your selection of devices for teachers and students.

Test a wide variety of devices before making a selection. One of the best ways to test devices is by creating a testing script, a list of actions for teachers and students to try on each device. If a school district will be using specific web-based systems, offer an online curriculum or have students regularly watch videos from a particular site; each of these functions should be tested on every potential type of device.

Do not compare devices by technical specifications alone. If you want students to make movies, test how well each device makes movies. If you want teachers to participate in online communities, test how well each device enables them to do so. If you want devices to last for a certain amount of time without having to be recharged, try using them for that amount of time. Your main evaluation criteria should be how responsive and usable devices and software are in helping students and teachers complete various tasks.

Tip

Visit the Federal Registry for Educational Excellence (FREE) for access to thousands of digital teaching and learning resources.

Issues of accessibility are of particular importance when considering which devices will best serve students' learning needs. Special education specialists should be an integral part of the device selection process. The Individuals with Disabilities Education Act (IDEA) ensures that children with disabilities have access to the general curriculum and that they will receive the services and supports needed to achieve their educational goals, and to prepare them for further education, employment and independent living.

Children must have full access to content and instruction required to effectively participate in educational environments and to meet their educational goals. Assistive and instructional technologies such as special software and devices, and accessible versions of curricular materials, textbooks and media are powerful tools that ensure full access to educational curricula and content. For more information about assistive and instructional technologies, media and accessible educational materials, visit the Center on Technology and Disability and Bookshare.org.

As with networks, it is important to compare the total cost of ownership for devices and peripherals, including keyboards, protective screens, cases, and any necessary software. A cheap device that requires an expensive case for protection from damage may cost more in the end than a device that is more durable but slightly more expensive.

Computing devices most frequently come in four different types: desktops, laptops, tablets, and smartphones. Generally, either laptops or tablets are the choice when providing devices to all students because they are portable, have large enough screens for most activities, and are available at prices that make them affordable for mass deployment.

Some districts involve a variety of stakeholders in device selection. In Rhode Island, for example, the devices used in the Chariho Regional School District's 1:1 initiative were chosen by a Device Selection Advisory Committee composed of administrators, superintendents, school committee members, teachers, students, the director of technology, and a community member.[37,38]

Inclusion of these stakeholders can help inform the decisions being made and begins to bolster community support as you roll out your plan and implementation to schools and the surrounding community. Above all else, as you evaluate devices, be sure that they align with the learning and use goals you drafted as part of Section 1 of this guide.

Ask these questions when deciding which devices are right for your schools:

- What are your expectations for extended battery life?
- How reliable is the device's operating system relative to privacy and data storage concerns, and does this align with your district's privacy policy?
- What level of durability are you looking for in the device(s)?
- To what extent are considerations of screen size, keyboard/mouse, and peripherals such as scientific probes important for device selection?
- Given the ages of the students who will be using these devices, what choices are most developmentally appropriate?

Here are some pros and cons to consider as you evaluate and plan for device purchases.

Tablets are relatively lightweight, offer a touch screen interface, and typically have longer battery life than laptops. They also have instant-on capabilities, meaning that as soon as they are turned on, they are ready to be used. Laptops may take a few seconds to wake up after they have gone into sleep mode. Some find that reading and interacting with text are easier on a tablet than a laptop. One disadvantage of tablets is that web-based educational apps (applications) that have not been designed specifically for a tablet may be difficult to use. A school already committed to particular digital learning content should make sure that tablets will accommodate the software including any media files it may include.

> **Definition**
>
> **Digital learning content** includes resources such as teacher-created websites, free and open digital resources, and purchased content such as digital textbooks. This content can be available via an Internet connection or downloadable to devices.

Pros

- Tablets tend to be cheaper and lighter and have simpler interfaces than laptops, which can be particularly useful for younger learners.
- The always-on nature of tablets makes information and tools more easily accessible.
- Several peripherals such as science probes can complement the mobility of tablets, making lab experiments in the field possible.

Cons

- Tablets typically do not have built-in keyboards, which can make longer writing assignments challenging.
- The smaller screen size may make it harder for students to create media.
- Not all learning resource providers have updated their products to be used on a mobile device, which may adversely affect functionality and interactivity.
- Tablets can lack the processing power necessary for productivity tasks such as multimedia creation that are available in many laptops.

Laptops, although slightly less portable than tablets, often have larger screens, more powerful processors, and full keyboards. Some laptops also include the touch screen functionality of tablets. For the CTO of Houston Independent School District, laptops made the most sense for his high school deployment because "We knew we wanted to have something that had a keyboard enabled with it, and we knew that for a majority of kids, when they go to college, a laptop is the tool they find most functional."[39] Some laptops have web-based operating systems that rely largely on cloud-based file storage. Whereas these are often less expensive, they also come with trade-offs regarding functionality and processing power. As with any decision about learning tools, consider what you want students and teachers to accomplish with these tools to help guide your thinking.

Pros

- Laptops have larger displays and more processing power for students to create their own media and use advanced software.
- They have built-in keyboards.
- They are compatible with a wide range of digital learning resources and educational software.

Cons

- Battery life is often less reliable than that of tablets.
- Their size and moving parts can diminish mobile use.

Determining Device Requirements

Requirements for devices depend on what your schools plan to do with them now and over the life of the devices. Consider requirements for assessments that may be delivered on the devices. Many state online assessments specify minimum screen sizes, speed, and keyboard and/or mouse requirements. Visit the PARCC or Smarter Balanced consortia websites for specific information on those assessments. If your state or district uses other assessment systems, check the technical requirements of those systems as well.

Use Single Sign-On when Possible

Some school districts are able to negotiate up front with vendors and content providers the ability to use a single-sign on (SSO) process. SSO is a user authentication process that enables a user (student, teacher, administrator, and/or parent) to enter one name and password to access multiple applications. The process eliminates further prompts when the user switches applications during the same session. To avoid trying to retrofit software, be proactive about establishing the SSO process up front. Sign-on should be as simple as possible so that students are not scrambling to remember passwords and wasting valuable class time.

Purchasing devices that barely meet minimum specifications for delivering assessments may not be in the best interest of the district's broader educational goals. Consider optimal rather than minimal standards because they allow devices to be used as intended, allow for growth and expansion over the device lifetime, and allow room for unexpected future developments. A 9-inch screen may be the minimum threshold for online assessments, but will a 9-inch screen serve other educational needs for your students? This does not mean that districts should feel compelled to purchase the latest and greatest. For example, San Diego County purchases devices that fall in the 55%–75% range of premium (0% being the minimum specification and 100% being the most above-specification technology). By following this purchase strategy, the county has been successful in purchasing devices that are above the minimum technical specifications, are acceptably premium, and are reasonably priced.

Bring Your Own Device (BYOD)

BYOD policies can provide students with greater choice and control of their technological habits. However, schools should be cautious when considering BYOD as a replacement for school-provided devices. BYOD policies alone can create several challenges:

1. Economic disparity—The ability to access digital learning materials is disproportionately distributed to students whose families can afford the devices. This can widen the very learning gaps that technology is capable of closing. It may also raise legal concerns because schools are expected to provide a free education for students. If devices are required materials, all students must have access to an equivalent device.[40]

2. Instructional burden—It can be increasingly difficult for teachers to manage learning activities when they have to support multiple platforms and devices (some activities may be incompatible with some devices). In this situation, teachers may revert to "lowest common denominator" activities that work on older and less robust devices at the expense of the learning experience.

3. Assessment security—Student-owned devices may not have the functionality necessary to support a secure testing environment. If your school participates in online assessments, student-owned devices will most likely not provide an acceptable assessment option.

When considering allowing BYOD at your school, consider four important lessons from leaders who have already undertaken these efforts:

> - Security measures (such as content filtering) must be managed at the network level rather than at the device level.
> - Cloud-based resources are helpful for managing the transition between school and home.
> - Students may need to log in to learning systems from BYOD devices. Be sure you support such log-ins.
> - Set minimum device requirements for BYOD devices or provide a list of preferred devices. This can drive family purchases and standardize more of the device environment.

Structuring Device Purchases

This section highlights three funding strategies commonly used by districts across the country.

Through **outright purchase**, a district buys and owns the devices until it decides to retire them via donation, salvage, or other forms of disposal. With this model, districts may purchase a warranty or service agreement from the manufacturer or retailer to repair or replace devices under certain circumstances. Although it allows for expedient purchases, there can be challenges in relying on an outright purchasing approach. Unless a school district specifically creates a yearly budget line item for technology on a per-pupil basis, the tendency is to use one-time funds or other nonrecurring budget sources to pay for the initial purchase. This line item is established by some districts as the result of amortizing the purchase across multiple fiscal years through the selling party or a third-party lending institution. This allows for outright purchase in schools and districts that do not have budgets allowing for a single bulk payment.

Request Proposals

To keep costs lower overall, be mindful of how you develop purchasing agreements. Issuing a request for proposal (RFP) instead of requesting a price quote makes vendors compete for your business, leading to more competitive prices for your district. For small districts that may not be requesting large enough proposals to attract bids, partnering with other districts or states on collaborative purchases is a good option.

Often, these devices end up being deployed to students and teachers for 5 or more years. This extended use can result in students using outdated technology and districts spending a lot on labor and parts to maintain older devices. Before leveraging nonrepeating funds for an initial technology purchases, decide how you will fund the replacement or update devices in subsequent years.

In a **leasing** model, the school district acquires devices in exchange for periodic payments instead of purchasing devices outright. The leasing company owns the equipment and provides an equipment refresh based on the terms of the lease. For example, a district may determine that a 3-year refresh is appropriate to ensure students are using modern devices. At the end of the 3-year term, the leasing company refreshes all the devices and potentially pays the district for the residual value in the devices. Relative to outright purchase, leasing addresses some of the challenges created by owning equipment, like regular budgeting, maintenance, and equipment replacement.

With **cooperative purchasing**, school districts in some states or regions may be able to buy from regional, state, or consortium-based purchasing contracts. These contracts can offer volume-purchase and discount pricing for smaller or medium-size school districts. These buying consortia may also grant access to bids and RFPs that can be piggybacked on by other agencies. These cost reductions, redirections, and reallocations are important steps in budgeting analysis before any funds are expended. Consult your state education authority for information on consortium purchasing available near you.

Funding Device Purchases

In the past, it has been acceptable for technology purchases to be seen as supporting resources outside the standard curriculum. As students' learning needs move toward a diverse learning ecosystem reliant on the presence of multiple technologies, such purchases can no longer be seen as extra. In addition to the possible funding sources outlined here, you should begin to adopt the mindset that technology purchases are normal parts of the operation of a school and recurring expenses within the budget.

Historically, school districts have paid for technology from general operating funds or special budget sources that are outside the general fund.

Special sources may include grants, donations, local categoricals targeted for specific purposes, lottery funds, special-purpose local-option sales tax (Georgia, North Carolina, Iowa), fines and forfeitures, and federal funding available through the Elementary and Secondary Education Act (ESEA) of 2001.

Make Every Dollar Count

This U.S. Department of Education Office of Educational Technology provides guidance and examples for leveraging federal funds to purchase educational technology: tech.ed.gov/funding/

Some school districts leverage short- and long-term bonds approved by voters to pay for technology. This approach is risky because taxpayers can be saddled with debt that outlives the devices by many years. In addition, it gives the appearance that device purchases are one-time expenses rather than recurring ones. Some have suggested using bonds with shorter lengths, closer to the expected life expectancy of the devices. In Ann Arbor, Michigan, voters passed a 5-year technology bond. School leaders should carefully evaluate the benefits of bonds because many devices can be more cheaply replaced than repaired in just a few years. In California, a new type of school bond was introduced to provide school districts with an ongoing funding source for education technology that also protects taxpayers from incurring long-term debt.[41] Contact your local government to see what funding options are available to purchase devices and other elements of school technology.

In addition to identifying new funding sources, district leaders are wise to consider costs that can be eliminated because of the evolving education model. For example, funds typically dedicated to textbooks, printed materials, or other instructional resources may be redirected to devices that make such resources obsolete. Several districts, such as Huntsville, Alabama, and Mooresville, North Carolina, stopped purchasing textbooks, allowing the redistribution of funds to support the transition to digital learning.

Schools and districts are increasingly using open educational resources (OER) to reduce licensing costs for digital content. As with any new curricular resource, the transition to OER will require professional development for teachers as well as time to curate and share those resources. In addition to the potential of long-term savings from the elimination of licensing fees, open resources may have the added benefit of allowing teachers to customize and share their materials with others without violating licensing agreements.

Setting a Refresh Cycle

Beyond 4 years, the combination of student wear and tear and software updates require devices to be replaced. "Within three to four years, it is less expensive to replace the device than repair it," says Doug Levin, the executive director of SETDA.[42] Devices should be disposed of by resale, donation, salvage, recycling, or other form of disposal to minimize harm to the environment. If you are considering resale, be sure first to check on local legal restrictions and any contractual language regarding such sales. Additionally, consult the Electronic Product Assessment Tool to better understand the environmental impact of your technology purchases and disposal of those products if they cannot be resold or donated. For information on more environmentally friendly technology, consult CoSN's SmartIT paper at www.cosn.org/smartIT.

When considering device purchases, account for the cost of battery replacement. Some states, such as Maine, include the replacement of any battery that no longer holds a useful charge plus the proper recycling of the spent battery in their annual cost per student because batteries often require replacement before devices reach end of life. Newer devices have longer battery lives, and some providers claim that batteries on their new devices will last 3 to 4 years before they need replacing.

Strategies for Managing Devices and Applications

Device management is both a technical and managerial issue that includes such aspects as deciding what content is allowed on the devices, remotely wiping stolen devices, and tracking devices reported missing. From a technical perspective, it is important to plan and implement procedures that employ system-level controls for device and application management. School district staff should be able to push out updates, security protocols, and other critical functions from a central location (versus physically touching each device). Most operating systems have built-in mobile device management tools or support third-party device management tools. *See Device Management in Section 5 for more information.*

192 Office of Educational Technology

Warrantees and Maintenance

Although educational technology implementations are and should be about learning and education, they become focused on technology each time something breaks. Make sure you have a plan for addressing inevitable device maintenance and repair. Whether you retain school employees or outside contractors for the job, you need a plan for how repairs will happen quickly and with minimal disruptions to learning. You can supplement your professional technical support with student support teams to handle less detailed recurring repair concerns. If equipment cannot be repaired fast enough, the situation can be disruptive to teachers and students.

Make Learning Justify Spending

Before engaging in discussions about funding options, have an answer to the question about how device investment contributes to student learning. Your district's finance officer also needs to be on board and understand what it means for long-term financial planning combined with your vision for teaching and learning. Auburn, Maine, is in year 4 of providing tablets to students in K–12. The district calculated the cost of remediation and found that if the devices can reduce remediation by even a small number of students, that reduction will pay for the devices.

Varying degrees of local or off-site maintenance may be needed depending on the expertise of staff. In addition, the strategy for maintenance needs to take into consideration continuity of learning such as providing students and staff replacement devices while theirs are being repaired or have been misplaced. Typically, schools operate along these lines:

TIER 1: Local – Repairs that can be handled by the local school or sent out for repair (lower warranty cost)
TIER 2: Off site – Repairs requiring the device be sent to a repair center. Consider these needs while negotiating warranties and contracts.

Clarify a plan for Tier 1 and Tier 2 maintenance before signing a contract to decide which repair issues will be handled in the district and which will be sent out. Buying a warranty can cover or lessen the cost of the repair, but it does not mean the repair is actually made. Schools should ensure that they have plans and contracts in place that take into account the time it takes to

Future Ready Schools 193

repair the devices. If outsourcing maintenance, then service-level agreements with the provider can clarify responsibilities for both parties. When performing in-house maintenance, check warranties first to see whether manufacturers cover needed maintenance at no or low cost.

Students as Tech Support

At Burlington High School in Massachusetts, the Student Help Desk is a resource for all students on their basic tech needs. The Help Desk also teaches students valuable lessons about digital citizenship and encourages them to take responsibility for their devices. Encouraging students to be a part of the solution gives them a sense of responsibility and ownership.

Try to make warranties match your refresh cycle unless it is cost prohibitive to extend a warranty program to the planned life of your devices. Some larger districts are moving to service center models of IT support, sharing resources across several districts. This reduces costs by eliminating such expenses as vendor-trained school staff and using cloud-based services. With the maturity of cloud-based technical services, school districts now have the option to outsource some infrastructure services to regional data centers.

District Devices at Home

Districts opting to send devices home with students are creating policies and expectations pertaining acceptable use and establishing agreements for handling a lost or damaged device. These policy considerations and others are addressed in Section 5.

Some districts are pursuing strategies for connecting students off campus to provide continuous connected learning opportunities. For example, according to a CoSN survey, 29% of districts provide or subsidize Internet access for low-income families, 50% have partnerships with community or business wireless hot spots for student use, and 13% provide students with filtered smartphones.[43] Some districts are choosing to provide students with a wireless router that acts as a mobile hot spot (aka wireless mobile data bridge)—a small portable device that provides wireless connectivity to nearby computers. For example, Irving Independent School District outside Dallas, Texas, began distributing mobile hot spots to qualifying families who lack Internet access in 2013.[44]

> ## Know Students' Home Access, and Craft Educational Experiences Accordingly
>
> Teachers who become accustomed to leveraging technologies in the classroom may not stop to consider students' access levels at home if devices are required to be left in the classroom or lockers. Even if students may take devices home, they might not have Internet connectivity. Students without access may need to worry about work-arounds. Some may download and upload content while they are at school. Such work-arounds caused by inequity negate the gains made by increasing school connectivity.
>
> Some districts provide wireless access on school buses or at community centers where students spend time after school. Others partner with local businesses, providing them with extra power supplies or other incentives in exchange for providing students with free wireless access. *See Section 3 for information on wireless networks available to the community and Path 4 in Section 2 for information on mobile broadband cellular services.*

As you consider allowing students to take district-provided devices home during the school year, start to anticipate family and student interest in taking devices home over the summer. For some 1:1 programs, schools delay the summer option until a year or two into the program so they better understand and meet repair needs. Others prohibit students from taking devices home over the summer entirely for fear of increased loss or damage when students are away from school. As you begin to deploy devices, anticipate questions from families and other stakeholders and have answers prepared.

> ## Determining Student Access at Home
>
> **Fairfax County Public Schools** in northern Virginia surveys families about home access and includes home access questions on emergency care forms that are updated annually. Fairfax's CTO offers some tips based on the district's experience.
>
> Fairfax initially distributed the district-wide survey via email. For families that did not respond, the district conducted an automated telephone survey (to home phones and cell phones). Then, for those who had not responded to the email or telephone surveys, schools followed up with individual phone calls and papers sent home in backpacks. "It may seem obvious, but if your survey is only email or web-based, you will likely miss

> the families you are most concerned about," notes Fairfax's CTO. In addition, Fairfax issued all the surveys (web, phone, paper) in multiple languages and individualized surveys based on the students' home language. Remember to be sensitive to the language divide as well as the digital divide.
>
> With regard to devices, the survey asked whether a family had adequate devices at home for their students to do homework rather than whether they had a computer/device at home because even if there is one computer in the home, it may be shared by multiple children and multiple adults. Finally, the district includes the survey information as required fields in the student information system (SIS). The questions, "Do you have Internet access at home?" and "Do you have adequate devices at home?" were added to the emergency information form families are required to update annually. Having the data in the SIS is advantageous because they are easy for teachers to access and easy to report, and it is easy to see which students' information is missing.
>
> Think of home surveys as spaces for parents to communicate their needs directly to schools as well. Consider including open items that allow for responses outside pre-identified data to increase your understanding of unidentified needs.

Choosing a Rollout Model

Four possible models for device rollout are outlined here. Each has the potential of being used in conjunction with the others, and you should design a rollout that best suits your schools' needs and capacities. Consider piloting whichever model you choose with a small sample to allow for necessary adjustments when you are ready to deploy to the full district or school.

Full school: The entire student body of a school receives devices at the same time.

Pros: Creates a cultural shift within the school. A concentration of resources are available for full professional development for faculty and teachers. High school rollouts can benefit from wholesale 9–12 deployment because multi-grade classrooms in high school make grade-by-grade implementation difficult.

196 Office of Educational Technology

Cons: Provides limited opportunity to work out the kinks at the school level and a great deal of pressure to ensure professional development and logistics are adequately planned.

Grade level: Over the course of several years or throughout a single year, devices are distributed to students one grade level at a time. Often in this model, devices are given to the youngest grade in a school each year. More specific educational goals drive which grades are selected. As students age up a grade, they take their devices with them. This cycle continues until all students have received devices. Be careful of using this in high school because of the concern mentioned above; this may work best for middle school and elementary school.

Pros: Allows you to buy fewer devices at a time as well as work out the kinks in a single grade and prepare a few teachers at the same time.

Cons: Runs the risk of losing funding for the next grade level. Creates inequity of access across grade levels.

Subject area: Devices are rolled out to a focused discipline or content areas within schools. This is effective if a school has a discipline focus, such as STEM or the arts, that will be implemented well with a device model. This is especially common with literacy in younger grades. Consider subjects for which you have buy-in about the potential for technology, along with educational need and determination.

Pros: Allows an additional focus on the educational requirements of a specific subject. Less expensive than a schoolwide rollout and allows time for lessons learned (similar to a grade-level rollout).

Cons: The student experience can be uneven across classrooms, teachers, and/or subject areas. Some teachers may lack interest or ownership in using devices for learning because they see them as belonging to other programs or subject areas. Other subjects may want to use the technology to support their subject areas as well.

Exemplar teacher model: Work first with the teachers who can and are interested in helping you build a program. Consider identifying these teachers by outlining the vision for utilizing digital learning resources, and the requirements for participation as an exemplar teacher. Ask interested teachers to apply for consideration and include past examples of work and learning that align with district plans.

Pros: Works through the process with power users and early adopters to develop policies, protocols, and procedures. Greater chance of success out of the gate, which can be helpful while building momentum. Allows for adjustments from lessons learned.

Cons: Risks non-pilot teachers feeling disconnected from the process. Could also result in policies and procedures that fail to take into account reluctant users.

Full-School Pilot Model

Consider which rollout strategy makes the most sense for your school or district. The **Houston School District** kicked off its $18 million 1:1 laptop PowerUp initiative in 2013. The district ramped up the initiative in phases throughout the school year so that the infrastructure capacity could be tested and adjusted. It used a full-school pilot model for the initial rollout. At the start of the 2013–14 school year, teachers at 11 pilot high schools received laptops. In January 2014, all students in the pilot high schools received laptops, with the program ultimately providing 130,000 students in grades 3–12 with laptops. Before implementing the program, the district superintendent and CTO observed several other 1:1 programs to learn from them and to brainstorm improvements. Their main advice for other districts considering 1:1 programs is to be flexible and willing to alter course if something is not working.[45]

PLANNING YOUR ROLLOUT

Planning must take place at the district and school levels to ensure a smooth rollout. In the same way that your district will need to develop a plan that is unique to your needs and context, your schools will most likely need some leeway in designing a process that suits their school populations. While the suggestions here offer guidance, providing schools with planning templates will require them to consider key issues while allowing for site ownership of the process.

Beginning an initiative that includes devices for all students will mean an influx of device inventory at all levels. Plan for a flow of responsibility for checking devices in and out. Many schools will use existing systems such as those in place in libraries or media centers to leverage existing capacities and system knowledge.

Consider parents to be partners in this process, especially if you will be providing devices for home use. Plan informational meetings in advance of handing out devices so you can walk parents through policies and procedures and address concerns without the distraction of new devices in students' hands. When scheduling these events, take into account the availability of your parent population so that you can meet face to face with as many parents as possible and avoid miscommunications with parents who are not able to attend.

When communicating with parents and community members, keep them informed of all aspects of the process. For many families, the shift to devices in classrooms and homes will require a great adjustment; providing as much information as you can will help to answer questions as they arise and show your district is operating in accordance with a clear vision and plan.

Professional development on the most effective ways to use digital learning resources will be an ongoing process, and it should begin before teachers receive devices. Plan an introductory course (online, in person, or blended) to help teachers learn basic functionality and troubleshooting before they can access devices. That same course could then be modified for students to ensure all district members have a foundational level of understanding before rollout.

While some students will be adept at device usage from the moment they receive them, some will need guidance, and all will probably require help accessing new digital learning resources. Have a document such as an electronic handbook preloaded on devices that explains account and sign-on procedures students will need to follow. This will be much easier if your district is using SSO for accessing resources.

Communicating With Stakeholders

In 2012, the **St. Vrain Valley School District** in Colorado formed an instructional technology advisory committee to plan the district's upcoming technology investment so that it would best serve learning goals. Throughout the technology planning and implementation process, the district's goal was to communicate often, build trust with the community through transparency, and to maintain the focus on learning. To keep lines of communication open, the district created a blog to communicate its story and to give stakeholders an opportunity to provide feedback. The technology department placed a shortcut on the home screen of every device to provide families with information and resources about the transition. The shortcut includes information for parents in both English and Spanish, as the district has a significant population of Spanish-speaking families (30%). In addition, the district reached out to community groups working with local families and partnered with libraries and businesses to provide opportunities for family events and trainings.

5. RESPONSIBLE USE, PRIVACY, AND OTHER CONSIDERATIONS

In This Section

- Device management
- Responsible use & digital citizenship
- Student privacy requirements
- Safeguarding against inappropriate content
- Policies for lost or damaged devices

Setting expectations that encourage device management, digital citizenship, and other policies that outline responsible use, including safeguarding student privacy are essential considerations to ensure technology effectively supports learning. Policies in these areas should be carefully considered before device rollout begins.

Device Management

Remote Management

Devices require ongoing management—including keeping software updated, adjusting filtering settings, and changing system preferences. Software tools can be installed on devices to make it easy to remotely update them without users having to take them physically back to the school each time an update is required. This software may also collect information about how devices are being used in order to better support students and teachers. The district is responsible for maintaining up-to-date security and privacy settings to prevent hacking and protect student data. As schools transition to online assessments, installation of special software may be necessary to ensure a secure testing environment.

Remote Locking

In addition to installing software to remotely update devices, you may also consider installing tools to remotely disable or erase a device in the event of loss or theft. This can increase the likelihood that lost devices are returned to the district as well as prevent data from being taken from a lost or stolen device. Publicly communicating that devices can be permanently locked may

200 Office of Educational Technology

also help deter theft. For example, you might put a sticker on the bottom of every device stating that if the device is lost or stolen it will be remotely disabled. Local law enforcement agencies may be good resources for determining how best to deter theft and address missing devices.

Student Access

Districts need to decide how much control students may have over school-provided devices. Less ability to modify or change the device settings can make it easier for IT staff to maintain devices but gives students less freedom to personalize devices for their needs. The decision to allow more control over a device may vary depending on the student. A multi-tiered model of permissions and restrictions gives students who demonstrate responsible behavior more privileges and restricts access for students who fail to show responsible behavior. As you consider these policies, remember that restricting a student's access in one class will affect that student's ability to participate in learning in subsequent classes as well.

Mobile Management for Device Configuration

In Maine's statewide laptop deployment, each student has full administrator access to his or her device, and students are fully responsible for their device's management. The state has a mobile device management system, which allows the state and individual schools to make software available to students and teachers as well as to remotely update software and settings.

Ensuring and Encouraging Responsible Use

Before students are allowed to access the Internet at school, whether via a school-provided or personal device, most schools ask parents and students to sign an Acceptable Use Policy (AUP), also known as a Responsible Use Policy (RUP). An AUP is a written agreement between parents, students, and school personnel that outlines the terms of responsible device use and consequences for misuse. AUPs traditionally cover topics such as guidance on how students are expected to interact with one another in digital spaces, what resources may or may not be accessed with district-provided devices, and standards for academic integrity when using digital resources for learning. Parents are asked to acknowledge that their child agrees to basic care and responsibility guidelines. Students are asked to sign a contract agreeing to follow rules governing their use of the Internet and online conduct.

Modify What Works

Defining digital citizenship for your district in the face of shifting technological landscapes can be daunting. Turn to organizations like Common Sense Media for resources to help guide your thinking on the kinds of digital citizens you want educators and students to be. Common Sense materials range from an outreach kit for a family engagement night to advice videos and family tip sheets in English and in Spanish.

AUPs should be written in plain language that is easily accessible for students, parents, and district personnel. For additional information on questions to consider when drafting an AUP, see CoSN's Rethinking Acceptable Use Policies to Enable Learning: A Guide for School Districts. Relying on strict policies and procedures for the use of devices can often have unintended negative consequences like preventing access to legitimate educational resources. Effective AUPs are an opportunity to teach students to create a positive digital persona. Learning responsible digital citizenship while in school helps students to thrive in a connected world. Digital citizenship can include aspects of students' online lives that range from online etiquette and safety to their rights to privacy and access.

Rather than try to mandate how devices will be used, schools and districts should set forth clear guidelines to parents, teachers, and students about how the devices should be used and about how and when the school/district will use student data. By implementing flexible policy recommendations, schools and districts can set expectations for responsible use.

AUPs as Learning Opportunities

AUPs can be written in plain language. For an example, see the AUP of **Austin** ISD in Texas. Another helpful approach is tailoring your AUP language to different grade levels of students, as **Boston Public Schools** in Massachusetts has done. Consider creating lesson plans or other materials to help teachers present AUP content in a meaningful way that makes understanding your AUP a learning opportunity.

In addition to providing acceptable use policies for schools, it is essential to provide families with guidelines to help them establish their own norms for acceptable use at home. Many districts hold a mandatory parent orientation before issuing students' devices, and may do so in coordination with parent organizations to lead classes on technology use in the home. Hosting parent and community nights to explain the school's approach to connected learning, ensuring clarity about policies, and presenting digital citizenship for all community members helps to share responsibility. Parents should be educated on use, responsibilities, digital citizenship, and how to manage devices at home.

Definition

An **acceptable use policy** (or **responsible use policy**) is a contract between districts, parents, and students that states the expectations and responsibilities of anyone using the school's network and devices. Signed AUPs typically are required before a student can gain access to a school-provided device or network.

Protecting Privacy

Schools officials, families, and software developers must be mindful of how data privacy, confidentiality, and security practices affect students.

Schools and districts have an obligation to tell students and parents what kind of student data the school or third parties (e.g., online educational service providers) are collecting and how the data can be used.

As you plan, be certain that policies are in place regarding who has access to student data and that families understand their rights and responsibilities concerning data collection. These policies should include not only formal adoption processes for online educational services, but click-wrap agreements as well. A user encounters click-wrap when asked to click on a button to accept the provider's terms of service before using an app or software. With click-wrap agreements, the act of accepting the terms of service enters the developer and the user (in this case, the school or district) into a contractual relationship akin to signing a contract. Be sure all teachers in your schools understand the implications and district policies governing the use of such software agreements.

Future Ready Schools 203

> **Consult PTAC Recommendations**
>
> The U.S. Department of Education established the Privacy Technical Assistance Center (PTAC) as a one-stop resource to learn about privacy related to student data. PTAC provides information and updated guidance on privacy, confidentiality, and security practices through a variety of means, including training materials and direct assistance. PTAC also provides guidance on the relevant privacy laws. PTAC recently provided additional recommendations on Protecting Student Privacy while Using Online Educational Services and Transparency Best Practices for Schools and Districts.

A number of statutes apply to student privacy in schools. More information on each is below.

FERPA (the **Family Educational Rights and Privacy Act**) gives parents the right to access and seek to amend their children's education records (these rights transfer to students when they reach 18 years of age or when they attend a postsecondary school at any age). FERPA protects personally identifiable information in education records from unauthorized disclosure, and requires prior written consent before schools share personally identifiable information from student education records. However, school officials with legitimate educational interests can disclose personally identifiable information from education records with vendors subject to certain requirements, including that the vendor performs an institutional service or function that would otherwise be performed by school employees.

The second statute is **COPPA** (the **Children's Online Privacy Protection Act**), which governs online collection of personal information from children under 13. Before an online organization can collect any information from students under 13, "verifiable parental consent" is required. The Federal Trade Commission, which enforces COPPA, has said that school officials can, in certain situations, provide consent on behalf of the parents in order to sign students up for online educational programs at school. Signing up for any online educational program entails some level of student data collection. This can become complicated when students use their own devices at school and sign up for educational services or programs and then take the devices home. For school-provided devices, the law is clearer and schools can collect data on those devices for educational purposes when the devices are at school or elsewhere.

204 Office of Educational Technology

Review Federal Guidance

For more guidance on FERPA, visit the US Department of Education's FERPA for School Officials.
The Federal Trade Commission enforces COPPA. See the FTC's Complying with COPPA FAQ for more details.
The FCC's CIPA Guide offers a more in-depth understanding of CIPA requirements.

CIPA (the Children's Internet Protection Act) imposes several requirements on schools or libraries that receive E-rate discounts for Internet access. Schools and libraries must certify that they have technologies in place to block or filter Internet access to content that is obscene, pornographic, or harmful to minors, and schools must also monitor the online activities of minors.

PPRA (the Protection of Pupil Rights Amendment) is intended to protect the rights of parents and students in two ways. The first is by seeking to ensure that schools and contractors make instructional materials available for parents' inspection if those materials will be used in connection with a survey, analysis, or evaluation funded by the U.S. Department of Education. Second, PPRA requires that a school district, with exceptions, directly notify parents of students who are scheduled to participate in activities involving the collection, disclosure, or use of personal information collected from the students for marketing purposes or for sale or provision to others for marketing purposes and give parents the opportunity to opt out of these activities. One important exception to PPRA is that neither parental notice and the opportunity to opt out nor the development and adoption of policies are required for school districts to use students' personal information for the exclusive purpose of developing, evaluating, or providing educational products or services for students or schools.

HIPPA (the Health Insurance Portability and Privacy Act) sets national standards for the security of electronic protected health information. In most cases, the HIPPA Privacy Rule does not apply to an elementary or secondary school because the school either: (1) is not a HIPPA-covered entity or (2) is a HIPPA-covered entity but maintains health information only on students in records that are by definition "education records" under FERPA and, therefore, is not subject to the HIPPA Privacy Rule. For a better understanding

Future Ready Schools

of the issue, see the jointly-published guidance from the US Department of Health and Human Services and the US Department of Education.

Safeguarding Against Inappropriate Content

It is the school's responsibility to protect students from inappropriate content when they are using the Internet. This can be done through technical approaches (filtering and blocking) as well as through establishing a digital citizenship curriculum and school culture that includes online safety.

Share Data Wisely

As a general rule, if the school provides the device, has an educational service contract with a vendor performing an institutional function or service, and the application has educational value; then collecting data for purposes of helping the student or teacher or improving the application itself is generally permitted. However, the requirements of FERPA's "school official" exception must be met, including that the data uses are authorized by the school and constitute a legitimate educational interest per the school's annual notification of FERPA rights. For districts that rely on the general terms of service (TOS) offered by outside providers, PTAC provides additional guidance regarding TOS and managing that process. You can find more information at tech.ed.gov/privacy.

Use Technical Filtering

Many tools are available to filter the content that can be accessed on the Internet. All connections to the Internet must be filtered in order to be in compliance with E-rate. However, filtering can be challenging because of the enormous volume of online resources.

When establishing technical filtering solutions, schools must balance protecting students from inappropriate materials with not limiting access to valuable educational content. If filters are set to be too strict, students and teachers may be prevented from using high-quality educational resources and collaboration tools, which would defeat the very purpose of investment in the technology.

Filtering is a partnership between teachers, students, and the people responsible for providing the technical filtering system. Decisions about what materials should be available or restricted should be made in consultation with teachers, and teachers should have an ongoing and streamlined way to request access to sites with educational value as well as to recommend sites that should be restricted.

One helpful strategy is to periodically audit content access. In this approach, websites being accessed by students are regularly reviewed and adjustments made. Inappropriate activity can be detected and consequences created for inappropriate behavior. Conversely, blocked sites that students regularly attempt to access can be reviewed in case they are educational sites that are inadvertently being blocked. This can be a powerful approach for maintaining a strong content filter without limiting educational access to a wide variety of sources.

No technical filtering tool is 100% reliable, and some objectionable content may still pass through, which is why building a curriculum and school culture that include digital citizenship is an essential component of keeping students safe.

Involve Parents

When it comes to content filtering, transparency with families and teachers is key. In general, schools are not required to provide filtering when a device is not used on a school-provided network. It is a good practice, however, to provide filtering on school-owned devices even when they are used on home or public networks. Make sure that you communicate clearly to parents where and how the school is providing filtering and inform them in what cases they are responsible for filtering (such as on personal devices connected to a home network). Give families guidance on both technical and human filtering options that can be put in place on devices they are responsible for. For more information on filtering on devices, see the FCC guide on Protecting Children from Objectionable Content.

Teach Responsibility

While technical filtering tools should always be in place, teaching students to be responsible Internet users is the best long-term strategy because students can develop judgment, which can ensure appropriate use even when students are using devices that may not have the same technical restrictions (such as home computers or personal smartphones). Approaching the guidance you offer students from this mindset can help them act like the online citizens you hope them to be when you are not in the room or monitoring a device. Failing

Future Ready Schools 207

to teach students responsible use and hoping they will automatically know the safest ways to behave when filters and security settings are no longer present is irresponsible and potentially dangerous.

The most successful approach to protecting students from inappropriate content is a combination of technical filtering and a strong digital citizenship curriculum.

Consider how you will filter content on nondistrict devices

If you are considering a BYOD program, you have additional filtering challenges to consider. Because schools have limited ability to control personal devices, filtering solutions must be implemented at the network level. Districts may require students with their own devices to use only the school's wireless network rather than the student's personal data plan to ensure that filtering is provided. If a district is issuing mobile hot spots for student home Internet use, the service provider for the mobile access must be filtered. Some schools have decided to require that students use their devices to connect to school filtered networks only and use only school-provided learning applications and software.46 For an example of a BYOD filtering success story, see the Fairfax County example in Section 3, on page 41.

Dealing with Lost or Damaged Devices

Districts should have a plan to address the inevitable issue of lost, stolen, or damaged devices and ensure that parents and students are aware of their responsibilities in these situations.

Preventing Device Damage or Loss

The best way to deal with device loss or damage is to prevent it from happening in the first place. Implementing the following suggestions can help you prevent and reduce rates of device damage and loss:

- **Teach students responsible practices.** Explicitly discussing with students how they can protect themselves and their devices will help them care for what is likely to be the most expensive learning resource they have ever received from a school. Practices like discussing what they would do in hypothetical situations, group brainstorms of tips to keep themselves safe, and periodically asking students to share what they have learned about taking care of devices are all good starts to the effort.

- **Allow students to customize their devices.** When students are allowed to customize their device, they have a greater sense of ownership of them. Customization may include putting stickers on the device and choosing a unique desktop background image. Customization also helps prevent students from accidentally taking someone else's device by making it easier to identify their own.
- **Require password lock when devices are not in use.** Many devices require a password after not having been in use for a certain amount of time. Requiring students to set a password on their device can help to make them unattractive to would-be thieves who lack the passcodes. This has the added benefit of preventing students from accessing other students' work and accounts.

Device Protection at All Grade Levels

Policies regarding device care can be made appropriate for even the youngest learners. A kindergarten teacher at Pachappa Elementary School in **Riverside Unified School District** in California said that not one of her 25 students' devices has been broken in the 2 years her classes have used them.[47] Each kindergartener uses a small plastic tub (the kind designed for leftovers) to store his or her device when not in use. The teacher tells the students, "That's their device's 'house.'" The plastic case that originally packaged the device is its "bed." Kindergartners are taught to tuck their device into bed, wrapped in a cloth, its "blanket." Then they put a "seatbelt" (a rubber band) around the case so that it will not "fall out of bed."[47] Children carry their device's "house" between school and home in their backpacks.

- **Prohibit students from carrying the device outside their backpacks.** In a school setting where all students carry devices from place to place, the chance of damage from being dropped is reduced if devices are moved only in backpacks. Asking students to stow devices in backpacks when moving outside the school can lessen the chances of device theft.
- **Install device-tracking software to locate a missing device and remotely render it inoperable.** If a device is lost or stolen from a

Future Ready Schools 209

student, tracking software can help you to alert authorities to the location for retrieval. This software can also help locate devices students may report as stolen that are actually misplaced. If such software is installed, establish clear policies that limit the use of this functionality to cases where the device has been reported lost or stolen or in an emergency.

- **Buy a protective case for the devices to protect them from accidental drops.** Before committing to a mass case purchase, ask manufacturers for trial versions and re-create the scenarios you envision occurring with students dropping devices. If purchasing cases is not part of your budget, this testing can help you supply families with a list of district-approved cases for guidance.

As you design the safety measures that make the most sense for your population, loop families in to your plan and ask for their feedback. This will make device safety everyone's responsibility.

Dealing with Device Damage or Loss

Whatever your strategy for dealing with lost or stolen devices, communicate it clearly and often with families and students to help embed safe practices across all stakeholders. Some of the strategies that districts use are:

- **Require payment.** Some districts require the student or family to pay for a device that is missing or damaged. The advantage to this approach is that it provides accountability for addressing the damage. However, it can also pose challenges for families who may not be able to afford the new device. For such families, if you choose this option have a plan for possible reduced or installment payments.
- **Contract insurance.** Establishing an insurance policy is the simplest but usually more expensive way to handle lost or missing devices. The insurance policy can either be paid by the district or by the families. If the latter, the district may need to have a solution in place for families who cannot afford the cost of device insurance. Consider a reduced rate or installment plan for these families.
- **Maintain extra inventory.** Some districts choose to self-insure by purposefully purchasing more devices than are needed for the initial rollout and keeping them in stock to replace broken or missing ones. If you self-insure, avoid use the term *insurance* when describing your program because it has legal meaning, and your district is not a

licensed insurance company. Establish clear guidelines defining when the school or district is liable for repairing a student's device and when the student is liable (e.g., because of intentional misuse).

Less Damage When Devices Went Home

In Maine, in the first 4 years of the Maine Laptop Initiative (2002–06) schools had a choice to send laptops home or not. Roughly 50% of schools sent the devices home across the state. Data collected showed that damage was *higher* in schools that did not send the devices home than in schools that did. Based on these data, in 2006 the state mandated that schools send the devices home with students. In addition, schools that allowed students to take the devices home generally had better examples of digital learning activities because teachers felt greater flexibility in assigning projects that required longer and deeper uses of the devices.

Districts may establish additional consequences for students with repeated problems with maintaining their device or when there is evidence of intentional damage. Examples may include losing the privilege of taking the device home or losing the use of the device altogether for a certain period. An older or less expensive device may be provided until the student can show he or she is able to properly maintain control over the original device. These decisions should balance accountability with the need to provide the student with the tools to complete schoolwork.

CONCLUSION

An essential element of providing equitable education for America's students is ensuring the existence of infrastructure to support personalized learning, collaboration, increased engagement, and creativity. Planning and providing infrastructure, both Internet connectivity and devices, should stem from a clear vision for how learning and teaching will be supported. This involves understanding a variety of technical options and legal requirements as well as seeking input from teachers, leaders, students, parents, and community members. This guide provides a list of options to consider and questions to ask to make sure you make the right choices when leading this change in your district.

Future Ready Schools 211

Our students live in a connected world where they will be expected to engage and interact with peers and experts online, create and design with digital tools, and be exemplary digital citizens. With vision, infrastructure, professional learning, and devices, our schools will be better able to support students with the opportunity to learn and thrive.

APPENDIX

Future Ready Schools: Quick Reference Guide of Key Questions

The questions listed below address many of the important considerations as you plan to bring and increase connectivity throughout your district and schools. Each set corresponds to further guidance within *Future Ready Schools: Building Technology Infrastructure to Support Learning*.

1. Getting Started: Assess Your Current Situation and Set Future Goals (*see Section 1*)
- What is the vision for learning that technology will be supporting?
- What digital learning resources will be needed?
- What kind of professional development will teachers need to become proficient with digital learning?
- What is your current network capacity?
- What is the current state of your physical infrastructure?
- How many and what type of devices does your network support now? What is planned for the future?
- What resources are available to fund the transition?

2. Getting High-Speed Internet to Schools (*see Section 2*)
- What are the options for high-speed Internet access in your area?
- Which of the connectivity path is best for your district's needs?
- What are the elements that will affect cost in your area?
- What funding sources are available to get Internet to schools?
- What resources are available for rural schools?

3. Getting High-Speed Internet Throughout Schools (*see Section 3*)
- What are the steps in planning a wireless network inside a school?
- What physical infrastructure considerations will impact the network?

- How should the network be provisioned, configured, and managed?
- How should security risks to the network be managed?

4. Getting Devices to Students and Teachers (*see Section 4*)
- Why are devices important?
- Which factors should be considered when selecting devices?
- What about BYOD programs?
- How will you pay for devices?
- What funding sources are available?
- How often will devices need to be replaced?
- How will devices be maintained?
- Should your school allow devices to be taken home?
- How should devices be rolled out?

5. Determining Responsible Use, Student Privacy, and Other School Policies (*see Section 5*)
- How should devices be managed?
- How can schools ensure and encourage responsible use of devices?
- What are school obligations for protecting the privacy of students?
- How should content filtering on devices work?
- Which policies for lost or damaged devices make sense?

Notes

[1] Fox, C., Waters, J., Fletcher, G. and Levin, D. (2012). The Broadband Imperative: Recommendations to Address K-12 Education Infrastructure Needs. Washington, DC: State Educational Technology Directors Association (SETDA).

[2] Federal Communications Commission. (2010). 2010 E-Rate Program and Broadband Usage Survey: Report. Available at http://transition.fcc.gov/010511 Eratereport.pdf

[3] Federal Communications Commission. (2011). Seventh Broadband Progress Report and Order on Reconsideration. Available at https://apps.fcc.gov/edocs public/attachmatch/FCC-11-78A1.pdf

[4] The White House. Office of the Press Secretary. (2013). Remarks by the President at Mooresville Middle School - Mooresville, NC. Available at http://www.whitehouse.gov/the-press-office/2013/06/06/remarks-president-mooresville-middle-school-mooresville-nc

[5] The White House, Office of the Press Secretary. (2013). President Obama's Plan for Connecting All Schools to the Digital Age. Available at http://www.whitehouse.gov/sites/default/files/docs/connected fact sheet.pdf

[6] Donahue, N. and Garcia, L. (2014, July 7). A Working Model for Blended Learning in an Urban School. *Edutopia.* Available at http://www.edutopia.org/blog/working-model-for-blended-learning-nicholasdonohue-lourenco-garcia

Future Ready Schools

213

[7] Foster, M. (2013). Netcraft Analysis: Online Speed Testing Tools. Available at http://www.setda.org/c/ document library/get file?folderId=353&name=DLFE-1647.pdf

[8] Project Tomorrow. (2013). From Chalkboards to Tablets: The Emergence of the K-12 Digital Learner. Available at http://www.tomorrow.org/speakup/pdfs/SU12-Students.pdf

[9] The White House, Office of the Press Secretary. (2013). President Obama's Plan for Connecting All Schools to the Digital Age. Available at http://www.whitehouse.gov/sites/default/files/docs/connected fact sheet.pdf

[10] Fox, C., Waters, J., Fletcher, G. and Levin, D. (2012). *The Broadband Imperative: Recommendations to Address K-12 Education Infrastructure Needs*. Washington, DC: State Educational Technology Directors Association (SETDA).

[11] Education Superhighway. (2014, April). *Connecting America's Students: Opportunities for Action*. Available at http://www.educationsuperhighway.org/uploads/1/0/9/4/10946543/esh k12 e-rate spending report april 2014.pdf

[12] California Executive Order S-21-06. (2006, October 27). *Twenty-First Century Government: Expanding Broadband Access and Usage in California*. Available at http://gov.ca.gov/news.php?id=4818

[13] NYC Information Technology & Telecommunications. (n.d.). Innovation: Broadband. Available at http:// www.nyc.gov/html/doitt/html/business/micro trenching.shtml

[14] CTC Technology and Energy. (n.d.) Dark Fiber Lease Considerations. Available at http://www.ctcnet.us/ DarkFiberLease.pdf

[15] Gonzalez, L. (2013, August 1). Dark Fiber Paying off in Florida's Lakeland. *Community Broadband Networks*. Available at http://www.muninetworks.org/content/dark-fiber-paying-floridas-lakeland

[16] Herold, B. (2014). Districts Get Creative to Build Faster Internet Connections. *Education Week*. Available at http://mobile.edweek.org/c.jsp?DISPATCHED=true &cid= 25983841&item=http%3A%2F%2Fwww.edweek.org%2Few%2Farticles%2F2014%2F01%2F15%2F17fiber ep.h33.html

[17] Birkenbuel, R. (2014). Butte Schools' Fiber Optics Switch Featured in Nationwide Magazine. *The Montana Standard*. Available at http://mtstandard.com/news/local/butte-schools-fiber-optics-switch-featured-innationwide-magazine/articled2cba792-826a-11e3-a083-001a4bcf887a.html

[18] Fatbeam. (2013, July 10). Fatbeam Launches Fiber Optic Network in Butte, Montana. Available at http:// www.bldc.net/wordpress/wp-content/uploads/2014/03/Community-Fiber-Optic-Network.pdf

[19] CSMG and Gates Foundation. (2011). *Connections, Capacity, Community: Exploring Potential Benefits of Research and Education Networks for Public Libraries*. Available at http://www.arkansased.org/public/userfiles/LegislativeServices/Quality%20Digital%20Learning%20Study/Reports/Connections%20 Capacity%20Community.pdf

[20] State Educational Technology Directors Association. (2012). *The Broadband Imperative: Recommendations to Address K-12 Education Infrastructure Needs*. Available at http://www.setda.org/web/guest/ broadbandimperative

[21] The Utah Education Network (2012). Welcome to UEN. Available at http://leadershipsummit.setda.org/wp-content/uploads/sites/5/2013/11/Welcome-to-UEN.pdf

[22] State Educational Technology Directors Association. (2012). *The Broadband Imperative: Recommendations to Address K-12 Education Infrastructure Needs*. Available at http://www.setda.org/web/guest/ broadbandimperative

[23] MCNC. (n.d.). About MCNC. Available at https://www.mcnc.org/about.html

214 Office of Educational Technology

[24] MCNC. (2013, April 9). North Carolina "Races to the Top" in the Cloud. Available at https://www.mcnc.org/news/nc-races-to-top-in-the-cloud

[25] AT&T. (2013). Lake Tahoe Hits the Jackpot with Technology-Rich Learning Environment. Available at http://www.corp.att.com/edu/docs/lake tahoe netbooks.pdf

[26] Lake Tahoe Unified School District (2012). *Lake Tahoe Unified School District Education Technology Plan.* Available at http://www.ltusd.org/userfiles/file/Tech%20Plan%202012-15%20FINAL%20without%20EETT%20Template.pdf

[27] Cavanagh, S. (2013, July 28). A Closer Look at the FCC's Ideas for Revamping the E-Rate. *Education Week.* Available at http://blogs.edweek.org/edweek/DigitalEducation/2013/07/a closer look at the e-rates n. html?print=1

[28] Fulton County Schools. (n.d.). Fulton County Schools SPLOST. Available at http://www.fultonschools.org/ en/SPLOST

[29] Navajo Nation Telecommunications Regulatory Commission. (2013). FCC Modernizing the E-Rate Program for Schools and Libraries: Comment from The Navajo Nation Telecommunications Regulatory Commission. Available at http://apps.fcc.gov/ecfs/ document/view?id=7520944058

[30] Consortium for School Networking (2013). E-Rate and Broadband Survey. Available at http://www.cosn.org/e-rate-broadband-survey

[31] Layton, L. (2013, September 11). Arne Duncan sells benefits of Common Core standards, technology to Arizona students. *The Washington Post.* Available at http://www.washingtonpost.com/ local/education/arne-duncan-sells-benefits-of-common-core-standards-technology-to-arizonastudents/2013/09/11/2485b58c-1b05-11e3-82ef-a059e54c49d0 story.html

[32] Veres, M. (2013, October 1). Personal communication, Sunnyside Office of Public Information.

[33] Sunnyside Unified School District. (n.d.). Available at http://www.susd12.org/

[34] Beasley, W. (2013, November 6). Personal communication.

[35] School 2.0. (n.d.). Available at http://etoolkit.org/etoolkit/

[36] Greaves, T., Hayes, J., Wilson, L., Gielniak, M. and Peterson, R. (2010). *The Technology Factor: Nine Keys to Student Achievement and Cost-Effectiveness.* MDR.

[37] Chariho School District. (n.d.). Chariho 1:1 - An Investment in the Future: Our Journey Toward a Vision for Technology Use. Available at http://www.chariho.k12.ri.us/ sites/default/files/1-1 vision.pdf

[38] Chariho School District. (n.d.) Chariho 1:1 Device Selection Advisory Committee. Available at http://www. chariho.k12.ri.us/sites/default/files/device selection advisory committee members.pdf

[39] Herold, B. (2014). Houston Launches Ambitious 1-to-1 Computing Initiative. *Education Week.* http://blogs.edweek.org/edweek/DigitalEducation/2014/01/houston launches ambitious. html

[40] Lhamon, C. U.S. Department of Education, Office for Civil Rights. (2014, October 1). Dear Colleague Letter: Resource Comparability. Available at http://www2.ed.gov/about/offices/ list/ocr/letters/ colleague-resourcecomp-201410.pdf

[41] CASBO (California Association of School Business Officials). (n.d.). New California bond solution developed to fund educational technology. Available at http://www.casbo.org/ ?NewSchoolBondSolutio

[42] Davis, M. (2013, October 29). Critics See Risks in Use of Bonds for School Tech Projects. *Education Week.* Available at http://www.edweek.org/ew/articles/2013/10/30/ 10bond.h33.html

Future Ready Schools 215

[43] Consortium for School Networking. (2013). E-rate and Broadband Survey 2013. Available at http://www. cosn.org/sites/default/files/2013EratebroadbandFinal.pdf

[44] Selk, A. (2013, Jan 13). School district giving out free wifi hotspots to families without Internet. *Dallas Morning News.* Available at http://irvingblog.dallasnews.com/ 2013/01/school-district-giving-out-freewifi-hotspots-to-families-without-internet.html/

[45] Herold, B. (2014). Houston Launches Ambitious 1-to-1 Computing Initiative. *Education Week.* http://blogs.edweek.org/edweek/DigitalEducation/2014/01/houston launches ambitious.html

[46] Norris, C. and Soloway, E. (2011). Tips for BYOD K12 Programs. Critical Issue in Moving to "Bring Your Own Device." Available at http://www.districtadministration.com/article/tips-byod-k12-programs

[47] Straehley, D. (2013, May 24). RIVERSIDE: District introduces textbooks on iPod, other tablets. The Press-Enterprise. Available at http://www.pe.com/local-news/topics/topics-education-headlines/20130524-riverside-district-introduces-textbooks-on-ipod-other-tablets.ece

RELATED NOVA PUBLICATION

NATIONAL EDUCATION TECHNOLOGY PLAN, 2011

Arthur P. Hershaft

ISBN: 978-1-61324-636-8   Publication Date: 2011

Education is the key to America's economic growth and prosperity and to our ability to compete in the global economy. It is the path to higher earning power for Americans and is necessary for our democracy to work. It fosters the cross-border, cross-cultural collaboration required to solve the most challenging problems of our time. The National Education Technology Plan 2010 calls for revolutionary transformation. Specifically, we must embrace innovation and technology which is at the core of virtually every aspect of our daily lives and work. This book explores the National Education Technology Plan which presents a model of learning powered by technology, with goals and recommendations in five essential areas: learning, assessment, teaching, infrastructure and productivity.

INDEX

2

21st century, 5, 9, 14, 38, 59, 78, 85, 105, 108, 114, 115, 125, 129, 167

A

academic success, 10
academic tasks, 39
access, 3, 5, 6, 7, 8, 9, 12, 19, 22, 24, 27, 29, 30, 33, 35, 37, 43, 47, 50, 51, 52, 53, 54, 55, 58, 59, 63, 64, 65, 66, 68, 69, 72, 75, 76, 78, 79, 82, 83, 84, 85, 86, 87, 88, 89, 90, 91, 92, 93, 94, 96, 97, 98, 99, 101, 102, 105, 106, 107, 125, 126, 131, 134,135, 136, 137, 138, 139, 141, 142, 145, 149, 151, 153, 154, 155, 156, 157, 158, 159, 160, 161, 162, 165, 167, 168, 169, 170, 171, 172, 173, 175, 176, 177, 178, 179, 180, 181, 182, 183, 186, 187, 189, 193, 194, 195, 196, 198, 200, 201, 202, 203, 204, 205, 206, 207, 211
access device, 97, 106
accessibility, vii, 1, 3, 24, 29, 69, 78, 99, 101, 102, 124, 183
accommodation(s), 3, 25, 72
accountability, 62, 127, 209, 210
achievement, 3, 11, 28, 36, 64, 70, 75, 78, 83, 118, 119, 127, 133, 141

action research, 110
adaptation, 10, 70
administrators, 5, 33, 42, 47, 51, 53, 77, 98, 99, 103, 104, 106, 107, 116, 124, 142, 145, 184
adolescents, 125
adult education, 36
adulthood, 127
adults, 89, 195
advertisements, 17
advocacy, 47, 103
age, 17, 19, 50, 84, 89, 93, 94, 109, 112, 116, 126, 130, 165, 196, 203
agencies, 74, 88, 123, 139, 153, 170, 189, 200
American education, vii, 2
American Educational Research Association, 130
anatomy, 8
animations, 68
annotation, 70
articulation, 48
artificial intelligence, 21
ASL, 25, 26
assessment, 5, 25, 45, 46, 51, 53, 55, 56, 62, 64, 65, 66, 67, 68, 69, 70, 71, 72, 73, 74, 77, 78, 79, 90, 102, 104, 105, 110, 115, 116, 129, 140, 142, 143, 145, 151, 171, 172, 186, 187, 218
assessment tools, 53, 66, 78, 105
assets, 114, 115
assistive technology, 3, 26, 42, 69, 124

220 Index

attachment, 180
attitudes, 7, 94
audit, 181, 206
authentication, 178, 181, 186
authority(ies), 61, 103, 189, 209
autonomy, 126
awareness, 7, 10, 21, 83, 94

B

bandwidth, 48, 135, 142, 143, 144, 145,
    146, 147, 150, 151, 152, 154, 155,
    156, 157, 158, 160, 166, 167, 168,
    171, 173, 178, 179
barriers, 3, 30, 74, 99, 111, 113, 168
base, 8, 13, 18, 27, 29, 38, 58, 60, 66,
    67, 68, 69, 73, 97, 101, 106, 111, 125,
    134, 137, 143, 182, 184, 185, 194
behaviors, 68, 76, 89, 94
benchmarks, 45, 55
benefits, vii, 1, 9, 40, 86, 88, 130, 135,
    141, 182, 190, 214
blogs, 33, 125, 214, 215
Bluetooth, 172
board members, 53, 55
bonds, 164, 190
broadband, 49, 51, 58, 85, 86, 87, 97,
    106, 112, 130, 135, 136, 137, 139,
    141, 144, 146, 147, 152, 154, 161,
    162, 164, 165, 167, 168, 179, 194,
    214
browser, 60, 143
budget line, 188
businesses, 19, 42, 57, 168, 194, 198

C

cable service, 152
cables, 149, 165, 173, 174
candidates, 41, 42, 47, 65, 100, 103
case study, 113, 130
certificate, 42
certification, 54, 154
CFR, 93, 94

challenges, 8, 13, 14, 20, 31, 39, 43, 46,
    51, 54, 66, 70, 71, 73, 74, 83, 86, 95,
    99, 107, 153, 167, 187, 188, 189, 207,
    209
chat rooms, 94
Chicago, 16, 18, 19, 20, 125
chief technology officer(CTO), 48, 58,
    140
children, 17, 50, 54, 62, 65, 84, 85, 93,
    94, 125, 136, 169, 183, 195, 203
circulation, 87, 88
cities, 18, 19, 85, 169
citizens, 9, 12, 54, 67, 92, 201, 206, 211
citizenship, 12, 43, 51, 76, 193, 199,
    201, 202, 205, 206, 207
civil rights, 53
class period, 72, 146, 179
classes, 22, 95, 200, 202, 208
classroom, 2, 4, 6, 13, 14, 15, 18, 21, 25,
    30, 31, 32, 34, 38, 39, 40, 41, 42, 45,
    47, 51, 60, 67, 68, 70, 73, 77, 89, 94,
    102, 103, 112, 117, 129, 134, 135,
    141, 145, 151, 173, 178, 194
classroom teacher, 2, 4, 32, 42
clusters, 28, 29, 61, 100, 101, 104
coaches, 51, 143
coding, 18, 20
cognitive development, 11
cognitive skills, 16, 78, 105
cognitive theory, 125
collaboration, vii, 1, 8, 9, 14, 18, 24, 29,
    30, 31, 43, 51, 52, 58, 62, 79, 89, 97,
    99, 101, 105, 106, 182, 205, 210, 218
colleges, vii, 1, 36, 55, 77, 78, 79, 90,
    104, 105, 106, 158
commercial, 86, 90, 155, 158, 161, 164,
    176, 177
communication, 9, 25, 53, 73, 78, 79, 82,
    92, 97, 99, 104, 105, 198
community(ies), vii, 1, 2, 3, 6, 7, 8, 14,
    16, 17, 18, 19, 22, 30, 31, 32, 52, 61,
    83, 85, 86, 87, 104, 108, 109, 111,
    114, 115, 118, 119, 135, 143, 155,
    168, 170, 183, 184, 193, 194, 198,
    202, 210

Index

221

community support, 61, 103, 140, 184
competition, 37, 51, 112, 130
competitive grant program, 58
compilation, 124
complement, 179, 185
complexity, 25, 178
compliance, 33, 205
complications, 168
comprehension, 54
computer, 8, 13, 19, 21, 56, 60, 91, 135, 143, 164, 166, 176, 182, 195
computer labs, 56, 166, 182
computing, 6, 109, 116
conceptual model, 21
conference, 43, 46, 135
confidentiality, 93, 95, 202, 203
configuration, 170, 177, 178, 179
connectivity, 5, 6, 8, 12, 17, 22, 23, 24, 37, 47, 48, 51, 53, 57, 58, 79, 83, 84, 85, 86, 87, 88, 89, 91, 97, 98, 99, 102, 106, 107, 134, 135, 136, 137, 138, 140, 141, 143, 144, 146, 147, 152, 153, 154, 155, 157, 159, 161, 162, 163, 164, 166, 167, 168, 169, 170, 174,176, 177, 179, 182, 193, 194, 210, 211
consent, 93, 94, 203
construction, 14, 164, 168, 171
consulting, 174
consumption, 6
conversations, 44, 50, 53, 61, 103, 142
cooperation, 10
coordination, 168, 202
cost, 6, 16, 36, 55, 56, 57, 59, 60, 78, 86, 90, 98, 105, 106, 138, 147, 148, 149, 150, 151, 152, 153, 155, 156, 157, 158, 159, 160, 161, 162, 164, 165, 166, 167, 168, 169, 173, 175, 176, 183, 189, 191, 192, 193, 209, 211
cost saving, 56, 90, 98, 106
creativity, 14, 17, 20, 43, 90, 210
credentials, 45, 76, 77, 111
crisis management, 13
critical thinking, 9, 14, 32, 38, 51, 81
CTO, 109, 140, 172, 185, 194, 195, 197

culture, 40, 50, 51, 76, 111, 205, 206
curricula, 32, 183
curricular materials, 183
curriculum, 12, 13, 22, 32, 41, 51, 55, 57, 60, 64, 67, 70, 81, 82, 115, 123, 182, 183, 189, 205, 206, 207
curriculum development, 57
customers, 87, 149
cyberbullying, 94
cybersecurity, 180
cycles, 61, 73, 104

D

data analysis, 65
data center, 160, 193
data collection, 8, 13, 34, 93, 202, 203
data rates, 154
data set, 20, 33, 51
data transfer, 136
database, 35, 98, 107, 112
DEA, 58, 183
deep learning, 33
democracy, 218
demonstrations, 62
Department of Agriculture, 130
Department of Commerce, 124
Department of Defense, 121
Department of Education, 1, 11, 25, 34, 35, 36, 43, 49, 52, 58, 68, 74, 76, 81, 83, 88, 89, 90, 92, 93, 94, 116, 117, 119, 121, 123, 124, 126, 129, 131, 133, 137, 139, 143, 147, 190, 203, 204, 205, 214
Department of Health and Human Services, 205
Department of Justice, 88
depth, 18, 204
designers, 15, 18, 31, 39, 51
detection, 175, 176
detection system, 176
digital divide, 7, 19, 22, 23, 37, 83, 86, 98, 100, 107, 111, 125, 126, 130, 195
digital text, 3, 43, 56, 169, 185
disability, 3

disadvantaged students, 9
disclosure, 93, 180, 203, 204
discrimination, 38
distance learning, 29, 87, 101
distribution, 73
diversity, 38, 85
donations, 86, 190

E

earning power, 218
economic growth, 218
economic status, 3, 47, 102
economics, 87, 125
economies of scale, 58, 161
ecosystem, 189
education, vii, 1, 2, 3, 5, 9, 12, 13, 16,
    19, 22, 24, 26, 27, 29, 30, 32, 33, 36,
    37, 38, 41, 42, 43, 47, 48, 53, 55, 58,
    59, 61, 62, 64, 65, 68, 74, 75, 85, 88,
    89, 93, 96, 97, 98, 99, 100, 101, 102,
    103, 104, 106, 107, 109, 111, 112,
    114, 117, 118, 124, 125, 126, 127,
    128, 129, 131, 134, 135, 136, 139,
    147, 153, 155, 157, 158, 169, 182,
    183, 187, 189, 190, 192, 203, 204,
    210, 214, 215
educational activities, 3
educational experience, 5, 24, 37, 63, 73
educational institutions, 93, 147, 155
educational materials, 29, 97, 101, 106,
    183
educational opportunities, 3, 8, 64, 88
educational programs, 94, 203
educational services, 93, 202, 203
educational settings, 124
educational software, 186
educational system, 64, 74
educators, vii, 1, 4, 5, 9, 12, 13, 18, 19,
    25, 26, 27, 29, 30, 31, 32, 33, 34, 35,
    36, 37, 38, 39, 42, 43, 44, 46, 47, 53,
    58, 61, 62, 64, 65, 66, 68, 69, 71, 73,
    75, 77, 78, 79, 92, 97, 98, 99, 100,
    101, 102, 103, 104, 105, 106, 107,
    116, 117, 120, 123, 129, 142,144, 201

e-learning, 114, 157
elementary school, 13, 21, 59, 118, 196
emergency, 174, 194, 195, 209
empathy, 10
employees, 192, 203
employers, 18
employment, 36, 183
encryption, 161
enforcement, 200
engineering, 13, 27
England, 109, 112, 114, 125
English language ability, 3
English language learners, 3, 39, 50, 83
entrepreneurs, 2, 18, 19
environment, 9, 10, 16, 37, 45, 77, 81,
    83, 114, 182, 187, 188, 191, 199
environmental conditions, 145
environmental factors, 171
environmental impact, 191
environmental influences, 37
environmental issues, 71, 154
environments, 3, 4, 8, 10, 16, 31, 37, 47,
    51, 66, 71, 79, 103, 105, 108, 111,
    127, 182, 183
equipment, 33, 51, 60, 95, 148, 149, 150,
    151, 165, 166, 169, 174, 175, 176,
    177, 180, 181, 189, 192
equity, vii, 1, 3, 9, 29, 38, 73, 75, 83, 84,
    85, 97, 99, 101, 106, 110, 124, 125,
    126, 141
etiquette, 12, 201
evidence, 3, 5, 6, 10, 33, 34, 36, 59, 62,
    68, 71, 76, 78, 105, 119, 124, 126,
    210
examinations, 94
execution, 61, 103
executive function, 10
Executive Order, 213
exercise, 90, 159
expenditures, 58
expertise, 8, 9, 16, 29, 30, 31, 41, 42, 47,
    78, 90, 99, 101, 102, 105, 123, 140,
    142, 165, 178, 192

Index

F

facial expression, 21
facilitators, 16, 35, 51, 55
faith, 111
families, vii, 1, 2, 4, 5, 7, 18, 30, 39, 50, 53, 61, 64, 65, 68, 69, 78, 89, 92, 93, 96, 99, 103, 105, 141, 187, 193, 194, 195, 198, 202, 206, 209, 215
family members, 42, 65
Federal Communications Commission, 23, 136, 212
federal funds, 58, 190
fiber, 86, 87, 148, 149, 150, 151, 152, 153, 155, 157, 158, 160, 165, 168, 169, 170, 171, 173, 174, 213
filters, 181, 205, 207
financial, 52, 55, 76, 82, 136, 138, 140, 167, 179, 192
financial planning, 192
financial resources, 167
financial system, 179
firewalls, 157, 160, 181
fiscal year, 124, 188
flammability, 173
flexibility, 13, 25, 28, 100, 171, 210
focus groups, 55, 86, 120, 124
force, 40, 47, 102
formal education, 16
foundations, 127
funding, 13, 18, 23, 34, 48, 54, 56, 57, 58, 59, 60, 61, 68, 98, 104, 107, 130, 137, 140, 147, 151, 155, 158, 164, 166, 188, 189, 190, 192, 196, 211, 212
funds, 56, 57, 58, 90, 94, 137, 164, 188, 189, 190

G

gender identity, 3
general education, 27
geography, 8, 47, 102
Georgia, 160, 168, 190

global economy, 7, 218
global education, 59
governance, 115
governments, 57, 168, 170
grades, 26, 95, 145, 160, 164, 180, 196, 197
graduate students, 42
grant programs, 58
grants, 60, 86, 147, 157, 190
growth, 7, 9, 11, 16, 21, 28, 36, 45, 68, 186, 218
guidance, 29, 49, 58, 78, 81, 92, 94, 99, 102, 104, 119, 139, 142, 167, 172, 181, 190, 197, 198, 200, 203, 204, 205, 206, 209, 211
guidelines, 16, 26, 92, 201, 202, 210

H

hacking, 175, 199
health information, 204
high school, 28, 40, 55, 76, 87, 129, 141, 158, 185, 195, 196, 197
higher education, 2, 30, 47, 58, 59, 74, 102, 111, 157
hiring, 41, 53
history, 15, 22, 27, 35, 38
homes, 3, 7, 53, 83, 85, 87, 98, 99, 100, 107, 136, 198
homework, 35, 73, 84, 169, 172, 195
hotspots, 83, 169, 193, 207, 215
House, 49, 121, 123, 130, 212, 213
housing, 85, 88, 131, 168, 181
Housing and Urban Development, 85
hub, 61, 104
human, 22, 49, 50, 165, 179, 181, 206
human capital, 165
human resources, 179

I

identification, 3, 123
identity, 3, 176
IDSs, 177

imagination, 17
immersion, 13, 117
impairments, 25, 26
improvements, 167, 197
income, 39, 50, 84, 85, 169, 193
incompatibility, 65
independent living, 183
individual learning, 3, 75, 89
individual students, 65, 69
Individuals with Disabilities Education Act, 58, 183
industry, 20, 29, 95, 101, 131, 149, 154
inequality, 126
inequity, 194, 196
infection, 181
inferences, 72
information technology, 118
infrastructure, vii, 5, 40, 49, 51, 55, 56, 57, 58, 59, 60, 71, 79, 80, 81, 82, 86, 87, 89, 90, 95, 98, 107, 112, 118, 123, 128, 134, 135, 137, 138, 140, 142, 143, 145, 146, 149, 151, 154, 157, 158, 160, 162, 165, 167, 169, 170, 172, 178, 179, 193, 197, 210, 211, 218
institutions, 3, 28, 29, 30, 36, 47, 50, 53, 58, 59, 61, 62, 79, 84, 89, 93, 96, 97, 98, 99, 100, 101, 102, 103, 106, 107, 135, 147, 149, 155, 157, 158
instructional materials, 3, 30, 57, 204
instructional methods, 137
instructional practice, 29, 46, 64, 78, 101, 102, 105
instructional time, 70
insurance policy, 209
integration, 65, 108, 110, 111, 112, 113, 118
integrity, 92, 200
intelligence, 21
interface, 67, 82, 96, 184
interference, 148, 149, 171, 172, 174
interoperability, 65, 70, 74, 76, 77, 95, 96, 104, 154
intervention, 24, 181

investment, 33, 40, 60, 82, 87, 108, 137, 138, 141, 192, 198, 205
issues, 19, 20, 38, 58, 65, 71, 97, 138, 141, 154, 176, 192, 197
iteration, 20

juvenile justice, 88

L

landscapes, 91, 201
language development, 83
languages, 26, 92, 195
laptop, 57, 108, 109, 145, 177, 184, 185, 197, 200
latency, 152, 153, 154
law enforcement, 200
leadership, 14, 15, 34, 35, 36, 45, 48, 49, 52, 54, 56, 57, 59, 83, 87, 99, 108, 109, 110, 111, 112, 114, 115, 117, 118, 123, 128, 129, 138, 139
learners, vii, 1, 2, 3, 4, 5, 6, 7, 8, 9, 10, 12, 13, 15, 16, 17, 18, 19, 24, 25, 27, 29, 30, 31, 33, 35, 36, 37, 39, 41, 42, 47, 50, 64, 65, 66, 68, 69, 72, 77, 78, 79, 83, 85, 97, 99, 101, 102, 105, 106, 125, 138, 185, 208
learning, vii, 1, 2, 3, 4, 5, 6, 7, 8, 9, 10, 11, 12, 13, 14, 15, 16, 17, 18, 19, 20, 21, 22, 24, 25, 26, 27, 28, 29, 30, 31, 32, 33, 35, 36, 37, 38, 39, 40, 41, 42, 43, 44, 45, 46, 47, 48, 49, 50, 51, 52, 53, 54, 55, 56, 57, 58, 59, 60, 61, 62, 64, 65, 66, 68, 69, 70, 71, 73, 74, 75, 76, 77, 78, 79, 80, 81, 82, 83, 84, 85, 87, 88, 89, 90, 91, 92, 94, 95, 96, 97, 98, 99, 100, 101, 102, 103, 104, 105,
learning environment, 4, 8, 9, 16, 37, 45, 47, 51, 81, 83, 103, 108, 111, 127
learning experiences, vii, 1, 3, 4, 6, 7, 8, 12, 18, 21, 25, 27, 29, 30, 31, 32, 35,

37, 38, 43, 46, 51, 65, 79, 80, 88, 90,
    100, 101, 102, 133, 135
learning outcomes, 5, 51, 70, 78
learning process, 42, 62, 73
learning skills, 17
lesson plan, 22, 37, 87, 201
librarians, 4, 42, 59, 60, 87, 88
life expectancy, 190
life sciences, 26
lifelong learning, 17
lifetime, 187
light, 149, 150
literacy, 15, 18, 38, 39, 42, 43, 46, 51,
    65, 76, 85, 102, 129, 196
local authorities, 61, 103
local educators, 46
local government, 168, 190
location information, 174
long-term debt, 190

M

majority, 39, 145, 148, 185
management, 7, 13, 74, 75, 92, 95, 96,
    157, 158, 160, 166, 170, 175, 176,
    177, 182, 191, 199, 200
mapping, 24, 29, 101
marketing, 94, 204
materials, 3, 9, 29, 30, 36, 57, 75, 88, 90,
    97, 98, 101, 106, 107, 130, 135, 140,
    155, 164, 182, 183, 187, 190, 201,
    203, 204, 205
mathematics, 13, 21, 28, 36, 57, 67
media, 8, 13, 14, 15, 17, 23, 25, 31, 37,
    43, 50, 52, 82, 91, 92, 107, 109, 111,
    114, 127, 151, 183, 184, 185, 186,
    197
medical, 180
membership, 158
messages, 87, 89
meta-analysis, 125
Miami, 53
Ministry of Education, 114
minors, 94, 204
misconceptions, 35

misuse, 92, 200, 210
mobile device, 22, 25, 33, 66, 79, 82, 89,
    93, 137, 145, 163, 166, 172, 185, 191,
    200
mobile phone, 154
models, 9, 12, 13, 19, 21, 27, 29, 42, 47,
    59, 61, 101, 102, 104, 127, 147, 155,
    158, 182, 193, 195
modernization, 22, 84, 98, 167
momentum, 196
Montana, 151, 213
motivation, 7, 11, 24, 39, 68, 75, 79, 106
multimedia, 9, 33, 72, 97, 106, 135, 136,
    138, 169, 185
multiple-choice questions, 62
museums, 15, 18, 30
music, 8, 15, 20, 89

N

National Assessment of Educational
    Progress (NAEP), 68
National Center for Education Statistics
    NCES, 74, 116
National Economic Council, 121
National Education Technology Plan
    (NETP), 2, 3, 5, 7, 12, 100, 119, 120,
    123, 124, 133, 134, 137, 217, 218
National Park Service, 15
National Research Council (NRC), 67,
    129
Navajo Nation, 168, 214
negative consequences, 10, 92, 201
negotiating, 152, 192
Netherlands, 119
networking, 32, 45, 94, 150, 171
New Zealand, 44, 114
next generation, 76, 78, 105, 129
No Child Left Behind, 54
nonprofit organizations, 2, 123, 139

O

Obama, President Barack, 48, 84, 130, 136, 137, 212, 213
obstacles, 168
officials, 92, 94, 98, 107, 142, 170, 202, 203
Oklahoma, 86, 130
online information, 35
online learning, 16, 33, 36, 47, 96, 102, 108, 151
openness, 54
operating system, 184, 185, 191
opportunities, 3, 7, 8, 9, 10, 13, 15, 18, 19, 21, 24, 29, 31, 32, 34, 36, 38, 42, 46, 47, 54, 56, 58, 59, 64, 65, 73, 75, 82, 83, 85, 88, 97, 101, 102, 106, 123, 128, 137, 140, 142, 143, 144, 161, 169, 193, 198
opt out, 204
organize, 5, 13, 18, 27, 72
outreach, 83, 86, 88, 120, 201
outsourcing, 193
ownership, 51, 54, 71, 78, 105, 141, 149, 165, 169, 177, 183, 193, 196, 197, 208

P

parental consent, 94, 203
parents, 17, 20, 50, 53, 55, 62, 64, 82, 87, 91, 92, 93, 117, 138, 141, 145, 195, 197, 198, 200, 201, 202, 203, 204, 206, 207, 210
participants, 8, 14, 15, 16, 18, 20, 27, 34, 43, 91, 124
password, 95, 179, 186, 208
pathways, 8, 13, 29, 47, 51, 65, 72, 73, 78, 101, 102, 105, 128, 144, 147, 154
pedagogy, 22
peer review, 32
perseverance, 7, 51, 68
personal learning, 44
personality traits, 125

Philadelphia, 46, 130
physics, 8, 71, 72, 129, 130
PISA, 67, 68
pitch, 117
platform, 18, 22, 26, 34, 35, 81, 96
playing, 17, 21, 72
policy, 35, 51, 94, 107, 110, 125, 126, 131, 145, 176, 179, 184, 193, 201, 202, 209
policymakers, vii, 2, 3, 46, 47, 64, 98, 99, 103, 106
population, 26, 69, 82, 87, 198, 209
population density, 87
portability, 76
portfolio, 36, 51, 135
positive behaviors, 76
post-secondary institutions, 3, 28, 29, 62, 97, 100, 101, 106
poverty, 7, 87, 146
preparation, 5, 6, 30, 40, 41, 42, 43, 46, 47, 78, 99, 100, 102, 103, 105, 116
President, 48, 53, 84, 120, 121, 122, 123, 130, 136, 137, 147, 212, 213
principles, 2, 12, 16, 19, 24, 25, 29, 78, 79, 101, 105
prior knowledge, 72
Privacy Protection Act, 94, 203
private sector, 85, 137
problem solving, 9, 10, 20, 71, 37, 67
problem-solving skills, 20
procurement, 28, 101
producers, 15, 29, 101
professional development, 5, 6, 13, 18, 30, 31, 34, 36, 43, 44, 46, 54, 55, 57, 59, 60, 65, 77, 81, 99, 100, 108, 110, 111, 112, 114, 115, 116, 117, 118, 119, 137, 138, 141, 142, 143, 144, 151, 165, 190, 195, 196, 211
professional growth, 45
professionals, 54, 61, 103, 178
programming, 19, 87, 100
project, 13, 15, 18, 21, 22, 27, 32, 34, 37, 38, 40, 43, 44, 45, 52, 54, 60, 75, 89, 111, 124, 129, 148, 169
proliferation, 98, 99

property rights, 149
prosperity, 7, 218
protected areas, 94
protection, 77, 94, 95, 98, 104, 107, 181, 183
psychology, 13, 125
public domain, 56
public education, 64
public housing, 88
public schools, 48, 55
public service, 14
purchasing power, 159, 161, 162, 164, 165

R

race, 3, 38, 53
reading, 11, 15, 17, 24, 28, 39, 54, 67, 88, 184
reading comprehension, 54
real time, 69, 74, 75, 136, 176
reality, 22, 34, 46, 102, 128, 134
recognition, 77, 115
recommendations, 3, 12, 75, 123, 124, 140, 171, 181, 201, 203, 218
recycling, 191
redistribution, 190
redundancy, 95, 156, 161, 162, 165, 166
Reform, 82, 108, 111, 130
Registry, 57, 183
regulations, 33, 77, 104, 168
relevance, 16
reliability, 154, 157
remediation, 41, 192
repair, 188, 191, 192, 194
requirements, 40, 93, 94, 95, 140, 143, 174, 186, 188, 196, 199, 203, 204, 205, 210
research institutions, 79, 106, 157
researchers, vii, 2, 12, 14, 22, 29, 33, 34, 47, 55, 78, 98, 99, 101, 102, 105, 107, 120, 123
resource allocation, 58
resources, 5, 6, 8, 11, 12, 13, 14, 17, 28, 29, 30, 32, 33, 34, 36, 40, 42, 43, 45,

47, 48, 49, 50, 51, 52, 54, 56, 57, 58, 59, 60, 61, 62, 65, 69, 71, 75, 76, 79, 81, 82, 83, 84, 87, 88, 89, 90, 92, 95, 96, 97, 98, 99, 100, 101, 102, 103, 104, 106, 107, 113, 115, 117, 123, 128, 133, 134, 137, 138, 139, 141, 142, 143, 144, 146, 147, 157, 163, 165, 167, 172, 175, 176, 179, 180, 181, 183, 185, 186, 188, 189, 190, 193, 195, 196, 198, 200, 201, 205, 211
response, 42, 64, 66, 67, 69, 78, 105, 147
restrictions, 153, 158, 191, 200, 206
rights, 38, 53, 93, 149, 153, 168, 201, 202, 203, 204, 205
risks, 33, 35, 39, 50, 75, 170, 181, 196, 212
rules, 74, 82, 92, 201
rural areas, 51, 86, 147, 155, 168
rural schools, 146, 211

S

safety, 66, 94, 98, 107, 173, 201, 205, 209
savings, 56, 90, 98, 106, 170, 190
scaling, 111
scholarship, 112
school, vii, 1, 2, 6, 7, 8, 9, 10, 11, 13, 15, 18, 20, 21, 22, 23, 24, 26, 28, 30, 31, 32, 33, 34, 40, 41, 42, 44, 46, 47, 48, 49, 50, 51, 52, 53, 54, 55, 56, 57, 58, 59, 60, 61, 62, 64, 65, 66, 68, 71, 75, 76, 77, 78, 79, 81, 82, 83, 84, 85, 86, 87, 88, 89, 91, 92, 93, 94, 95, 96, 97, 98, 99, 100, 102, 103, 104, 105, 106, 107, 108, 109, 112, 113, 114, 115, 117, 118, 125, 127, 129, 130, 133,
school community, 141
school culture, 205, 206
school improvement, 115
school learning, 6, 18
school performance, 125

science, 8, 13, 19, 32, 33, 36, 60, 91, 118, 185
secondary education, 13, 47, 93, 103, 118
secondary schools, 146
security, 30, 33, 41, 51, 65, 66, 74, 78, 90, 93, 104, 138, 142, 157, 160, 162, 165, 176, 177, 178, 181, 187, 191, 199, 202, 203, 204, 207, 212
security practices, 93, 202, 203
security threats, 176
self-assessment, 45
self-awareness, 7, 10
self-efficacy, 16
self-reflection, 44, 62
self-regulation, 10
September 11, 214
servers, 169, 177, 180
service provider, 85, 86, 93, 148, 150, 154, 157, 162, 174, 202, 207
services, 51, 56, 59, 93, 94, 96, 135, 145, 150, 153, 157, 160, 162, 166, 167, 168, 169, 175, 176, 179, 180, 183, 193, 194, 202, 203, 204
signal quality, 148
signals, 171, 172
Silicon Valley, 122
simulation, 21, 67
simulations, 21, 33, 35, 66, 79, 105
skill competencies, 10
social interests, 39
social justice, 19
social learning, 76, 114
social network, 32, 94
social participation, 117
social skills, 125
society, 8, 43, 85, 115
software, 6, 16, 21, 22, 24, 26, 33, 51, 52, 83, 90, 92, 93, 94, 97, 106, 112, 137, 138, 142, 144, 155, 161, 175, 177, 180, 181, 183, 184, 186, 191, 199, 200, 202, 207, 208
software providers, 138
solution, 16, 32, 72, 88, 138, 152, 155, 164, 177, 193, 209, 214

special education, 26, 27, 42
specialists, 183
specifications, 74, 171, 183, 186
spending, 56, 167, 189, 213
spreadsheets, 117
staff development, 164
staff members, 45, 52, 59, 181
staffing, 59, 95
stakeholder groups, 61, 78, 98, 103, 105, 107, 123
stakeholders, vii, 2, 29, 50, 54, 55, 68, 75, 78, 99, 100, 101, 104, 105, 120, 124, 138, 141, 168, 184, 194, 198, 209
state, 3, 20, 30, 38, 40, 46, 47, 48, 53, 55, 56, 57, 58, 59, 60, 61, 74, 81, 84, 87, 88, 95, 98, 99, 102, 103, 104, 106, 107, 111, 124, 129, 135, 139, 142, 155, 156, 157, 158, 160, 169, 178, 186, 189, 200, 210, 211
statistics, 59, 84
statutes, 203
stock, 61, 104, 209
storage, 57, 166, 177, 184, 185
storytelling, 10, 40, 91
strategic planning, 60, 61, 103
structure, 20, 22, 43, 111, 152, 155
student achievement, 28, 64, 118, 119, 127, 133, 141
student populations, 83
supervisor, 62
support services, 169
suspensions, 10
sustainability, 52, 98, 107
synthesis, 29, 101, 109, 114, 116
systemic change, 5, 100

T

target, 70, 84, 137, 143, 147, 167
taxes, 168
taxpayers, 190
teacher preparation, 5, 6, 30, 40, 41, 42, 43, 46, 47, 78, 99, 100, 102, 103, 105

Index 229

teachers, vii, 2, 3, 4, 5, 6, 7, 14, 15, 22, 26, 29, 30, 31, 32, 33, 34, 35, 36, 37, 38, 39, 40, 41, 42, 44, 45, 46, 49, 50, 51, 52, 53, 54, 55, 57, 60, 64, 65, 72, 73, 81, 82, 83, 86, 88, 90, 91, 95, 96, 99, 101, 111, 112, 116, 118, 123, 126, 127, 128, 129, 130, 134, 135, 136, 137, 139, 141, 142, 143, 144, 145, 146, 151, 155, 165, 168, 173, 177, 182, 183, 184, 185, 187, 189, 190, 192, 195, 196, 197, 198, 199, 200, 201, 202, 205, 206, 210, 211
teaching effectiveness, 109
teaching strategies, 113
teams, 34, 45, 53, 65, 124, 139, 192
technical assistance, 119
technical support, 95, 165, 166, 192
technology, 1, 2, 3, 5, 6, 7, 9, 12, 13, 18, 19, 20, 22, 23, 24, 26, 27, 28, 29, 30, 31, 32, 33, 34, 35, 36, 37, 38, 40, 41, 42, 43, 45, 46, 47, 48, 49, 50, 51, 52, 53, 54, 55, 56, 57, 58, 59, 60, 61, 62, 64, 65, 66, 67, 69, 70, 72, 73, 76, 79, 80, 81, 83, 84, 85, 88, 89, 91, 92, 94, 97, 98, 99, 100, 101, 102, 103, 104, 106, 107, 108, 110, 111, 112, 113, 114, 116, 117, 118, 120, 123, 124, 125, 126, 127, 128, 133, 134, 136, 137, 138, 139, 140, 141, 142, 143, 144, 145, 146, 151, 163, 164, 165, 168, 173, 176, 177, 182, 184, 187, 188, 189, 190, 191, 192, 196, 198, 199, 202, 205, 211, 214, 218
technology in education, vii, 99
technology infrastructure, vii, 51, 55, 57, 80, 81, 97, 134, 142
telecommunications, 148, 151, 158, 167, 169, 173
telephone, 130, 148, 149, 150, 151, 165, 194
test items, 70, 73
test scores, 28, 87
testing, 3, 38, 68, 70, 73, 78, 105, 142, 166, 178, 179, 182, 187, 199, 209
testing program, 68

textbooks, 49, 56, 57, 59, 90, 137, 151, 166, 169, 183, 185, 190, 215
text-to-speech, 3, 24, 69
theft, 175, 199, 208
threats, 148, 176, 180, 181
time periods, 22
Title I, 2, 57, 90, 110
Title II, 57, 90
Title IV, 2
trade-off, 153, 185
training, 30, 35, 41, 42, 49, 85, 91, 93, 137, 142, 148, 203
training programs, 42
traits, 125
trajectory, 72
transformation, 3, 54, 81, 133, 138, 218
transformational learning, 12, 21, 79, 100
transformations, 99
translation, 83, 92
transmission, 135, 149, 152
transparency, 198, 206
trial, 209
troubleshooting, 38, 198
tuition, 55
tutoring, 179

U

United States, 5, 7, 19, 38, 51, 84, 90, 110, 124, 130, 147, 169
universal access, 59
universities, vii, 1, 13, 36, 55, 78, 79, 87, 105, 106, 155, 158
updating, 59, 82
up-front costs, 149, 150
urban, 18, 31, 42, 118, 124, 168
urban schools, 168
US Department of Health and Human Services, 205

V

valuation, 62

vandalism, 175
Vice President, 120, 122
video games, 39, 71, 129
videos, 14, 15, 20, 33, 35, 38, 44, 52, 56, 87, 135, 141, 178, 183, 201
virtuous cycles, 61, 104
vision, vii, 1, 2, 5, 7, 30, 48, 49, 50, 52, 54, 55, 56, 60, 61, 74, 81, 86, 99, 100, 103, 104, 117, 123, 134, 137, 139, 140, 146, 182, 192, 196, 198, 210, 211, 214
visions, 48
visualization, 98, 107
VoIP, 154, 165, 173, 174, 177

W

Washington, 20, 68, 90, 91, 98, 106, 109, 110, 112, 113, 114, 115, 116, 117, 118, 119, 120, 124, 125, 126, 129, 212, 213, 214
web, 20, 107, 115, 134, 142, 143, 169, 182, 184, 185, 194, 213
webpages, 20
websites, 13, 20, 24, 25, 36, 72, 82, 94, 143, 172, 181, 185, 186, 206
White House, 49, 121, 123, 130, 212, 213
White Paper, 108
Wi-Fi, 27, 55, 86, 136, 145, 147, 164, 167, 171, 172, 177, 179
wireless connectivity, 23, 137, 193
wireless networks, 87, 194
wires, 5, 148
Wisconsin, 45

X

XML, 96